Comedy in Context: Essays on Molière

Comedy in Context:
Essays on Molière

By H. GASTON HALL

UNIVERSITY PRESS OF MISSISSIPPI

Jackson

Library of Congress Cataloging in Publication Data

Hall, H. Gaston.
  Comedy in context.

  Bibliography: p.
  Includes index.
  1. Molière, 1622–1673—Criticism and interpretation—
Addresses, essays, lectures. I. Title.
PQ1860.H35 1984   842'.4   83-21729
  ISBN 0-87805-200-3

To the memory of Albert Sanders

Contents

Introduction

This volume brings together a dozen essays devoted to aspects of Molière's stagecraft. Though originally written at various times for different readerships, each illustrates in its way the overall theme of the volume: *Comedy in Context*. The first seven essays are devoted to questions and themes common to a number of plays, while the last five deal successively with individual comedies: *L'Ecole des femmes*, *Tartuffe*, *Dom Juan*, and especially *Le Misanthrope*. These four comedies were all first performed within a few years of each other at the height of Molière's career in Paris between 1662 and 1666, a period of struggle. The essays relating to them are placed in chronological order—that is, in order of first performance. Otherwise the essay on *Tartuffe*, which was not performed and published in the five-act version we know until 1669, or the one on *Dom Juan* (not published until 1682, nine years after Molière's death), might have been placed last. The order chosen allows the essays on *Le Misanthrope* to be grouped together while the last essay in the volume looks outward towards the fortunes of that comedy on the English Restoration stage and in the eighteenth century.

There was no such obvious way of ordering the first seven essays; and the reader quite unfamiliar with Molière's career might be advised to begin with chapter 6, which contains a brief biographical outline related to Molière's experience and satire of contemporary medicine. "Satire of Medicine" certainly illustrates the theme of comedy in context, but I thought that the opening chapter should treat some important aspect of the theatrical context in which Molière worked. "Comedy and Romance in the *dépits amoureux*" looks again at some undervalued scenes in a number of Molière's plays—scenes too often judged simply as lines on a page and not for their potential as scenes with warm bodies, hesitant movement and poignant moments on a stage—in the context of *commedia dell'arte*, seventeenth-

century French comedy and conventions of stage proprieties the special nature of which contrast so sharply with
stage conventions permissible since about 1968. The argument is not simply to reevaluate those scenes, but to suggest
that they encapsulate Molière's distinctive blend of comedy
and romance which allows us—insensitive comic theory
notwithstanding—to sympathize with characters at whom
we also laugh. "Comic Images" is more concerned with
comic theory and looks at moments in a number of comedies in relation to their implications, arguing (without
prejudice to Molière's mastery of "absolute comedy" and
the celebratory humor of the great carnavalesque *comédies-
ballets*) that humor, wit, and laughter in Molière's comedies
is often significant. Some similar conclusions are reached on
the basis of a less theoretical analysis in chapter 5, "Wordplay," a previously unpublished paper read at a conference
at the University of Wales, Aberystwyth, in 1973, marking
the centennial of the university and commemorating the
tercentennial of Molière's death. Readers who find chapters
2 to 4 more difficult than the others might proceed to
"Wordplay" directly from "Comedy and Romance."

Chapter 3, "Ce que Molière doit à Scaramouche", reex-
amines Molière's debt to the great *commedia dell'arte* artist
with whom he shared his principal theatre during the years
in which he was writing most of the comedies by which he
is remembered today. From the context of theatre and acting styles in chapter 3 I move in chapter 4 to the context of
Molière's original printers: not all of them, because one at
least was dishonest and others were careless. But in the
main Molière's original printers seem to have been more
careful, and their conventions more meaningful in terms of
guiding a theatrical reading of the plays, than the reorgani-
zation of the punctuation in most current editions—
including those used for quotations in other chapters in this
book—allows modern readers to see for themselves.
"Dramaturgie et ponctuation" suggests that the "acciden-
tals," especially the punctuation, of the best original editions constitute important neglected evidence of the
breathing, rhythm and tone of important roles. As part of

the discussion in both of these chapters is somewhat technical, it was judged suitable to republish them in French as
written. Details of chapter 4 could hardly apply to a translation, requiring a close reading of the original French text
of comedies discussed; and there is a more developed tradition of textual criticism in English than there is in French,
in which language this contribution is likely to be more
valuable.

"Characterism of Vices," chapter 7, presents further evidence for stressing the moralist dimensions in Molière's
comedies, especially those first performed between 1664
and 1670, in relation particularly to Urbain Chevreau's
translation of Joseph Hall's *Characters*, the subtitle of which
for the relevant section we borrow for this chapter. It also
introduces the attention to the literary context of individual
comedies developed in the following chapters. By "literary
context" I sometimes mean *source*, in the old-fashioned
scholarly acceptation of the word, which is especially appropriate to Molière study, because he is known to have
recycled so many of his dramatic subjects, such as *Dom
Juan*, *L'Avare* and *Amphitryon*. In such recycling, and in
more independent forms of composition, he seems also to
have drawn more or less closely on other written sources
and plays on other subjects. But identification of a source
never does the work of analysis. It merely establishes a
point of comparison by which to measure achievement
within the context in which the plays took shape. We have
access to so little of the total context that it is not always
possible to establish sources, nor is such accreditation necessary for every use to which literary context may be put.
Any single play or scene has always been elaborated and
perceived as part of a larger experience, all of which is in
some degree contextual. The great advantage of literary
context, including scripted dramatic literature, is the relative ease of access to reliable contemporary witnesses; and a
text need not be a proven source for intertextual comparisons to be of value.

The examples and arguments which follow must speak
for themselves, but I would add an illustration relevant to

chapter 10, on " 'La Scène du Pauvre' " of *Dom Juan*." It has been established by various scholars that there are multiple sources for this play besides the plays on the subject by Cicognini, Dorimond and Villiers on which Molière manifestly drew for his own. Sganarelle's rejoinder to his master "vous parlez tout comme un livre" (Act I, scene 2) is based on a passage in Charles Sorel's *Polyphile ou l'amant de plusieurs dames* (1663). The double seduction scene in Act II is adapted from a similar scene in Dorimond's *L'Inconstance punie*, not his *Festin de Pierre*. The prominence of Sganarelle in Molière's version of the subject doubtless owes a great deal to the fact that he wrote that role for himself, but arguably he was partly guided in that redistribution of the subject's structure by the important role of Sancho Panza in Guérin de Bouscal's trilogy of plays from Cervantes's *Don Quijote* if not in the novel itself. In chapter 7 I argue that the contrast of Sganarelle as the Superstitious with Dom Juan as the Profane, which had not been a feature of the dramatic subject before Molière, is traceable to Urbain Chevreau's *L'Ecole du sage*, which includes his version of Hall's *Characters*.

In chapter 10 I stress theatrical context, including the "marché de décors" which discloses important aspects of the original staging and the comic potential of Sganarelle as a third presence throughout the "Scène du Pauvre," as well as elements in the scene and in its social background which show the extent to which Molière situates his foreign and legendary subject in relation to the historical present of his own time and country. I will suggest here, but cannot prove, that the "Scène du Pauvre" derives part of its dramatic power through a *contaminatio* or blending with the Don Juan legend of the famous encounter in antiquity between Alexander the Great (to whom Dom Juan compares himself in Act I, scene 2) and the philosopher Diogenes the Cynic who had stripped himself of virtually all material possessions to live unconventionally in extreme poverty. There are several channels through which the story may have reached Molière. A plausible one occurs in Desmarets de Saint-Sorlin's *Les Délices de l'esprit*, dialogues between

Philédon (a hedonist) and Eusèbe (a man of piety) published in a sumptuous folio volume in 1658, the year Molière returned to Paris with his troupe. Eusèbe enquires who was more fortunate, Diogenes who needed nothing, or Alexander who needed everything because he wanted everything, "et qui mesme desiroit plus que tout, puisque toute la terre ne luy suffisoit pas." Philédon replies that Alexander was more fortunate, because he was a powerful king and Diogenes a mere beggar. Eusèbe points out that nevertheless "ce Roy tres-puissant, voyant que ce gueux n'avoit besoin de rien, envia son repos, et la gloire et la hauteur de son esprit, qui dédaignoit toute sa pompe; et dit, 'Si je n'estois Alexandre, je voudrois estre Diogène.'" Philédon cannot see any sense in Alexander's saying, but Eusèbe explains as follows: "Alexandre se trouvant engagé dans ses vastes désirs, avec lesquels il ne pouvoit jamais se satisfaire, et dont il ne pouvoit se défaire; pensa en voyant Diogène si tranquille, qu'il eust esté plus expédient d'estre débarrassé de tout comme luy . . . (Part I, p. 21).

It is not extravagant to imagine that Molière might have noticed this passage, near the beginning of the most lavishly produced book of an author whose comedy *Les Visionnaires* was in Molière's repertory, whose plays and ballets had been the great theatrical innovations on the Paris stage in the years immediately before Molière turned to professional theatre as a way of life, whose adaptation of Saint Gregory of Nazianzus's *Maximes du mariage* he parodies in *L'Ecole des femmes*, who—to judge from a passage in Desmarets's *Ariane*—had participated in the design of the stage on which *Dom Juan* was produced and the installation of the machines which made the spectacular scene changes in *Dom Juan* possible. But I cannot show the passage as a source, because the texts themselves are not sufficiently close in expression. The encounter in any case was widely cited, for instance by Perrot d'Ablancourt in his *Apophtegmes des anciens*: "Il disoit, Que s'il n'estoit Aléxandre il voudroit estre Diogéne. *C'est qu'il part d'vne mesme ambition, de tout mépriser, ou de tout avoir*" (Paris, 1664, quarto ed., p. 29). The value of the *rapprochement* is in the light it throws on "la scène du

Pauvre." Behind Molière's imaginary encounter between the seducer of limitless desires and the Mendicant who has renounced all treasures of this world lurks a legendary encounter, actively discussed by contemporary moralists, opposing a character content with nothing because he wants everything and another character living hand-to-mouth who has everything because he wants nothing.

Arguably "la scène du Pauvre" has mythic dimensions because it reenacts, *mutatis mutandis*, a legendary encounter juxtaposing limit cases in the evaluation of the world. As so often in Molière's comedies, the incompatible characters brought on stage together to show each other off and to show each other up are linked by a common passion, in this case ambition. Contextual intertextuality thus points not only to secure historical interpretation related to issues relevant to Molière's time but to those larger issues whose dilemmas, decisions, and drama are still with us. It is hoped that similarly in chapters 9 and 11 aspects of the literary context of *Tartuffe* and of *Le Misanthrope* discussed will interest in this broader way as well as in the historical interpretation of those comedies. Finally, chapter 8, "Parody in *L'Ecole des femmes*," examines devices of style, literary and theatrical, relevant to the historical appreciation not only of that comedy, but of the other major plays discussed in the second half of this volume.

As a reviewer of most of the Molière literature published in the past twenty-five years I have contracted debts to other *Moliéristes* too numerous to be mentioned here. But I am still conscious of debts to the late A. G. Sanders, who introduced me to Molière at Millsaps College; to the late W. G. Moore, who encouraged my interest in Molière when I was his pupil at St. John's College, Oxford; and to Jacques Guicharnaud, who let me audit his Molière course in the Yale University Graduate School. To Jacques Guicharnaud I am also grateful for specific advice related to the publication of this volume, especially in chapter 5. Other *Moliéristes* who in conversation, correspondence or reviews of the previously published articles have guided improvements on particular points include J.-P. Collinet, Georges Couton, Marcel Gutwirth, Roger Herzel, W. D. Howarth, Roger Laufer, and Jeanne Veyrin-Forrer. Any errors or infelicities of expression which remain would certainly be more numerous but for their interventions, in some cases before the original publications, in some cases in response to one or more of them.

Except for chapter 5, the other essays in this volume have been published before in whole or in part. I have gathered them here in hopes of reaching a wider readership. Most have been republished substantially as originally written, but I have taken the opportunity to correct or restate specific points in chapters 3, 6, 10 and 11, I. The annotation of chapter 6 has been brought into line with that of other essays in the volume, while that of chapters 7 and 11 has been reduced or introduced into the text. Chapters 8 and 9 on *L'Ecole des femmes* and *Tartuffe* have been recast and extended. Parts of chapter 12 have been rephrased.

I am grateful to the following periodicals and publishers for permission to reprint copyright material: *Australian Journal of French Studies* for chapter 1, reprint from vol. 8 (1971), pp. 245–58, and chapter 9, reprint from vols. 10 (1973), pp. 119–29, and 13 (1976), pp. 179–80; Centre National de la Recherche Scientifique, Paris, for chapter 4, reprint from *La Bibliographie matérielle*, 1983, pp. 125–41; Edinburgh University Press for most of chapter 10, reprint from *The Art of Criticism: Essays in French Literary Analysis*, ed. P. H. Nurse, 1967, pp. 69–87; *French Studies* for chapter 7, reprint from vol. 29 (1975), pp. 398–410; University Press of Kentucky for chapter 11, part II, reprint from *Kentucky Romance Quarterly*, vol. 19 (1972), pp. 347–63; *Modern Language Review* for part of chapter 8, reprint from vol. 57 (1962), pp. 63–65; Oxford University Press for chapter 2, reprint from *Molière: Stage and Study. Essays in Honour of W. G. Moore*, ed. by W. D. Howarth and M. Thomas, 1973, pp. 43–60; *Papers on French Seventeenth Century Literature* for chapter 12, reprint from vol. 10, no. 19 (1983), pp. 787–806; Royal Society of Medicine, London, for chapter 6, reprint from *Proceedings of the Royal Society of Medicine*, vol. 70 (1977), pp. 425–31; Editions Slatkine, Geneva, for most of chapter 3, reprint from *Mélanges à la Mémoire de Franco Simone: France et Italie dans la culture européenne, vol. 2, XVIIᵉ et XVIIIᵉ siècles*, 1981, pp. 257–67; and *Studi Francesi* for most of chapter 11, part I, reprint from vol. 14 (1970), pp. 20–38.

Chronology

1622   Jean-Baptiste Poquelin (hereafter Molière, the stage name he adopted in 1644) born in Paris, first son of Jean Poquelin ("marchant tapissier") and of Marie Cressé.

1628   Jean Poquelin (Molière's grandfather) dies.

1629–30   Corneille's *Mélite* performed at the Théâtre du Marais in Paris.

1632   Marie Cressé dies. Jean Poquelin (Molière's father) becomes "tapissier ordinaire du roi." Molière enters Collège de Clermont.

1633   Jean Poquelin remarried to Catherine Fleurette.

1636   War with Spain begins. Small theatre in Palais-Cardinal opens.

1637   First mention of "lettres de provision" concerning the *charge* "tapissier et valet de chambre du roi" in favor of Molière as heir to his father. Corneille's *Le Cid* and Jean Desmarets's *Les Visionnaires* performed at the Théâtre du Marais and published. Descartes's *Discours de la méthode* published.

1638   Louis de Cressé (Molière's maternal grandfather, said to have taken him to the theatre) dies. The dauphin (future King Louis XIV) is born.

1639   Desmarets's *Ballet de la félicité sur l'heureuse naissance de Monseigneur le Dauphin* danced in February and March at Court theatres including the Palais-Cardinal.

1640   Jansenius's *Augustinus* published.

1641   Performance and publication of Desmarets's *Mirame* and *Ballet de la prospérité des armes de la France* for the opening of the great theatre in the Palais-Cardinal, which became Molière's principal theatre in 1661.

1642   Cardinal Richelieu dies. The Palais-Cardinal becomes the Palais-Royal. Cardinal Mazarin becomes "premier ministre." The London theatres are closed.

1643   Molière joins with members of the Béjart family and

others to found L'Illustre Théâtre, "entretenu par Son Altesse Royale" (Gaston d'Orléans, brother of Louis XIII who becomes Lieutenant général de France at the beginning of the regency in May). They rent the "jeu de paume des Mestayers" (an indoor tennis court on the left bank of the Seine in Paris) and adapt it to make a theatre along traditional French rectangular lines, with the stage at one end, elevated, and two tiers of boxes along the sides. Artificial light only used (mainly candles and oil lamps). King Louis XIII dies. His widow, Anne of Austria, becomes regent. Scarron's comedy *Jodelet ou le Maître valet* performed at the Théâtre du Marais.

1643–44   Corneille's *Le Menteur* performed.

1644   Théâtre du Marais burns down in January, reopens modernized in October. L'Illustre Théâtre moves to the "jeu de paume de la Croix noire" on the right bank, in a more fashionable quarter than the Mestayers. The Elzevirs of Leiden publish *L'Illustre théâtre de Monsieur Corneille* containing five of his tragedies (*Le Cid*, *Horace*, *Cinna*, *La Mort de Pompée* and *Polyeucte*), plays likely to have represented Corneille's tragic theatre in the repertory of L'Illustre Théâtre, given (a) Corneille's unsuccessful efforts in 1643 to prevent performance of the last three of these by troupes not of his choosing, and (b) pictorial and other evidence that Molière performed roles in these plays.

1645   L'Illustre Théâtre fails. Molière is imprisoned for debts soon paid by his father.

1646   Molière and the Béjart family begin their wagon days by joining with the touring company of actors led by Dufresne and protected by the duc d'Epernon, governor of Guyenne.

1648–53   Scarron's *Le Virgile travesti* (books one through seven) published.

1648–53   Civil wars in France known as La Fronde.

1653   Molière has become the leader of his troupe, which performs Corneille's semi-opera *Andromède* in Lyons and later, at Pézenas, receives the protection of the young Prince de Conti, the new governor of Languedoc.

1655 *L'Etourdi* performed in Lyons.

1656 *Dépit amoureux* performed in Béziers for the Etats de Languedoc.

1656–57 Publication of Pascal's *Lettres provinciales:* "il y a bien de la différence entre rire de la religion, et rire de ceux qui la profanent par leurs opinions extravagantes" (eleventh *Provinciale*, 1657).

1657–58 Various portraits made of Molière as an actor, as a reader and (if indeed the eighteenth-century portrait by Coypel really is in this respect a faithful witness to a lost contemporary portrait by Nicolas Mignard) as a writer.

1658 Molière's troupe returns to Paris after performing in Rouen; becomes the "troupe de Monsieur" (Philippe d'Orléans, only brother of Louis XIV); performs Corneille's *Nicomède* for king and court October 24 in the Petit-Bourbon (a great hall used for ceremonial occasions in which the Italian players led by Scaramouche had a theatre) and follows it with a successful address to the king and performance of a one-act farce, *Le Docteur amoureux*. Molière's troupe allowed to share the theatre in the Petit-Bourbon with the Italian players already established there. From November performances of *L'Etourdi* and *Dépit amoureux* "ne contribuèrent pas peu au succès de la Troupe" (La Grange).

1659 *Les Précieuses ridicules* performed at the Petit-Bourbon November 18. Peace of the Pyrenees ending the war with Spain (November 7).

1659–62 Molière reported by the abbé de Marolles and by Jean Chapelain working on a (lost) translation of Lucretius's *De rerum natura.*

1660 *Les Précieuses ridicules* published in January. *Sganarelle ou le cocu imaginaire* performed at the Petit-Bourbon May 28 and pirated editions published in the summer. "Le théâtre du Petit-Bourbon commença à être démoli par M. de Ratabon, surintendant des bâtiments du roi, sans en avertir la troupe qui se trouva fort surprise de demeurer sans théâtre" October 11 (La Grange). Molière is offered use of the great theatre in the Palais-Royal, then in disrepair. Corneille's semi-opera *La Toison d'or* performed in connection with celebrations over the marriage of King Louis XIV with the Spanish infanta Maria Teresa. Three-volume edition of Corneille's *Théâtre* published October 31. Deaths of Scarron, Jodelet, Vincent de Paul, and Gaston d'Orléans. Restoration of King Charles II of England and reopening of theatres in London.

1661 Reopening of the theatre in the Palais-Royal with *Dépit amoureux* and *Sganarelle* January 20. *Dom Garcie de Navarre* performed at Palais-Royal February 4. *L'Ecole des maris* performed at Palais-Royal June 24. *Les Fâcheux* performed as part of courtly *fête galante* at Vaux-le-Vicomte August 17 in the presence of king and court. Nicolas Foucquet (the *surintendant des Finances* who had organized the *fête*) arrested September 5. *Les Fâcheux* performed at the Palais-Royal November 4. Cardinal Mazarin dies. Mlle de la Vallière becomes the king's mistress. Louis XIV embarks on his personal reign.

1662 In January "les comédiens italiens ont recommencé à jouer alternativement avec nous les jours extraordinaires, c'est-à-dire lundis, mercredis, jeudis et samedis" (La Grange). Marriage contract between Molière and Armande Béjart (sister of Madeleine Béjart with whom he had formed L'Illustre Théâtre, born around 1642 or 1643) signed January 23 provides "communauté de biens," specifies a dowry for Armande of 10,000 *livres tournois* and a marriage settlement on her of 4,000 *livres*. The marriage took place February 20 at Saint-Germain l'Auxerrois, "vis-à-vis le Palais-Royal" and more directly opposite the site of the Petit-Bourbon on which the great colonnade of the Louvre (its east front) was being constructed. The company was enlarged by two shares to fifteen shares in June, spent seven weeks from June 24 to August 11 performing at Court at Saint-Germain-en-Laye, earning 14,000 *livres*. *L'Ecole des femmes* was performed at the Palais-Royal December 26. The repertory this year included (besides Molière's own plays among which it seems possible to identify the early farces *Le Médecin volant* and *La Jalousie du barbouillé*) Corneille's *Sertorius*, *Rodogune*, *Héraclius*, *Le Menteur*, and *Cinna*; Scarron's *L'Héritier ridicule, Jodelet ou le Maître valet* and *Dom Japhet d'Arménie;* Thomas Corneille's *Jodelet Prince;* Tristan L'Hermite's *La Mariane;* Rotrou's *La Soeur;* Guérin de Bouscal's *Sanche Pansa;* Prade's *Arsace* and Boyer's *Oropaste*, the two last being new plays. Lully becomes a French subject. Pascal organizes the first public omnibus system in Paris and dies.

1662–64 "La querelle de l'Ecole des femmes."

1663 *L'Ecole des femmes* published March 17. *La Critique de l'Ecole des femmes* performed at the Palais-Royal June 1, published August 7. *L'Impromptu de Versailles* performed during visit to Versailles between October 16 and 21, and at the Palais-Royal November 4. First collected edition of *Les Oeuvres de Monsieur Molier* (sic) in two volumes. Molière advises Racine on composition of his first tragedy, *La Thébaïde*. Pierre Mignard completes his fresco *La Gloire des bienheureux*, on the cupola of the Val-de-Grâce Church.

1663–64 First editions of the *Maximes* of La Rochefoucauld.

1664 *Le Mariage forcé* performed January 29 in the Queen Mother's apartments in the Louvre, the king dancing in the performance; libretto of the ballet published; public performance at the Palais-Royal February 15. Baptism February 28 of Louis, Molière's son born January 19, with Louis XIV as godfather and Henriette d'Angleterre, duchesse d'Orléans, as godmother. *Plaisirs de l'île enchantée* produced at Versailles May 6 to 13, including *La Princesse d'Elide* performed May 8 and three acts of *Tartuffe* performed May 12. After September 24, Molière composes sonnet *A La Mothe Le Vayer sur la mort de son fils*. *La Princesse d'Elide* performed at the Palais-Royal November 9. *Tartuffe*, apparently in five acts, performed at Le Raincy, the Princess Palatine's pleasure house near Paris for the Prince de Condé November 29. "Marché de décors pour *Dom Juan*" agreed by Molière with the painters Jean Simon and Pierre Prat. Two-volume edition of Molière's *Oeuvres* published. Reconstruction of Versailles begun. Molière produces Racine's *La Thébaïde* June 20.

La Fontaine's *Nouvelles en vers* and Perrot d'Ablancourt's *Apophtegemes des Anciens* published.

1665   *Les Plaisirs de l'île enchantée* (containing *La Princesse d'Elide*) published. *Dom Juan* performed at the Palais-Royal. Molière's daughter Esprit-Madeleine baptized August 4 (the future Mme de Montalant); comte de Modène, godfather, and Madeleine Béjart, godmother. At Saint-Germain-en-Laye August 14 Louis XIV assumes protection of Molière's company as "la troupe du Roi au Palais-Royal" and presents it with a *pension* of 6,000 *livres*. *L'Amour médecin* produced at Versailles September 14 and at the Palais-Royal September 22. *Tartuffe* and *L'Amour médecin* performed for Prince de Condé at Le Raincy. Molière writes religious quatrains for La Confrérie de l'Esclavage de Notre-Dame de la Charité, included in an engraving by François Chauveau. Molière produces Racine's *Alexandre-le-Grand* at the Palais-Royal December 4, but Racine removes the production (and the actress Mlle Du Parc) to the rival Hôtel de Bourgogne.

1665–66   The "Querelle des *Imaginaires*"

1666   *L'Amour médecin* published January 15: "il n'est pas nécessaire de vous avertir qu'il y a beaucoup de choses qui dépendent de l'action: on sait bien que les comédies ne sont faites que pour être jouées; et je ne conseille de lire celle-ci qu'aux personnes qui ont des yeux pour découvrir dans la lecture tout le jeu du théâtre" (Molière, *Au lecteur*). *Les Oeuvres de M. Molière* in two vols. published. *Le Misanthrope* performed at the Palais-Royal June 4. *Le Médecin malgré lui* performed at the Palais-Royal August 6. *Le Ballet des Muses* (containing *Mélicerte*, two acts only) performed at Saint-German-en-Laye December 2. *Le Misanthrope* and *Le Médecin malgré lui* published December 24. Fashion for coffee drinking begins in Paris. Death of Anne of Austria (the queen mother). Publication of d'Aubignac's *Les Conseils d'Ariste à Célimène* and Boileau's *Satires* (I through VII).

1667   *La Pastorale comique* performed at Saint-Germain-en-Laye January 5. *Le Sicilien ou l'Amour peintre* performed at Saint-Germain-en-Laye February 9 or 10. "Deux nouvelles entrées de Turcs et de Mores" added to *Le Ballet des Muses* at Saint-Germain-en-Laye for performances February 14 and 16 *(Gazette)*. Rumors of Molière's death from an acute illness in April. *Le Sicilien* performed at the Palais-Royal June 10. *Tartuffe* performed once in public at the Palais-Royal August 5 and again banned; August 11 Archbishop Hardouin of Paris posts notices of excommunication of such as may "représenter, lire ou entendre réciter la susdite comédie", an ecclesiastical sanction apparently challenged at law the same day and in any event lifted by November, though the legal ban on public performance continued. Molière's company produces Corneille's *Attila* March 4: "On a tort de dire en tous lieux /Que ce n'est point leur fait que le jeu sérieux" (Subligny). Racine's *Andromaque* and *Les Plaideurs* are produced at the Hôtel de Bourgogne. Pope Alexandre VII dies. Madame de Montespan becomes the king's mistress.

1667–68   The War of Devolution

1668   *Amphitryon* performed at the Palais-Royal January 13. "Molière surpasse Plaute dans son *Amphitryon*, aussi bien que Térence dans ses autres pièces" (Saint-Evremond). Molière writes sonnet *Au Roi, Sur la conquête de la Franche-Comté* probably in February. *Tartuffe* performed for Prince de Condé at the Hôtel de Condé and again for him at Chantilly September 20. *Amphitryon* published March 5, dedicated to Prince de Condé. *George Dandin* performed July 18 as part of *Le Grand Divertissement royal de Versailles*, and the *intermèdes* for that *comédie-ballet* are published in the program. The doorman at the Palais-Royal is murdered August 19. *L'Avare* is produced September 9 at the Palais-Royal. *George Dandin* is produced at the Palais-Royal November 9. Molière publishes in December *La Gloire du Val de Grâce*. La Fontaine's *Fables* (books one through six) and Scarron's *Oeuvres complètes* in eight volumes are published.

1668–69   *Les Oeuvres de Monsieur de Molière*, Paris: Jean Ribou, vol. 3 (1668), vols. 4 and 5 (1669), are published. Also *Les Nouvelles Oeuvres de Monsieur J. B. P. Molière*,

Paris: Pépinglé, 4 vols., a collected edition including wrong attributions.

1669   *Tartuffe* performed at the Palais-Royal February 5 and published March 23. *Monsieur de Pourceaugnac* performed at Chambord October 6. Jansenist bishops and nuns at Port-Royal accept settlement proposed by Pope Clement IX known as "la Paix de l'Eglise" February 15. Henriette de France dies.

1670   *Les Amants magnifiques* performed at Saint-Germain-en-Laye February 4 as part of *Le Divertissement royal* and the *intermèdes* are published in the program. *Monsieur de Pourceaugnac* published March 3. *Le Bourgeois Gentilhomme* performed at Chambord October 14 and a full descriptive program of the *comédie-ballet* published; performed at the Palais-Royal November 23. Molière produces Corneille's *Tite et Bérénice* at the Palais-Royal November 28. Guilleragues's *Lettres portugaises* published. Jean Poquelin (Molière's father) and Henriette d'Angleterre die. Louis XIV's armies occupy Lorraine.

1671   *Psyché* performed at the Tuileries Palace January 17 and the program published. La Grange notes repairs and modifications of Palais-Royal theatre March 15. *Le Bourgeois Gentilhomme* (text) published March 18. Molière stands as godfather to Jean-Baptiste-Claude Jannequin, son of the actor Rochefort, March 30. *Les Fourberies de Scapin* performed at the Palais-Royal May 24. *Psyché* performed at the Palais-Royal July 24. *La Comtesse d'Escarbagnas* performed December 2 at Saint-Germain-en-Laye as part of *Le Ballet des Ballets.*

1672   Madeleine Béjart dies February 17. *Les Femmes savantes* performed at the Palais-Royal March 11. Lully secures in March from Pierre Perrin the patent for opera in Paris, severely limiting the use of music and dance in other theatrical performances and ending the long collaboration with Molière on *comédies-ballets* for Court performances begun in 1661 with *Les Fâcheux;*Molière and company object, with limited success. Molière takes communion at Easter at Saint-Germain-l'Auxerrois. *Les Femmes savantes* published December 10. Louis XIV begins Dutch War, invades the Netherlands in June, begins the systematic persecution of Huguenots leading in 1685 to the Revocation of the Edict of Nantes.

1673   *Le Malade imaginaire* performed at the Palais-Royal February 10. Molière is stricken while completing the role of Argan at the fourth performance February 17, taken to his home in the nearby rue de Richelieu where he dies the same evening of a pulmonary hemorrhage. Lully takes over and refurbishes the Palais-Royal theatre, produces a series of seventeen grand operas there before his death in 1687, beginning with *Cadmus et Hermione*. Survivors of Molière's troupe are merged with the Théâtre du Marais and assigned to a new theatre on the left bank, the Théâtre Guénégaud, rue Mazarine, a reconstructed *jeu de paume*.

1680   Théâtre Guénégaud merged with Hôtel de Bourgogne to form La Comédie Française.

1682   *Les Oeuvres de Monsieur de Molière*, Paris: Denys Thierry, 8 vols., edited by La Grange and Vivot, are published. Volumes seven and eight contain previously unpublished works.

Comedy in Context: Essays on Molière

I
Comedy and Romance
in the *dépits amoureux*

Dépit amoureux is the title of one of Molière's early five-act comedies in verse. It is also that of his translation of Horace's ode *Donec gratus eram tibi*, incorporated in the third *intermède* of *Les Amants magnifiques*. But the phrase is probably better known in connection with the "scènes de brouille et de raccommodement" between lovers in *Tartuffe* and *Le Bourgeois Gentilhomme*. These scenes are commonly regarded as accessory to the main action of the comedies in which they occur. The late Antoine Adam remarks on *Le Bourgeois Gentilhomme*, for instance:

> La matière manque tellement que Molière recommence pour la troisième fois [*sic*] la scène du double dépit amoureux, qu'il avait déjà reprise en 1667 pour meubler le vide du IIe acte de *Tartuffe*.[1]

One also reads, in his edition of Molière's *Œuvres*, the observation by Eugène Despois that the title of the early comedy "ne convient nullement au fond de la pièce et ne s'applique qu'à ces scènes de *dépit amoureux*" (Act IV, scenes 3 and 4) which have no basis in the Italian comedy—Secchi's *L'Interesse*—from which so much of Molière's play is adapted, "et simple accessoire dans la pièce française."[2]

As far as the early comedy is concerned, this accessory is—with supporting lines—the only part of the play to have survived the eighteenth century in performances at the Comédie-Française. Its formal qualities—construction, rhythm, and movement—are appreciated by Adam (III, 258), whatever his reservations about reuse. When Despois states this early *dépit* "n'appartient qu'à Molière; et Molière y est déjà tout entier" (ed. cit., I, 381), his enthusiasm is clear, though one could wish he had researched the first

3

statement more carefully. It seems possible to amplify the second.

For we lack any sustained effort to explore in depth the sorts of dramatic appeal Molière sought to make in his *dépit amoureux* scenes. Why, precisely, did he include the first *dépit amoureux* in his adaptation of *L'Interesse?* Since he repeated it—or, more accurately, recast and varied it—in two of his greatest comedies, can we be sure that this was merely or even mainly to fill in? Should we not rather ask what sort of dramatic impression the scenes make in the different contexts? What they contribute to a performance? How they guide responses? What indeed can Molière have hoped to achieve dramatically in these few minutes? What precisely happens in a *dépit amoureux?* Is it always the same thing? And what do we learn, by all the complex means of theatrical communication, from a *dépit amoureux?* What effects are sought? What tones and associations are created? And what are those that Molière seems deliberately to have excluded?

Answers to such questions, to the extent that answers are possible in the performing arts, seem vital to any critical appreciation of the scenes themselves and their relation to the plays in which they occur.

Despois's view that the first *dépit amoureux* belongs exclusively to Molière was formulated in full awareness of his debt to the ode of Horace later translated and of the general currency of Terence's idea, "Amantium irae, amoris integratio." But it seems to have escaped general notice that for the basic idea of the *dépit amoureux* as a dramatized test of love Molière had the specific example of Corneille's *La Galerie du Palais*, Act II, scenes 6 to 8, in which Célidée sounds out Lysandre's true feelings for her by means of a "dédain forcé": "Ma feinte éprouvera si son amour est vraie." Célidée counts upon Lysandre's reaction to clarify her own feelings for him. Nor perhaps should we neglect the somewhat analogous scene in Corneille's *La Suite du Menteur*, Act V, scene 3, to which the conflicting emotions of Dorante and Mélisse give a rhythm comparable to that of a *dépit amoureux*, while at the dénouement of that comedy

Philiste comments to Mélisse (pertinently for our argument):

> J'ai voulu voir vos pleurs pour mieux voir votre flamme,
> Et la crainte a trahi les secrets de votre âme.

Affected disdain precipitates the title scenes of Molière's *Dépit amoureux*. As in other comparable scenes in Molière's comedies, we see the lovers together for the first time. Eraste has been jealous of Lucile from the beginning of the play, while Lucile had protested perhaps too much in Act II, scene 3, that she would prefer Valère, later rejected. It is only in the *dépit amoureux* of Act IV that Lucile and Eraste together confirm—to each other and to the audience—that they do indeed love each other; and it is the affected *dépit* that reveals the extent to which they are genuinely *amoureux*.

A principal function of the *dépit amoureux* thus appears to be the dramatization of a serious commitment to each other on the part of the lovers, a commitment that can stand this test; and this is no less true of *Tartuffe* and *Le Bourgeois Gentilhomme* than it is of *Dépit amoureux*. It is true also of *La Galerie du Palais*, where the resolution of the *dépit* is deferred to Act V, scene 4:

> Lysandre . . .
> Que j'aime ces dédains qui finissent ainsi!
> Célidée
> Et pour l'amour de toi, que je les aime aussi!

This French example in an author well known to Molière does not obviate the vexed question of the relation of his *dépits amoureux* to *commedia dell'arte*. The influence—suggested in the eighteenth century by Luigi Riccoboni and by Cailhava—of the scenario *Gli Sdegni amorosi* and other scenarios in the *commedia* tradition is rejected by Despois, on the sensible grounds that the analogies are insufficiently precise and in any case involve dramatic commonplaces (ed. cit., I, 384 ff.). Vito Pandolfi in fact lists three scenarios with the title *(Gli) Sdegni Amorosi*, none of which seem promising for our present purpose.[3]

Of more interest is the *Sdegno e pace* dialogue cited by

Perrucci in 1699 to illustrate the sort of material *innamorati* might memorize in order to enhance moments of an improvised performance. The following lines from the beginning and near the end of this dialogue—published in French in 1950 by Gustave Attinger—suggest its symmetry and high stylization:

> Lui. Eloigne-toi
> Elle. Disparais
> Lui. de mes yeux,
> Elle. loin de ma présence,
> Lui. Furie au visage céleste!
> Elle. Démon à masque d'amour!
> Lui. Que je maudis
> Elle. Que je déteste
> Lui. le jour où je t'admirai!
> Elle. l'instant où je t'adorai!
>   .   .   .
> Lui. L'espérance trompeuse me pousse . . .
> Elle. Ta beauté m'engage . . .
> Lui. à te découvrir fidèle.
> Elle. à ne pas te trouver coupable.
> Lui. Tu mens, car je ne le fus pas!
> Elle. Tu te trompes, car je me vante de l'avoir toujours été!
> Lui. Et ton amour pour d'autres?
> Elle. Et ton penchant pour une autre femme?
> Lui. Tu te trompes!
> Elle. On t'a trahi!
> Lui. Je t'aime!
> Elle. Je t'agrée!
> Lui. Je t'adore!
> Elle. Je t'idolâtre![4]

These fragments hardly show, however, the extent to which the genius of the passage is in the movement from irritation and recrimination to hesitation, then to guarded and conditional declaration, renewed recrimination, and a final reconciliation.

Striking too is the abstractness of the dialogue, the quasi-pastoral isolation of love from any social and economic factors that might dilute it and from any coarseness that might contaminate it. With the implied grace and beauty of the actors, the spectator's emotions are opened to romance. At the same time the dialogue is comic, probably in a variety of ways. Comic (and not *ridicules*, as Duchartre suggests); comic, mindful of Mic's view, rightly endorsed by Attinger, that "l'emploi des amoureux était *grave*."[5] On my reading the romance related to the *emploi grave* is not incompatible with laughter on a variety of levels. Doubtless at the beginning of the *dépit* it involves some superiority feelings, from above the vexation, together with awareness of incongruity: *innamorati* who make war, not love. Perhaps too, depending on the case, laughter already depends upon the consciousness of a masquerade, of the incompatibility of each lover's deep feelings and affected manner, and beyond that of the incompatibility of our natures in which the sincerest love is never quite free of vexation and spite: an incompatibility accepted joyfully for the love, and not tragically rejected for the spite.

Almost certainly the emotional balance changes with the lover's hesitations:

> Lui. Je ne sais ce qui me retient!
> Elle. Une force inconnue m'arrête!
> Lui. Mais, vois-tu, ce n'est pas l'amour.
> Elle. Sois sûr que ce n'est pas l'affection.

Depending within a certain range on interpretation, the discrepancy between words and manner must be heightened, so that there is more comedy of incongruity. But it seems to me that superiority feelings will have diminished, making way for laughter that is not derisive, but sympathetic: as when one asks, isn't that just like lovers? and just like ourselves? For we laugh without derision sometimes at what fulfills expectations. Nor does such fulfillment preclude the laughter of surprise at the speed with which hesitation follows renunciation, since the surprise—like the sense of incongruity—is related to the immediate context of recrimination, whereas the sense of fulfillment arises from underlying expectations concerning *innamorati*, and love itself.

I doubt whether much is left toward the end of the scene of any feelings of superiority, but the erotic appeal is stronger and more direct and with it a more intense sense of fulfilment and a more sympathetic involvement with the lovers. Though neither surprise nor incongruity seem to me to have disappeared entirely, the main level of appeal must be a sense of rightness and of well-being, of an ideal attained, an ideal full of romance but wide open to the laughter of well-being, of joy in life. Such a dialogue would stand out in the context of a scenario like a love duet in Italian opera, and if we compare it with the love duet in Act I of Donizetti's *Lucìa di Lammermoor*, it has something of the expansiveness of emotional appeals that makes the latter so powerful. But the phrases are shorter, and there is no shadow of external threat like that cast by the eavesdropping in *Lucìa*. Above all, the reconciliation foreshadows the symbolic marriages of comic dénouements in which the reconciliation not only suggests renewal, rebirth, a new life in the spiritual sense, but also new life, regeneration, in the biological sense, confidence and hope in the future based on a tested commitment.

Though this dialogue of *Sdegno e pace* probably shows the spirit of Molière in *commedia dell'arte* rather than the reverse, research might find a *commedia* precedent—perhaps in the dialogue of *Sdegni placati* listed among Domenico Bruni's *Dialoghi scenici* for *innamorati* in an undated, but probably early seventeenth-century, manuscript in the Biblioteca Burcardo, Rome (Pandolfi, II, 47). However, the community of inspiration is more important. For the comedy of disdainful, jealous, angry, or quarrelsome and yet romantic lovers, also features in the work of other great European dramatists deeply influenced by *commedia* between the Renaissance and the French Revolution: Beatrice and Benedick in *Much Ado About Nothing*, Lélio and La Comtesse in Marivaux's first *Surprise de l'amour*, Goldoni's *Gl'Innamorati*. . . .

The foregoing remarks on the *Sdegno e pace* raise questions relevant to the *dépit amoureux* concerning sensibility, deep-seated cultural attitudes and assumptions connected with the quality of love that stands the test. They also venture aesthetic judgments concerning the style and tones in which those cultural values are dramatized and projected, the manner of aesthetic appeal to an assumed or shared or provoked sensibility. The value shifts in recent years in every area of sexual morality and theatrical decorum may have made some of Molière's stylized conventions like the *dépit amoureux* seem more artificial and placed barriers between the ideal of love they express and the theatregoer or reader of today. But these same shifts have also disclosed latent values in his work which the new distance shows up in sharper relief. This is as true in some ways of the other great comedies mentioned above as it is of Molière's *dépits amoureux* and the cited *Sdegno e pace*. But the remaining points I wish to make about the sensibility reflected in the *dépits amoureux* and their aesthetic evaluation—though closely related to the general conception of the lover roles—can best be made through analysis of the scenes themselves in comparison or contrast with other specific expressions of love in the theatre.

The following remarks concern Molière's lovers. That is, the masters. In *Dépit amoureux* the lover's tiff and reconciliation is followed by a parallel, or rather burlesque, tiff between Marinette and Gros-René, that hero of farce. In *Le Bourgeois Gentilhomme* the burlesque *dépit amoureux* of Nicole and Covielle is skillfully interwoven with that of Lucile and Cléonte, giving it a new and original quaternary rhythm. Such doubling of scenes is a characteristic device of *commedia dell'arte*, and one which Molière exploits to different effects elsewhere.

In *Dépit amoureux* and *Le Bourgeois Gentilhomme* the effect of this doubling is not only to provide a broader humor, but also to underscore important differences between the lovers' language and vision and the servants', as illustrated by these parallel lines from the scene leading to the *dépit amoureux* proper in *Le Bourgeois Gentilhomme* (Act II, scene 9):

Cléonte. Tant de larmes que j'ai versées à ses genoux!
Covielle. Tant de seaux d'eau que j'ai tirés au puits pour elle!
Cléonte. Tant d'ardeur que j'ai fait paraître à la chérir plus que moi-même!
Covielle. Tant de chaleur que j'ai soufferte à tourner la broche à sa place!

It is not difficult to see that Cléonte's vocabulary excludes buffoonery while opening hearts to romance and the wish fulfillment associated with pastoral love (pastoral lovers wept copiously while they burned). At the same time the regret for tears shed, unconvincingly expressed in the very home of Lucile, turns the pastoral romance to comedy—not contaminated, but high-lighted by the low burlesque of Covielle's *seaux d'eau*, *chaleur*, and *broche*, which however exclude high romance in his own role. The parallelism of this dialogue intensifies the comic while heightening the romance in Cléonte's role by means of a structured differentiation. This is a dramatic technique later exploited by Marivaux, notably in the double disguises and parallel courtship scenes in *Le Jeu de l'amour et du hasard*. The qualities there revealed by the disguises markedly heighten the romantic appeal of the roles of Silvia and Dorante. The coarseness particularly of Arlequin sets off the refinement of their feelings and manners in sharp relief while contributing to the general comic atmosphere. As La Rochefoucauld reflected nearer to Molière's time: "Un honnête homme peut être amoureux comme un fou, mais non pas comme un sot."[6]

That even in *Dépit amoureux* Molière is already aiming at a peculiar blend of romance and comedy by the burlesque contrast of Gros-René's tiff with Marinette in Act IV, scene 4, is confirmed by analysis of his adaptation of Secchi's *L'Interesse*. There is no doubt that *Dépit amoureux* shares the Italian comedy's novelistic atmosphere. Molière retains transvestism and secret marriage. In *L'Interesse* Pandolfo had wagered a large sum that his pregnant wife would have a son; and in order to win that wager even when a daughter is born, he had brought up the latter as a boy. Molière substitutes a rich uncle's will; and, remarks Despois, "il a compliqué encore cette donnée, déjà assez singulière, en ajoutant à ce travestissement de la jeune fille une substitution d'enfant" (ed. cit., I, 382). This is not the only case in which Molière redoubles the implausible to make it more theatrically acceptable, and it is significant that the child-swapping does not merely intensify the novelistic atmosphere, but also protects Lucile from contamination by an ambiguous situation. This is part of a characteristic purification and idealization of Molière's lover roles, especially that of his *jeunes premières*. Despois remarks also that Molière "a supprimé heureusement les grossièretés les plus intolérables de l'original," containing "des indécences . . . dans le rôle même de l'héroïne, qui défient toute citation" (ed. cit., I, 382). But his approval of what Molière had done in the way of the *bienséances* did not lead him to analyze what this means in terms of cultural and dramatic values.

Nor can such analysis be compassed by dismissing the *bienséances* as inhibitions, though this, for better or for worse, is what to some extent they were. For we know that Molière repeatedly shocked the community in which he worked in a number of ways, and this can only mean that he deferred selectively to the *bienséances*, as for instance when he allows Dorine—but not Mariane—to pronounce the low word *roter* in *Tartuffe*, explaining in the first edition: "C'est une servante qui parle" (Act I, scene 2). A host of further examples, in *Dépit amoureux* and elsewhere, could be adduced to show that—within limits stricter than those prevailing in European capitals and the United States since the late 1960s—Molière observed the *bienséances* he chose and for the effects he desired.

Depois was shocked by four lines of Gros-René's dispute with Marinette (ed. cit., I, 496):

> Gros-René: J'oubliois d'avant-hier ton morceau de fromage:
>   Tiens. Je voudrois pouvoir rejeter le potage
>   Que tu me fis manger, pour n'avoir rien à toi.
> Marinette: Je n'ai point maintenant de tes lettres sur moi;
>   Mais j'en ferai du feu jusques à la dernière.
> Gros-René: Et des tiennes tu sais ce que j'en saurai faire?

And he applies here Voltaire's commentary on Corneille's *La Suite du Menteur*, Act V, scene 1:

> Ces scènes où les valets font l'amour à l'imitation de leurs maîtres, sont enfin proscrites du théâtre avec beaucoup de raison. Ce n'est qu'une parodie basse et dégoûtante des premiers personnages.

One can imagine the sort of gesture that must have accompanied Gros-René's last line. But Despois was surely wrong to accept that this tiff is only a parody. For it is also a contrast, a negative outline, a *dépit* devoid of *honnêteté*, one exploiting the comedy of gifts returned at levels Voltaire and Despois did not wish to explore, but which for Molière's public must have helped characterize the lovers and situate the romance of the preceding scene.

For this servants' quarrel dramatizes a quite different sort of love from that of the masters. The successive *dépits* disclose aspects of different sorts of relationship. Obviously, the bracelet returned by Eraste belongs to a higher style than the cheese returned by Gros-René and the soup he offers to regurgitate. Obviously, Gros-René's lines are a parody of Eraste's, and the idea of vomit is provocative. But bracelet and soup symbolize different relationships. Eraste and Lucile return only symbols of affection, symbols incidentally having associations of class and wealth (a diamond and an agate seal as well as the bracelet and love letters), but no connection with the appetites fed on cheese and soup, which are carefully excluded. It is not simply that the *bienséances* have been applied more strictly to the lovers than to the servants, a relationship has been dramatized at a more idealized level of invention, in which emetic and scatological humor is not appropriate. Such humor belongs rather to the depiction of a love relationship imagined largely in terms of biological appetites.

There are of course many levels on which love relationships can be dramatized, just as there are many sorts of love relationship, ranging from the "platonic" to the pornographic. Robert Joffrey's ballet *Astarte* (New York City Center Joffrey Ballet, 1967) combines strobe lighting, complementary film, pop music, and the dancing skill of classical ballet to project a high positive evaluation of the act of love, strongly erotic, but transmogrified, aesthetically recreated. As the couple dancing—at any rate in the autumn of 1970—were racially mixed, the act of love in *Astarte* is also politicized, offering a symbolic ideal of mutual acceptance to a racially mixed and divided community. But the erotic and the political are so strong that they exclude romance, doubtless intentionally.

What strikes me in this example—which could be multiplied with reference say to the naked dancing of *Oh! Calcutta*, to films of the *He and She* (1970) type—is not so much the greater freedom of expression, though this obviously is important, as the desire to express something altogether different from the sort of love that passes the test of Molière's *dépits amoureux* and which had a European following for three centuries and more.

It is not that eroticism is lacking in Molière's lover roles, or generally in the theatre of his time. For my suggestion of an erotic aspect of the *Sdegno e pace* applies, *mutatis mutandis*, to the *dépits amoureux*. Eroticism was in fact one of Molière's Jansenist enemy Pierre Nicole's principal objections to theatre as a whole. In the *Traité de la comédie* (written chiefly against Corneille's tragedies, probably in the 1650s, but published in 1667 after a "querelle du théâtre" in which Molière was involved), Nicole objects particularly to the refined lovers in theatre, since these by their refinement cause the scrupulous Christian to lower his guard and make what he calls sin more attractive by decorous presentation. Even the framework of anticipated marriage seems dangerous to him in the context of the love relationships presented by the theatre of his time, because from his point of view even marriage does not excuse the sort of erotic urges such lovers arouse.[7]

Yet eroticism is clearly not the dominant appeal of any seventeenth-century French theatre *amoureux* known to me. In the *dépits amoureux* that is in part because eroticism is not emphasized dramatically, and in part because the emphasis is placed elsewhere: on innocence and purity, on mutual sympathy, and—since uncertainty and jealousy feature in every *dépit*—particularly on fidelity. Though sexual pleasure is tacitly implied, or implicitly anticipated, as Nicole complains, this is always within a context of commitment, of engagement, the permanency of which is symbolized by marriage.

This convention of marriage, however, as Nicole saw,

has little to do with the Christian sacrament, let alone Jansenist views of it. Obviously it could be a mere pretext for portrayal of unmarried love, though Molière sails very close to that wind when he wishes, as in *Le Mariage forcé*, *George Dandin*, and *Amphitryon*. On the other hand, Molière's comedy clearly rejects abuse of the cruder forms of the secular *mariage de convenance*, even if some of the marriages seem to symbolize a reconciliation of class interests where gaps are not too great: Cléonte (a *noble de robe*) and Lucile in *Le Bourgeois Gentilhomme*, Henriette (another *bourgeoise*) and Clitandre (a *gentilhomme*) in *Les Femmes savantes*. Yet it certainly is also distinct from the tradition of courtly love to the extent that courtly love is adulterous. What remains is a secular ideal, rooted in pastoral, but more aware of the economic and social facts of life: a monogamistic ideal in which marriage is much more a contract between individuals than a sacrament, an acceptable framework in the right circumstances for a relationship, spiritual and physical, whose chief values are derived neither from the teachings of the Church on marriage nor from the immediate class and economic structures of contemporary French society. In the presentation of love leading to such an ideal marriage, the *bienséances* undoubtedly play an important part. But however restrictive they may later have been felt, here they are a convention that corresponds to—and should not conceal—a cherished, long-lived, influential and rather attractive ideal.

The *dépit amoureux* as a test for love and marriage can be made to disclose more clearly its essential characteristics by comparison with the dramatic exchange of kisses, which in Molière's youth was an established symbol of mutual affection on the French stage, as of course it has been on many Western stages before and since, e.g. in *Romeo and Juliet* and countless Hollywood film romances of the vintage years. But from Molière's point of view, the kiss presented a number of problems in addition to the moral one of the effect on the actors themselves of such sex play.[8] To begin with, a kiss dramatizes sexual interest to any desired degree better than it dramatizes commitment (though this can be made part of the convention, as in the vintage years of Hollywood). Or so one might deduce from Corneille's comedy *Mélite*, performed around 1629–30, published in 1633. There is no need to assume that Molière knew precisely how many directions for kisses between lovers disappear in successive editions until by 1660 not one of the thirteen kisses indicated in the first edition remains. The revision of *Mélite* evidences the shift in decorum against the exchange of kisses between lovers on the Paris stage, and it is well known that no kisses are ever exchanged between lovers in Molière or in Racine.

Yet other equally important facts connected with stage kisses in seventeenth-century French theatre have been neglected. It is difficult to tell to what extent the kisses in *Mélite* were originally intended to be frankly erotic. But clearly they do not prove fidelity, for many are exchanged between Cloris and Philandre, who later betrays her. It is clear too that when Tirsis interrupts one of their kisses in the last scene of Act I, jesting: "Voyla traitter l'amour justement bouche à bouche," eroticism associated with the kiss is turned by Tirsis's jest *en raillerie*, toward playful comedy and not toward high romance.

Such facts have a particular significance when assessed in connection with Molière's selective deference to the *bienséances*, and in particular with his use of burlesque kisses for low comedy: kisses received by Vadius "pour l'amour du grec," kisses proffered in *Le Malade imaginaire* by Thomas Diafoirus to Béline and by Béline to Argan. . . . These kisses are all given—not exchanged—by grotesque characters in situations of low comedy, and their comedy arises precisely from their lack of eroticism and their even more explicit lack of romance. A Sganarelle can make a pass at a Jacqueline, "en voulant toucher les tetons de la Nourrice" *(Le Médecin malgré lui)*. Tartuffe demands on stage *réalités* and *d'assurés témoignages* in his adulterous courtship of Elmire (Act IV, scene 5), and there is rich comedy both in the circumstances of this test of the hypocrite and in his own treacherous quest for authenticity. But no authentic lover in Molière ever makes such a demand, although the coherence of several comedies depends upon the sincerity of the lovers; that is, upon Molière's having found dramatic symbolism capable of conveying such an impression of commitment.

In his lovers, then, and particularly in the *dépits amoureux*, Molière is obviously seeking a different register from the burlesque kisses of a Béline or the amorous passes of a Sganarelle or a Tartuffe, and not just deferring to *bienséances:* a different level of comedy with other associations, stylistic and emotive harmonics blending other tones and overtones. As in the dramatic pastoral (*Aminta, Il Pastor fido, Les Bergeries* of Racan), in the *dépits amoureux* the erotic is diffused in the romantic and linked to an ideal marriage as indicated above. The *bienséances* are vital to the peculiar blend of sensuality and romance combined in this ideal, because they help to elevate it, to mark its uniquely human quality (in contrast with the bestial, ever part of the immediate background of pastoral), to guarantee its durability, and to show the lovers' respect for themselves and for each other, measurable in terms of social values and other human relations.

In terms of such values, it is significant that each of Molière's three *dépits amoureux* represents a justification as well as a test. Lucile in *Dépit amoureux* is suspected of having accepted Valère as a lover in all senses. No kiss or sex play could testify so well as anger to her innocence. When Mariane meets Valère in *Tartuffe*, doubt exists in both minds as to the status of their engagement, since word has reached Valère that Orgon has ordered Mariane to marry Tartuffe. In such circumstances, a kiss might show passion, but at some cost to the romance by which Mariane embodies an ideal of anticipated fidelity in love and marriage. In *Le Bourgeois Gentilhomme*, Cléonte is jealously suspicious of Dorante's visits to Lucile's father's house. He has not yet asked for her hand, and her other loyalties include an aunt "qui veut à toute force, que la seule approche d'un homme déshonore une fille" (Act III, scene 10).

In each of these cases kissing or other overt sex play is inappropriate, not simply because the *bienséances* preclude it, but because kisses do not carry so rich a charge of dramatic symbolism as a lovers' quarrel, or a compatible comic tone. A century later Beaumarchais could allow Figaro to kiss Suzanne—briefly—in the opening scene of *Le Mariage de Figaro*, where not only is the wedding imminent, but the characters belong to different *emplois*. But how quickly Beaumarchais—whose *parades* are salacious when he wishes—interrupts the kiss and diffuses the erotic in laughter for reasons no less pertinent to our argument than to the themes of his comedy: "Et qu'en dirait demain mon mari?" asks Suzanne. In these circumstances, flirtatious teasing can imply fidelity while arousing laughter. But there is less romance than in Molière's lovers, or in those of *Le Barbier de Séville* reflecting the same tradition, and a far more practically defined prospect of practical marriage. Molière's lovers, less central to his conception, are more pastoral and more abstract.

In other respects, however, the first scene of *Figaro* functions like the *dépits amoureux* in *Tartuffe* and *Le Bourgeois Gentilhomme*, by establishing a basis—moral and human—for judging the Count's plans for Suzanne in terms of the theatrical "droit du seigneur." By dramatizing from the beginning and on a level of high romance the serious nature of the lovers' commitment to each other—and thus establishing a suitable alternative to the marriage plans of Orgon and of M. Jourdain for their daughters—the *dépits amoureux* furnish a touchstone for assaying the moral extravagance of the bigot and the snob. A dramatic touchstone, both in the scope for non-literary theatrical resources (mime, movement, symbolic gesture) and in their quite different functions in the rhythm of performances.

For the *dépit amoureux* averts a potentially tragic *malentendu* in the early comedy and lifts the imbroglio it resolves toward high romance. In *Tartuffe* it relaxes tension and restores morale *after* Orgon's refusal, while in *Le Bourgeois Gentilhomme* it helps lay the ground for the *coup de théâtre* of M. Jourdain's refusal. The broader comic effects of the integrated double *dépit* are appropriate to this timing in the action, as is the more stylized movement of the two couples back and forth across the whole stage fully exploiting the theatrical medium of the *comédie-ballet* in its most synthesized form. The judgment that such a scene represents mere padding neglects the theatrical nature of Molière's writing and the relation of the idiom he chose to the moral content of his theatre. I might repeat in this connection that those who feel

> that Molière is simply filling in with these scenes . . . , have never suggested how he might have dramatized more economically the sincerity of Cléonte's affections for Lucile (showing he is not a fortune hunter) and at the same time make it comic.[9]

For, in conclusion, the *dépits amoureux* are also comic, properly played for laughs: and it is this dimension that sets them—like the related *Sdegno e pace* examined above—apart from pastoral lovers, who voice similar aspirations, but without any of the quality of vision conferred by Molière's comic perspective. Lovers in the pastoral tradition are not parodied, but more ambivalently depicted in a wider scheme of things. In such a perspective Molière has ordered mime of feigned disdain and injured innocence, of youthful doubts about the other's integrity and certainty about one's own. He deploys an angle of vision capable of depicting recrimination that shows affection, and love that teeters—but not heroically or perilously or desperately—toward scorn. Here the inherent impurity of love is not portrayed as dangerously destructive, like that of *Andromaque*. Nor is Molière content, like La Rochefoucauld, simply to acknowledge the impurity:

> S'il y a un amour pur et exempt du mélange des autres passions, c'est celui qui est caché au fond du cœur, et que nous ignorons nous-mêmes
>
> (ed. cit., 69: cf. 68).

Transparent hesitations and quick reversals are gladly embraced by his comic vision. Capitulations come without shame; and reconciliations, without regret. Far from degrading the lovers, or contaminating the high romance, the comedy of the *dépit amoureux* combines the wish fulfilling idealism of pastoral love with an ironic perception of its limitations. Quite apart from the *bienséances* it is difficult to see by what other dramatic symbolism Molière could have achieved so much.

2
Comic Images

This essay responds to a problem of practical criticism. Some of the scenes of Molière's comedies—passages in the text, moments in the action—which have made me laugh or smile, openly or inwardly, seem also to call for reflection on specific moral issues—that is to say, issues involving the quality of life and of human relations. Such scenes often culminate in or include statements or action (or both together) of special density, particularly in Molière's later comedies. The statements are characteristically absurd; the action, farcical or burlesque, which is why I venture the designation "comic images." Such images would certainly include statements by Alceste and by George Dandin, beatings in *Le Médecin malgré lui* and *Amphitryon*, Harpagon's capture of himself at the end of Act IV of *L'Avare*, Le Philosophe's attack on the masters in *Le Bourgeois gentilhomme*, mime by Argan and part of the advice Argan receives from Toinette in her burlesque doctor's disguise in the last act of *Le Malade imaginaire*. Many of these moments, or the scenes in which they occur, have embarrassed warm admirers of Molière for whom the farcical seems *ipso facto* frivolous. On the other hand, the significance of some of these same moments has been extolled by other critics, but interpreted as pathetic or tragic.

Authority exists for both attitudes. In the *Critique of Judgment*, Kant observes that "that which arouses laughter affords no satisfaction to the understanding and is merely a 'play with aesthetical ideas or representations of the understanding through which ultimately *nothing is thought*.'"[1] An assumption of this nature often colors attitudes toward laughter, and thus toward comedy. Specifically, some such assumption would appear to underlie not only the negative evaluations of the farcical aspects of Molière's theatre by J. Arnavon and G. Michaut, but also René Bray's positive acclaim of Molière's showmanship at the expense of what he disparagingly dismisses as "une prétendue fonction morale inventée par la critique."[2] It is well known, however, that in his conversations with Eckermann, Goethe called Harpagon's relations with his son tragic to a high degree, while anyone teaching Molière knows how frequently inexperienced readers resort to words like *pathetic* and *tragic* to express a legitimate concern for problems raised by Arnolphe and Alceste, Harpagon and Argan: roles which we know to have been laughed at on Molière's own stage, when he acted them. For "il y a beaucoup de choses qui dépendent de l'action," Molière wrote in the "Au lecteur" of *L'Amour médecin*, which he hoped would be read by people "qui ont des yeux pour découvrir dans la lecture tout le jeu du théâtre."

Conciliation of these divergent attitudes does not appear to lie—as admirers of Beckett and Ionesco might be tempted to suppose—in the concept of tragic farce, though Robert Hirsch's brilliant new interpretation of Sosie's terror in the first act of *Amphitryon* at the Comédie-Française in the 1967–8 season clearly showed the theatrical viability of such a reading. For everything we know about the hierarchy of styles and the separation of genres in seventeenth-century French literary theory and practice, as well as contemporary testimony on Molière's own acting style, argues against the historical validity of an interpretation which implies a protest over the human condition itself. This seems entirely lacking in Molière's comedy, where deviations are ridiculed within a framework implying rather a joyful acceptance of human limitations.

In his article "Molière's Theory of Comedy"[3] Will Moore proposes a more promising scholarly approach. Facing the partial truths and obvious flaws in the attitudes indicated above, he derives mainly from the *Lettre sur la comédie de l'Imposteur* (1667)[4] a theory which would preserve both the significance of the controversial scenes and their comic implications:

> In Molière's view it would seem that the most disastrous of human errors, errors we might wish to call tragic, may be

envisaged by the mind as comic. That this view of things often induces or sparks off laughter, no sane person would deny. But to assume that anything which does not provoke laughter is not comic is contrary to our text [the *Lettre*] and is perhaps the worst of all misunderstandings which have bedevilled Molière studies. . . . We consider lies and deceptions tragic when great, and comic when small or "not serious." Molière's language knows nothing of this distinction. It suggests that the difference between tragic and comic consists not in the gravity of the case but in the angle of perception.[5]

The hypothesis that the angle of perception of our scenes is comic, and their implications serious, seems to offer a reasonable prospect of conciliating divergent interpretations too important to be neglected. But Moore has achieved this conciliation only at the cost of separating the *comic* from the *funny*, a distinction which leaves a gap between stagecraft and literary implications reflected in comments like the following: "An actor might make me laugh as he said this, 'Le Seigneur Harpagon est de tous les humains l'humain le moins humain', but the statement itself is poetic, deep, suggestive, serious".[6] Since the provocation of laughter is viewed as distinct from "the statement itself," our problem really returns through another door. This is apparent in the invitation to look for the comic in *L'Avare* beneath the laughter and "apart from the amusing." Or in the view that George Dandin's line "J'enrage d'avoir tort lorsque j'ai raison" is "more than funny (if indeed it is funny at all), it is poetic, symbolizing a human position, the position in which what is right and expected just does not happen."[7] Unless once again we are assuming that the funny is by its very nature insignificant, it is not clear why such lines cannot be taken as both funny and symbolic, an approach which would lead us toward a closer definition of their poetic quality.

Thus, suggestive as it is, "Molière's Theory of Comedy" fails to solve a basic aspect of our problem. Different actors guide their publics to different reactions to the same text, and we cannot preempt future decisions as to the tone of delivery. Such decisions can only be taken in the light of given theatrical circumstances.

Comedy and tragedy consist, however, not in incidents or in statements or events, but in the perception of such incidents, and a dramatic text is designed to guide such perception either directly (when it is read) or through the mediation of performers. When an incident in life is called funny or comic, properly speaking a statement is being made, not about the incident itself, but about the way it is perceived; when an incident in a play is called comic, however, although the statement may have a similar status, it may also designate a literary intention, the angle into which perception is guided, the particular sort of emotional response sought by the playwright with the sympathetic collaboration of performers, or in the case of readers without them.

To a problem of aesthetics, we require a solution which does not divorce the significance of a dramatic statement from the mode of its delivery. If, therefore, a distinction is to be made between the *funny* and the *comic*, the distinction should be one of quality, not one of category. It should be a normative distinction, according to which one would no more argue that every incident that may seem funny is properly called comic in the literary sense than one would claim—loose colloquial and journalistic usage notwithstanding—that every incident which may seem sad or terrible or piteous is tragic. Granted then that *comic* as a term of dramatic criticism may have a normative value, implying an intellectual awareness and complexity not always discoverable in what is found merely funny, it is none the less important that such complexity—such seriousness—is achieved within the same angle of perception and without prejudice to the funny. The comic implies serious laughter—σπουδο-γέλοιος.

By taking the comic, not as distinct from, but as a more sophisticated form of the funny, we can resolve some of Moore's hesitations. It is unnecessary to doubt that Dandin's "J'enrage d'avoir tort lorsque j'ai raison" is meant to be funny simply because we feel it to be more than funny. The laughter invoked rather suggests the register in which this funny—this absurd—statement is also poetic. It indicates the mode in which the statement symbolizes not merely the position in which "what is right" does not happen, but all the relativity of any individual's assumptions as to what in a given social context constitutes right or wrong. Nor are Dandin's words a mere statement. In context, and with the invitation to comic mime of irrelevant anger which Molière's stagecraft has written into the line ("J'enrage . . ."), Dandin's statement has both the complexity and the tonality of what I have called the comic image.

But Dandin is not the only character in Molière to mime anger when expectations are upset, to mention only the cuff Mme Pernelle gives Flipote in the opening scene of *Tartuffe*, Orgon's fury at Dorine's opposition to his plan to make Mariane Tartuffe's bride in Act II, scene 2 ("Ah! vous êtes dévot, et vous vous emportez!"), and Oronte's fury at a sonnet scorned in the first act of *Le Misanthrope*. No less than Dandin, these characters—and many more—are furious to be wrong when they feel sure they are right. Yet the best parallel to Dandin's line may be Alceste's displeasure when what is "right" does not happen, but what he misanthropically expects does: "J'ai pour moi la justice, et je perds mon procès."

The unified complexity of this line with its double-edged satire can be brought out by two comparisons. In Corneille's *La Galerie du Palais*, Act I, scene 7, Dorimant suggests that a good book can be unsuccessful "comme avec bon droit on perd bien un procès," a remark destined to illustrate the caprice of individual judgments. Dorimant's comparison shows awareness of imperfections in the judicial system, but it is scarcely satirical. By stressing the ambiguity of the word *justice* ('law', 'justice'), Molière makes Alceste voice an idealism and a sense of outrage entirely lacking in Dorimant's line. And the satirical force of Alceste's line as social criticism is felt by all those who stress the ideal of justice in Alceste's word *justice*.

That there is more to Alceste's line than facile satire of corrupt institutions, however, immediately strikes anyone who reflects upon *justice*—law—as a social convention intended among other things precisely to decide upon the relative merits of disputed claims, claims which two or more opposed litigants believe to be just, to be right. Litigants *(Les Plaideurs)* and special pleaders *(La Femme juge et parti)* are a frequent theme of French comedy. Measured against a moralist tradition aware of the relativity of the merits of individual claims, which Pibrac's line "Juge en ta cause sentence ne donne" can illustrate as well as any, the self-righteousness of Alceste's assertion is patently absurd. Alceste never connects society's problems with his own nature. Molière does, which is why I call this line too a comic image.[8]

Both elements of this concept may now be defined. If we allow for extension to include theatrical dimensions such as mime and stage decoration, we may take over Ezra Pound's famous definition of an image as "that which presents an intellectual and emotional complex in an instant of time," "a unification of disparate ideas."[9] On stage, of course, an image will normally have a visual as well as a verbal component. It may even be wholly in mime, like the cuff Mme Pernelle gives Flipote, which farcically signifies the violence and urge to dominate overlain by her show of piety, foreshadowing much in the characterization of Orgon and his relation to others. But the function of the image remains less to picture than to evoke and to correlate.

Nor should we overlook the possibility that in Molière's time even stage decoration might in this sense be symbolic, not so much representing, for instance, a bourgeois interior as symbolizing the preoccupations of a miser, of a hypochondriac, of pedantic ladies. Pound's definition of the image is consonant with French Classical literary theory. In the preface to his translation of Vergil's *Aeneid*—published in the year in which *Amphitryon*, *Dandin*, and *L'Avare* were first performed—Segrais refers to "l'esprit de la grande poésie et du roman sérieux, qui ne doivent pas tant dire les choses que les signifier."[10]

On one level, to be sure, Segrais merely means that the detailed descriptions found in the French epics and gallant novels of the 1650s should be avoided, and the application of his remark to comedy may be questioned. But in *La*

Critique de l'École des femmes, Molière's Dorante explicitly challenges the idea that "tout l'esprit et toute la beauté sont dans les poèmes sérieux, et que les pièces comiques sont des niaiseries qui ne méritent aucune louange." In that same scene Dorante also uses the verb *peindre* to mean "signify" or "symbolize." For he explains that Arnolphe's repetition of Agnès's question "Si les enfants qu'on fait se faisaient par l'oreille" was not included "pour être de soi un bon mot, mais seulement pour une chose qui caractérise l'homme et *peint* d'autant mieux son extravagance. . . ." Here is surely, in Molière's own critical thought, a basis for the notion of the "comic image."

The image then for our purposes is the technique, literary and dramatic, by which at a privileged moment in the action Molière unifies the elements of a scene, presenting an intellectual and emotional complex, the focusing of which signifies a moral insight derived from what the *Lettre sur la comédie de l'Imposteur* calls his "méditation profonde sur la nature de l'âme."[11]

Neglecting the pages of this *Lettre* (pp. 554–8) which evidence a high degree of social commitment in Molière's art, we find in the Neoplatonist rationalism of its closing section a philosophic framework in which the sort of imagery outlined above is not only a possible but an obvious technique for any writer determined, as Dorante suggests in *La Critique* (scene 6), to "peindre d'après nature." For if nature is assumed to have endowed mankind with an innate capacity to apprehend [ideal] reason intuitively, nature has further provided "quelque marque sensible qui nous rendît cette connoissance facile" in "quelque sorte de forme extérieure et de dehors reconnoissable" (p. 559). Within such a framework, to use in a comedy what Dorante calls "une chose qui . . . peint . . . [l'] extravagance" would therefore seem to be imitating nature in one of its most significant aspects. A "chose qui peint" on stage provides, like nature, a perceptible correlative of a moral reality, an image not unlike what T. S. Eliot calls an "objective correlative."

However, it is with the comic nature of the image that

the *Lettre* is most helpful. Since the concept and term "nature" refer to a moral order quite as much as to a physical one, the *Lettre* confirms the link between ethical thought and comedy by reference to *le ridicule* as "une des plus sublimes matières de la véritable morale" (p. 559). What the *Lettre* calls the perceptible form of reason is "quelque motif de joie et quelque matière de plaisir que notre âme trouve dans tout objet moral." Within the mind *(esprit)* a "complaisance délicieuse" is aroused by the apprehension of truth and virtue. But when such pleasure comes from "la vue de l'ignorance et de l'erreur, c'est-à-dire de ce qui manque de raison, c'est proprement le sentiment par lequel nous jugeons quelque chose ridicule" (p. 559). Thus, once again, in order to "peindre d'après nature" the writer needs to devise in his comedy some such "vue de l'ignorance et de l'erreur," a moral dimension of *le ridicule* in art to reflect the moralist implications of *le ridicule* in nature, as the word *extravagance* in the phrase adapted from Dorante independently attests.

If the perspective indicated by the *Lettre* implies a comic theatre in which ethical judgments, symbolically expressed, are a form of "realism" or "naturalism" as conceived at the time, the *Lettre* is no less helpful in suggesting the areas of aesthetic response to comedy so conceived:

> Or, comme la raison produit dans l'âme une joie mêlée d'estime, le ridicule y produit une joie mêlée de mépris, parce que toute connoissance qui arrive à l'âme produit nécessairement dans l'entendement un sentiment d'estime ou de mépris, comme dans la volonté un mouvement d'amour ou de haine (pp. 559–60).

In other words, *le ridicule* arouses both joy and scorn, a complex emotional response involving not only rejection by both intellect and will, but also an inner elation, which helps situate the aesthetic response.

It should be noted in passing that comedy is not limited to *le ridicule*. For the *Lettre* indicates two sorts of *joie* which may be taken as springs, not so much of laughter in the abstract, as of differentiated forms of laughter (not *le rire*, but *les rires*): "joie mêlée d'estime" and "joie mêlée de mépris." To these may be added also a third *joie*, unmixed, the basis of laughter of well-being, of high spirits. That at least three such categories of laughter are required for sound criticism of comedy cannot be demonstrated here, but is abundantly confirmed in modern terminology in such useful studies of laughter as those by Hector Munro and Charles Mauron.[12] To these three states of joy we may relate different types of laughter, and thus different aspects of the comic, just as Racine relates a particular concept of the tragic to the qualified sadness which he designates "tristesse majestueuse" in the preface to *Bérénice*.

Pure elation could be argued as the spring of laughter exploited by the ebullience of certain characters (Nicole's infectious laughter on her first entry in *Le Bourgeois gentilhomme*), the exuberance—the fun, the play—of many happy stratagems, much by-play, and certain denouements. Similarly, "joie mêlée d'estime" may form the psychological basis for characterization and response in the idealizing aspects of Molière's comedy which, because they are conceived to represent an ideal nature, provide wish-fulfillment: the romantic love of the lover roles, for instance, together with the general reconciliation and the regeneration symbolized by many denouements, when a character embodying some aspect of the *ridicule* may also be driven out or disarmed. This is the laughter of assent, of joyful acceptance; and perhaps even the comedy of carefully prepared extravagance (like the entries of Tartuffe and of M. Jourdain) can be related on one level to laughter of this sort, as we laugh not only at the *disconvenance* or the incongruity of the extravagant, but also at a gesture or a remark that seems 'just like' a snob or a hypocrite, a blunderer or a bore, a plain-dealer or a miser. It does not follow from the need to differentiate divers springs of laughter that such springs can only be tapped separately. Jacques Guicharnaud suggests that entries like Orgon's and Tartuffe's, within their rigidly typifying characterization, occasion not surprise but satisfaction.[13] But, given Molière's hyperbolic presentation, in my experience of performances they provide *both* surprise *and* fulfillment, together with feelings of aesthetic rightness and moral rejection.

The *Lettre*'s definition of *ridicule* as "joie mêlée de mépris," however, is particularly helpful in situating the main areas of response sought by those moments in Molière's comedy we have called comic images. The adverse intellectual sensation and the emotional rejection which it implies quite clearly preclude responses in the pathetic or tragic registers, since there is no basis of pathos or empathy or pity, fear, and sadness. If *le ridicule* is the mainspring of most of Molière's comic images, the joyful adverse sensation in the mind and the emotional rejection which it implies clearly show the images to be derisive, satirical, to involve a moralist manipulation of laughter which Molière's comedy avowedly shares with classical satire.

The comic image, then, is a special sort of poetic image implying both laughter and a moral judgment. It is the literary and dramatic device by which Molière imitates on stage *le ridicule* in life, defined by the *Lettre* as "la forme extérieure et sensible que la providence de la nature a attachée à tout ce qui est déraisonnable, pour nous en faire apercevoir, et nous obliger à le fuir (p. 560)."

Among the many scenes which could illustrate this theory of the comic image, and against which its usefulness may be tested, none perhaps is more challenging than Harpagon's soliloquy at the end of Act IV of *L'Avare*. Actively pursuing the thief of his "chère cassette" ("Où courir? Où ne pas courir?"), Harpagon suddenly arrests himself: "N'est-il point là? N'est-il point ici? Qui est-ce? Arrête. Rends-moi mon argent, coquin . . . *(Il se prend lui-même le bras.)* Ah! c'est moi." The mobility and mime indicated by Harpagon's repeated questions, the familiarity of his orders, his preoccupation with money and use of the word *coquin* bring together comic stagecraft, comic style, a comic theme, and comic vocabulary which cannot be satisfactorily accounted for in any other register. Moreover, since Harpagon's self-arrest implies a contorted position, his following statement, closely adapted from Plautus—"Mon esprit est troublé, et j'ignore où je suis, qui je suis, et ce que je fais"— may in its context either be taken as a confidence to the audience, in which case the comedy is that of litotes or understatement, or else stand in the parodic relation to tragic *égarement*, like that experienced by Hermione in *Andromaque*, Act V, scene 1: "Où suis-je? Qu'ai-je fait? Que dois-je faire encore?"

The scene goes on to develop both sorts of comedy. Harpagon's apostrophe to his missing money, "Hélas! mon pauvre argent . . .", travesties the sort of apostrophe addressed to the gods, to personified wishes, to one's heart or eyes, etc.—frequent in French tragedy, to cite only Ildione's soliloquy occupying the same position at the end of Act IV of Corneille's *Attila*, performed the year before by Molière's troupe, or the more famous soliloquy in Act IV of *Horace*, in which the bereaved Camille proffers a *sentence* against which Harpagon's lamentations may be measured:

> En un sujet de pleurs si grand, si légitime,
> Se plaindre est une honte, et soupirer un crime.

Harpagon's laments are not tragedy, but parody. His declaration, "C'en est fait, je n'en puis plus; je me meurs, je suis mort, je suis enterré," beginning with an idiom frequent in French tragic death scenes, significantly amplifies Molière's sources, whether we look directly at Plautus, or at Larivey, or indeed at Cahaignes's *L'Avaricieux*.[14] Significantly, because the added words "je suis mort, je suis enterré" reflect the progressive stages of burlesque dying and death which Molière's stagecraft has written into the text to guide comic mime. Staggering, collapsing, Harpagon lays out as it were his own corpse and pretends to have buried it. Harpagon's pantomime is foreshadowed by his mime of death at the end of Act III, when he is knocked over by La Merluche and where his line "Ah! je suis mort" is clearly to be delivered from a position prone on the floor—a position which, in his soliloquy, he exploits by a direct appeal to the audience: "N'y a-t-il personne qui veuille me ressusciter. . . ?"

Such a mock burial in a comedy can I think only be properly read as burlesque. It can be compared with the mime of death that Molière wrote into the role of Argan in *Le Malade imaginaire*, Act III, scene 6, following Argan's excommunication from medicine by M. Purgon. Argan uses some of the same vocabulary as Harpagon ("je suis mort. . . . Je n'en puis plus"). His mock death is anticipated by Louison's in Act II, and it will be amplified later in Act III in the exposure of Béline, while Béralde's reaction to Argan's imaginary death in Act III, scene 6, confirms the burlesque register in which it is mimed: "Ma foi! mon frère, vous êtes fou, et je ne voudrais pas, pour beaucoup de choses, qu'on vous vît faire ce que vous faites." Béralde's next line indicates moreover that the mime of imaginary death is to be held for a noticeable period: "Tâtez-vous un peu . . ." and no doubt prepares a comic resuscitation.

That in Harpagon's soliloquy, to return to *L'Avare*, Molière exploits anti-illusionist as well as burlesque techniques of comedy is further evidenced by Harpagon's question to the audience about the thief: "N'est-il point caché là parmi vous?" By this question (also derived from the *Aulularia*), Harpagon re-establishes a *rapport* with the audience, as Molière's actors are meant to do from time to time in his early farces, in *L'Étourdi*, and doubtless in many asides in later plays. Molière transposes Harpagon's "Ils me regardent tous, et se mettent à rire" into the third person, but he could not have retained the line had he felt unable to hold on to his audience until they really do laugh. Some producers have deleted it. One actor at least has made it illusionist by speaking through a window into the wings. But surely it is evidence that in this scene Molière wanted Harpagon to be funny, to make people in the audience laugh, and that he succeeded.

That different moments in this scene are also morally significant seems to me equally likely. The miser who deprives himself through avarice is certainly a current moralist theme. Cotin's epigram "Sur un avare" in the *Œuvres galantes* of 1663 (from which Molière took Trissotin's two poems in *Les Femmes savantes*) reads:

> Le chagrin, la melancholie,
> Sont l'vnique fruit de son bien,
> Et par vne estrange folie
> Ce qu'il possede n'est pas sien.[15]

There is also La Fontaine's fable "L'Avare qui a perdu son trésor" (IV. 20) in the *premier recueil* of 1668, which begins: "L'usage seulement fait la possession." It does not therefore seem either farfetched or anachronistic to argue that Harpagon's self-arrest implies that the miser—in a far deeper sense than he realizes—is his own thief, that his avarice deprives him of his wealth, as Cotin and La Fontaine also suggest. But Molière's mime goes further in suggesting that avarice as a vice of the mind deprives the miser of his senses, his judgment, that it destroys him, buries him alive. The parallel moment in *Le Malade imaginaire* seems likewise to use the technique of burlesque imaginary death to suggest that, like avarice, hypochondria is a form of spiritual suicide. A stagecraft more developed than Plautus' or Larivey's conveys a meaning richer than Cotin's or La Fontaine's. Each of these moments is "une chose qui peint l'extravagance," a comic image that caricatures and rejects a self-destructive attitude, an image no less joyous because of its scorn and no less scornful because of its joy.

The implications of Argan's mime in *Le Malade imaginaire*, Act III, scene 6, appear to be confirmed by verbal images in Toinette's pseudo-medical advice in scene 10 of the act:

TOINETTE: Que diantre faites-vous de ce bras-là?
ARGAN: Comment?
TOINETTE: Voilà un bras que je me ferais couper tout à l'heure, si j'étais que de vous.
ARGAN: Et pourquoi?
TOINETTE: Ne voyez-vous pas qu'il tire à soi toute la nourriture, et qu'il empêche ce côté-là de profiter?
ARGAN: Oui, mais j'ai besoin de mon bras.
TOINETTE: Vous avez là un œil droit que je me ferais crever, si j'étais en votre place.
ARGAN: Crever un œil?
TOINETTE: Ne voyez-vous pas qu'il incommode l'autre, et lui dérobe sa nourriture? Croyez-moi, faites-vous-le crever au plus tôt, vous en verrez plus clair de l'œil gauche.
ARGAN: Cela n'est pas pressé.

It may be, as J. D. Hubert suggests in his *Molière and the Comedy of the Intellect*,[16] that Toinette's burlesque advice directly or indirectly parodies part of the Sermon on the Mount:

> And if thy hand offend thee, cut it off. And if thine eye offend thee, pluck it out: it is better for thee to enter the kingdom of God with one eye, than having two eyes to be cast to hell fire (Mark 9:43, 47; cf. Matthew 5:29–30).

And in any case Toinette's disguise as a doctor of farce, the indicated by-play ("ce bras-là," "ce côté-là," "Vous avez là . . ."), and the nonsense of what she says indicate the tonality of burlesque or farce.

But each of Toinette's recommendations is also "une chose qui peint l'extravagance," a correlative of Argan's hypochondria. The images symbolize moralist reflection on hypochondria and perhaps also on the spiritual hypochondria of puritanism which assumes that life is somehow better if half of it is rejected, an attitude that cuts and plucks away at life until what remains is hardly worth living. Toinette's extravagant prescriptions are images of the extravagance of self-mutilating fear and self-pity which Argan had comically dramatized in the opening scene of the play, comic images joyfully scornful of a self-destructive vice which is not looked upon as the fault of fate or of society, but as Argan's own individual responsibility. It is one of the ironies of literary history that Arnavon[17] should have chosen to delete this particular scene so that the "realism" of others could be better preserved. One might say with Argan: "Me couper un bras, et me crever un œil, afin que l'autre se porte mieux! J'aime bien mieux qu'il ne se porte pas si bien. La belle opération, de me rendre borgne et manchot!" For even an Argan can take a moral point when it is given "quelque marque sensible" and "quelque sorte de forme extérieure."

To conclude, three further points seem worth making, two to limit the application of what is here proposed, a third to raise further questions.

It is not argued, to begin with, that every image in Molière is a comic image with moralist implications, as for instance I would claim for Alain's line in *L'École des femmes*,

Act II, scene 3: "La femme est, en effet, le potage de l'homme," where Alain's metaphor signifies an attitude which would reduce Agnès or any woman to an *objet de consommation* in the service of a male appetite. With Alain's metaphor I would contrast a famous metaphor at the beginning of *Le Sicilien:* "le ciel s'est habillé ce soir en Scaramouche," a line admired by Hugo and often quoted out of context as if it were lyrically expansive. In the mouth of a clever valet, Hali, in context, it strikes me rather as burlesque: "Il fait noir comme dans un four; le ciel s'est habillé ce soir en Scaramouche, et je ne vois pas une étoile qui montre le bout de son nez." For in the *commedia dell'arte*, with which Molière and his public were thoroughly familiar, Scaramouche was a comedian. In 1667, the *commedia* had not been idealized by Watteau, or by Verlaine. The sky's disguise as a comedian fits into a series of three images, carefully graded from the commonplace dark of the oven to the burlesque conceit of stars not showing their noses. By this complex of imagery, and doubtless by supporting mime, Molière evokes the kind of imaginative stage "darkness visible" required for the action and for the audience to be able also to follow the action. Hali's images also contribute to the creation of a comic atmosphere, which they would not do if any of them were affective or lyrical. Thus in Hali's line I see not a lyrical, but a comic image, one with dramatic implications, but without any moralist ones.

In the second place, it is not argued that every extravagant line, every pun, every joke, every slapstick gesture in Molière is a comic image. I am convinced, on the contrary, that many are not. The quarrel between Sganarelle and Martine, Sganarelle's jokes, and the beating that Martine receives at his hands in the opening scene of *Le Médecin malgré lui* usually seem funny to me, but I cannot discover any special significance apart from motivation of the dramatic action to follow. When, however, in Act I, scene 5, of that comedy Sganarelle is beaten by Valère and Lucas until he agrees to be called a doctor, the farce does seem to me significant. The elements of the action are not unified in quite the tidy instant of time required of an image, but Sganarelle's line "J'aime mieux consentir à tout que de me faire assommer" could be argued to fall within the definition. For it focuses a relationship between fact, belief, force, and confession to which Molière returned several times in the late 1660s. It is by coercion in the first act of *Amphitryon* that Mercure obtains from Sosie a "confession" that he is not himself, but only after the clarifying protest:

> Tes coups n'ont point en moi fait de métamorphose;
> Et tout le changement que je trouve à la chose,
>   C'est d'être Sosie battu.

And later Sosie answers Amphitryon's threats (Act II, scene 1):

> Si vous le prenez sur ce ton,
> Monsieur, je n'ai rien à dire,
> Et vous aurez toujours raison.

It is hardly possible to demonstrate that these moments—with other related scenes like the one in which Maître Jacques is beaten for his sincerity in *L'Avare*, Act III, scene 1—are related to the contemporary French system of investigation by judicial torture—*la question*—or to the use of coercion in obtaining conversions to the established Catholic faith. That such scenes constitute an overt attack on the brutal system of so-called *justice* or on the uncharitable pressures which Protestants were inheriting temporarily from Jansenists could not be seriously maintained. But the parody of a tragic stance in Arnolphe's interrogation of Agnès in *L'École des femmes*, Act II, scene 5,

> O fâcheux examen d'un mystère fatal,
> Où l'examinateur souffre seul tout le mal!,

implies an inversion of *la question*, which suggests that Molière was well aware of the institutional violence officially justified as 'inquiry.' And it can hardly be denied that the scenes cited from *Le Médecin malgré lui* and *Amphitryon* focus, comically but clearly, the view that coercion can obtain almost any statement it requires, together with the fact that such a statement may be unrelated to the facts in question or to the belief of the speaker.

Thus in conclusion I would ask whether in certain comedies in which Molière has reconstructed folklore or myth there are not comic images containing ideas of such wider implications? It is not necessary for a play to be a *pièce à thèse* in order for it to contain ideas, nor are its ideas and images the less powerful for a certain abstraction, for having no explicit application. Specialist concentration in recent years on theatrical and aesthetic considerations in Molière studies has obtained rich, often brilliant results, of which some of the best are still to be found, after more than twenty years of intensive study, in Moore's *Molière: A New Criticism*. It is, however, also an aberration of the recent past, particularly of Bray's epigoni, to assume that the aesthetic and theatrical qualities of Molière's plays are somehow dependent upon a moral insignificance. Neither the critical writings of Molière himself nor those of his close associates suggest any such incompatibility of ethics and aesthetics: on the contrary. Only ten years after the publication of Bray's book, Vivian Mercier could write: "*Le Misanthrope* is one of the purest examples of the drama of ideas, a member of that very small group of plays which tease the mind long after one has left the theatre."[18] Perhaps not every play mentioned in this essay could be called a drama of ideas; but if my theory of comic images is acceptable in its general outline, more than three of Molière's comedies could be included in Mercier's "very small group," and others placed honorably near it. For if there is a danger in reading into the great works of the past the ideas, the concerns, and—yes—the fun of the present, there is surely a greater danger in reading into them a poverty of ideas, a lack of concern, and a humorless dullness. Either to trivialize the past or to deny its laughter can only impoverish the present, and the future.

3

Ce que Molière doit à Scaramouche

"Il fut le maître de Molière, Et la nature fut le sien," peut-on lire au frontispice de la *Vie de Scaramouche* (1695) d'Angelo Costantini. Et qu'à partir de 1660 environ Molière devait effectivement certains aspects de son art à Tiberio Fiorilli ou Fiorillo (1608–94), le plus célèbre des Scaramouches, aucun moliériste ne l'ignore. Un autre frontispice bien connu des moliéristes, celui d'*Elomire hypocondre* (1670) de Le Boulanger de Chalussay, représente les deux acteurs, "Scaramouche enseignant, Élomire étudiant"; une légende pose la question ironique: "Qualis erit? tanto docente magistro." Molière a pu connaître Scaramouche lors d'une des visites de l'Italien a Paris aux années 1640, mais l'essentiel reste sans doute le fait qu'à partir du retour de Molière à la capitale en 1658 ils partageaient le même théâtre. Ce fut d'abord au Petit-Bourbon, du 2 novembre 1658 jusqu'à la démolition de l'édifice en octobre 1660, ensuite au Palais-Royal depuis le retour à Paris des Italiens (partis après la démolition de l'autre salle) jusqu'à la mort de Molière, avec cette différence: au Petit-Bourbon la troupe de Molière avait joué les jours dits "extraordinaires"—c'est-à-dire les lundis, mercredis, jeudis et samedis—après avoir donné aux Italiens la somme de 1500 livres pour l'usage de leur théâtre; au Palais-Royal, au contraire, c'étaient les Italiens qui jouaient les jours "extraordinaires," et ils avaient dû rembourser à la troupe de Molière la somme de 2000 livres, soit la moitié des frais de l'établissement de la salle.

Si nous avons bien compris certains documents publiés en 1963 par Mmes Jurgens et Maxfield-Miller, il s'agirait du même théâtre, que Molière a fait reconstruire dans la grande salle de spectacles du Palais-Royal, alors en ruine: autrement dit, le théâtre des Italiens, reconstruit en bonne partie avec le même bois, et par conséquent d'après un plan

Scaramouche enseignant, Elomire estudiant (frontispiece of
Elomire hypocondre (1670).

sans doute assez semblable—circonstance à laquelle les historiens du théâtre n'ont pas prêté l'attention que son importance mérite. On a mis en valeur le caractère rectangulaire et élevé de la salle du Petit-Bourbon. Mais cc sont dcs détails quelque peu étrangers à la question, car les documents du Minutier Central suggèrent qu'à l'usage des Italiens on avait fait aménager un théâtre beaucoup plus petit à l'intérieur de cette vaste salle. Pour se donner une idée du théâtre de Molière au Palais-Royal, on s'est fortifié des pages connues des *Antiquités de Paris* (1733) où Henri Sauval décrit la grande salle de spectacles du Palais-Cardinal ouverte en janvier 1641 avec la représentation de *Mirame* de Desmarets de Saint-Sorlin. Mais il est évident que Molière, dont le théâtre n'occupait pas tout l'espace de cette salle, n'a guère respecté la disposition originale de ce théâtre et que sa troupe a joué jusqu'en mars 1671 "sous une grande toile bleue suspendue avec des cordages," ainsi qu'il résulte du *Registre* de La Grange. Cette toile limitait l'espace vertical alors que l'équipement apporté du Petit-Bourbon limitait l'espace horizontal. En comparaison avec le théâtre des

Stage setting of *Mirame*, Act III, Palais-Cardinal, 1641.
Engraved by Stefano della Bella.

représentations de *Mirame*, le théâtre de Molière construit à l'intérieur de la grande salle de spectacles du Palais-Royal était un théâtre intime.

Précisons. Dans une communication d'un très haut intérêt pour l'histoire de la mise en scène à Paris, Agne Beijer publia en 1963 une maquette inédite du *Ballet de la Prospérité des armes de la France* dansé en février 1641 au Palais-Cardinal (devenu après la mort du cardinal de Richelieu le Palais-Royal) avec une savante étude qui met au point les caractères de la grande salle de spectacle et les capacités des machines utilisées pour les représentations. Il rappelle que l'on peut voir dans les gravures faites par Etienne de la Bella pour l'édition in-folio de *Mirame* (1641) "la structure technique de la scène ainsi que la plantation des décors . . .: toile de fond, châssis latéraux, 'terrains' et frises, ces dernières, selon l'usage, non indiquées par le graveur, mais indispensables."[1] A l'ouverture de cette grande salle une mise en scène parisienne rejoint la conception baroque du décor théâtral fixée depuis des années à Londres comme en Italie. Et grâce à cette technologie théâtrale alors nouvelle en France, Desmarets a su unir dans la mise en scène de *Mirame* les changements à vue des grands spectacles baroques aux fameuses exigences des trois unités dramatiques dites classiques, unités de temps et de lieu surtout que les changements à vue soulignent. A Beijer revient aussi le mérite d'avoir su identifier, dans une grisaille du Musée des Arts Décoratifs à Paris qui montre une scène d'intérieur du Palais-Cardinal au cours d'une représentation d'une entrée du *Ballet de la Prospérité*, ballet dû à l'auteur de *Mirame*.[2]

Cette grisaille est connue surtout par une gravure de van Lochon, graveur au service du roi Louis XIII depuis 1625, mort en 1647. Intitulée "Le Soir" et parfois attribuée à Abraham Bosse, cette gravure montre, au milieu de la salle en face de la scène, le cardinal de Richelieu, le roi Louis XIII, la reine Anne d'Autriche, le futur roi Louis XIV qui paraît sensiblement plus âgé que les deux ans et demi qu'il avait en janvier 1641, un enfant qui doit être Philippe d'Orléans né en 1640, un chien de chasse, etc. Or cette

gravure a été remaniée, car il en existe plus d'un état. Un
état montre la même scène, mais après la mort du cardinal
de Richelieu; et plusieurs détails de l'état que fait repro-
duire Beijer lui-même sont plus faciles à expliquer à une
date postérieure à la mort de Richelieu qu'en février 1641:
l'âge des deux enfants royaux, par exemple, et les fleurs-de-
lys qui remplacent au proscenium les armes du cardinal que
l'on voit dans les gravures de della Bella. Les colonnes ap-
parentes du haut de la salle, peinte en trompe-l'oeil selon
Sauval; les degrés qui mènent du parterre au théâtre élevé;
les balcons et surtout la scène du *Ballet de la Prospérité* por-
tent à croire que la gravure représente la grande salle en
1641. Mais s'il s'agissait d'une reprise des décors de ce ballet
lors d'une représentation plus tardive, ainsi que le
suggèrent les fleurs-de-lys et l'âge apparent des enfants? Ou
bien, si la représentation avait été peinte, non d'après une
représentation effective du ballet, mais d'après une maquette de décor? Surtout si l'on compare "Le Soir" avec les
planches de *Mirame*, les dimensions de la scène ne sont pas
du tout les mêmes, à les estimer selon la hauteur des acteurs
qui y paraissent. La scène illustrée dans *Mirame* est énorme.

"Le Soir" *(Musée des Arts décoratifs)*

Le proscenium—à en juger selon les acteurs représentés—correspond bien aux indications données par Sauval pour l'espace affecté à la scène: elle serait large de neuf toises (17,60 m. environ). Mais les plans publiés par Beijer suggèrent que della Bella exagère les dimensions du proscenium (mais non pas celles de la scène). La scène montrée dans "Le Soir" ne paraît pas avoir les mêmes dimensions. L'artiste porte l'attention sur le groupe de spectateurs royaux, qui occupent au centre de la salle en face de la scène une position favorisée qui rappelle celle occupée par la famille royale espagnole aux grandes représentations de cour à Madrid.[3] Mais la largeur du proscenium ne serait que trois fois la hauteur d'un acteur qu'on y voit à droite, trois toises au maximum, même s'il s'agit d'un géant, alors que la largeur effective de ce proscenium a dû être cinq toises (30 pieds ou 9.5 m.). Je n'accepte pas par conséquent qu'à cet égard "Le Soir" donne une idée nette de l'aspect de la salle.

Or il exista au Palais-Cardinal une salle de spectacles plus petite, celle inaugurée en 1636. Cette salle pouvait accueillir 600 spectateurs en comparaison avec 3000 pour la grande salle. Avec d'autres détails, et surtout le plancher uni du parterre et l'absence de l'échaffaut (la tribune royale) dont il est fait mention dans la *Gazette de France* pour les cérémoniaux de la grande salle, les dimensions de la scène qu'on voit dans "Le Soir" m'avaient amené à conclure, dans la version primitive de cette étude, que la gravure montre cette petite salle. C'est une hypothèse qui rencontre autant de difficultés que celle plus traditionnelle selon laquelle "Le Soir" montre fidèlement la grande salle lors d'une représentation. Sans doute faut-il se méfier de toute interprétation trop littérale des éléments qu'on y voit: Les colonnes en trompe-l'oeil, par exemple, sont-elles effectivement de l'ordre corinthien précisé par Sauval, auquel on a l'habitude de se fier pour de tels détails? "Le Soir" comporte peut-être des éléments puisés non seulement à des moments différents, mais à des salles de spectacles différentes: des motifs décoratifs de la grande dans les dimensions de la petite. Quand bien même cette gravure ne représenterait pas une salle composite, l'absence des vingt-sept degrés "qui montent mollement et insensiblement" vers le fond de la grande salle dans la description de Sauval—disposition structurale de la plus haute importance pour les rapports entre la scène et la salle, car elle plaçait avantageusement tant de spectateurs dont la vue n'auraient été que partielle d'un parterre uni—confirme à quel point il faut être prudent dans la supposition que "Le Soir" donne une image exacte de la grande salle du Palais-Cardinal héritée par Molière. Ce qui est certain, c'est que le théâtre de Scaramouche qu'il y fit ériger en 1661 avait une toute autre allure. car il fit reconstruire les loges de Scaramouche à l'intérieur de la salle de Mercier, ainsi que nous l'indiquerons ci-après.

Le théâtre même où jouait Molière à l'apogée de sa carrière nous intéresse ici moins que les effets qu'il permettait d'abord à Scaramouche et puis à Molière de produire. Soulignons d'abord que—fait méconnu—la première dette de Molière envers Scaramouche vers 1660 était la disposition matérielle de son théâtre. De cette circonstance découlerait une dette reconnue, le jeu de Molière acteur, modelé sur celui de Scaramouche. Toutefois, cette dernière dette n'ayant pas été exactement ce qu'on dit communément, nous tâcherons de la préciser en mettant l'accent sur la grimace, l'usage sémiotique fait du visage par les deux comédiens—aspect de leur jeu qui s'expliquerait mal dans les salles rectangulaires de Paris comme l'Hôtel de Bourgogne, le Théâtre du Marais, ou les tripots où avait débuté l'Illustre Théâtre. Il nous semble infiniment probable que cet élément de leur jeu dépendait en partie de la disposition matérielle du théâtre qu'ils partageaient, disposition qui devait favoriser la vue des spectateurs, et que le nouveau style du jeu de Molière, compris de cette manière, est d'une importance considérable pour les rôles qu'il écrivait pour lui-même à partir de 1660 environ—c'est-à-dire les principaux rôles de son théâtre.

Notre but n'est pas de minimiser d'autres influences italiennes sur l'activité théâtrale de Molière, dont l'œuvre illustre mieux qu'aucune autre l'influence italienne. Deux dramaturges italiens—Secchi et Barbieri—lui ont fourni les modèles de ses premières comédies, le *Dépit amoureux et l'Etourdi*, dette que la monographie récente de Philip Wadsorth, *Molière and the Italian Theatrical Tradition* (1977), nous dispense d'analyser davantage ici. D'importants aspects de sa dramaturgie sont impensables sans le précédent—voire à l'occasion la collaboration et même la méchanceté—des machinistes italiens Torelli et Vigarani, et l'on sait bien que la plupart de ses comédies-ballets ont été représentées en collaboration avec le musicien italien Lully (Lulli). Mais nous estimons qu'on n'a pas remarqué à quel point l'activité de Molière illustre des thèses chères à notre maître disparu, Franco Simone: conscience d'une renaissance, persistance de traditions françaises médiévales, assimilation de solutions italiennes d'ordre surtout technique et esthétique, alors que d'importantes idées morales sont prises à la Renaissance du nord. Mais rien n'est plus évident. Témoigne la représentation en août 1661 à Vaux-le-Vicomte des *Fâcheux*, "un mélange," dit Molière, "nouveau pour nos théâtres, et dont on pourrait chercher quelques autorités dans l'antiquité." Mais sait-on s'il pense aux chœurs de la comédie grecque plutôt qu'a Plaute? La célèbre relation écrite par La Fontaine à Maucroix à cette occasion traduit une pareille conscience d'une renaissance. Car les amis avaient conclu que Molière "allait ramener en France / Le bon goût et l'air de Térence"—allusion perplexe dont on n'a peut-être pas approfondi la signification essentielle. Bornons-nous cependant à souligner ici non seulement cette conscience d'une renaissance où la participation italienne joue un rôle efficace ("L'un des enchanteurs," dit La Fontaine, "est le sieur Torelli"), mais celle aussi d'une véritable *translatio studii* effectuée par le décorateur du spectacle, Le Brun,

> Rival des Raphaëls, successeur des Apelles,
> Par qui notre climat ne doit rien au romain. . . .

On n'a qu'à ajouter à cette revendication d'une *translatio studii*, due en partie à l'exploitation de solutions techniques et esthétiques italiennes, une influence moraliste inspirée par la Renaissance du nord pour retrouver toutes les grandes lignes du système simonien, tel qu'il est exposé surtout dans *Il Rinascimento francese*. Et quand la mode ne sera plus de sous-estimer la pensée morale du philosophe— le mot est d'un contemporain—qu'était Molière homme de théâtre, on méditera la portée de certains faits que nous signalons depuis quelques années. De beaux sujets dramatiques de Molière, dont *Le Bourgeois Gentilhomme* et *Les Femmes savantes*, sont pris à des pièces de Chappuzeau basées sur les *Entretiens* d'Érasme, dont Chappuzeau lui-même avait publié en 1662 la première traduction en prose française. Et la caractérisation de ses personnages les plus célèbres— Tartuffe, Dom Juan, Sganarelle de *Dom Juan*, Alceste, Harpagon entre autres—reflète "les Caractères des vices" que, dans son *Ecole du sage* (1646), Urbain Chevreau avait traduits des *Characters* (1608) du moraliste anglais Joseph Hall, par la suite évêque d'Exeter et puis de Norwich. Même les portraits satiriques des *Fâcheux* relèvent d'une intention moraliste évidente dans l'épître dédicatoire de Molière "Au Roi," tandis que les souvenirs d'Horace, de Régnier, de Scarron entre autres attestent les continuités littéraires et *l'étude* dont parle Molière dans cette lettre. Car Molière ne doit à Scaramouche ni la qualité littéraire de ses comédies ni leur portée moraliste.

Les dettes de Molière envers son collègue italien s'inscrivent dans une activité théâtrale déjà mûre et depuis longtemps ouverte à d'autres modes, à d'autres modèles, à des suggestions et à des influences de plusieurs catégories, dont les divertissements de cour d'un italianisme en partie naturalisé en France et les traditions de la farce française, parfois italianisées elles aussi. C'est le cas notamment de la farce en un acte et en prose de Dorimond, *l'Ecole des cocus, ou la précaution inutile* (1661), dont les personnages—Le Capitan, Le Docteur, Lucinde, Léandre et Trapolin surtout— rappellent ceux d'un scénario de la *commedia dell'arte*, bien que son intrigue soit basée comme *l'Ecole des femmes* sur une nouvelle tragicomique traduite de l'espagnol par Scarron.[4] Ce fait est important, car l'imitation du jeu de Scaramouche a dû remplacer chez Molière non seulement un jeu tragique—celui que reflètent plusieurs portraits de ses années de tournées—, mais un jeu comique, et vraisemblablement bouffon, inspiré en partie au moins par celui de Jodelet, qui avait brillé notamment dans des rôles de *gracioso* adaptés du théâtre espagnol par P. Corneille, Scarron et d'autres depuis les débuts de Molière au théâtre. C'est Jodelet que Molière associait à sa troupe, sinon pour la représentation du *Docteur amoureux* devant la cour le 24 octobre 1658, du moins pour *les Précieuses ridicules* l'année suivante, peu avant la mort de Jodelet.[5] Sans doute Molière n'avait-il pas oublié les succès obtenus par Jodelet dans *le Menteur* (1642) et dans *le Maître valet* (1643), comédies dont le succès précède de peu l'ouverture de l'Illustre Théâtre. Le *Registre* de La Grange montre que ces deux comédies étaient bien au répertoire de la troupe de Molière peu après son retour à Paris, et c'est sans doute Molière qui tenait alors les rôles de Clarin et de Jodelet.

Il nous semble donc peu probable que, selon la formule de Bray, Molière se fît bouffon à l'école de Scaramouche (p. 190). Car sans parler de ses premières farces, ni du caractère burlesque de ses plus grands rôles qui peut devoir davantage à Jodelet et à Scarron qu'à Scaramouche, songeons au rôle burlesque de Mascarille joué par Molière en face de Jodelet. C'est le premier rôle important créé par Molière après son retour à Paris, mais un rôle dont l'effacement en face de Jodelet symboliserait, selon C.E.J. Caldicott, "la modestie de l'élève devant son maître."[6] Quand bien même Caldicott forcerait un peu la note, l'on ne saurait récuser le témoignage de Christian Huyghens, qui note à propos d'une représentation des *Précieuses ridicules* en janvier 1661: "Mascarille masqué, le [vi] comte enfariné." Dès les premières représentations Mlle des Jardins souligne, dans son *Récit en prose et en vers de la farce des Précieuses*, le caractère burlesque du rôle de Mascarille:

> . . . sa perruque était si grande qu'elle balayait la place à chaque fois qu'il faisait la révérence, et son chapeau si petit, qu'il était aisé de juger que le marquis le portait bien plus souvent dans la main que sur la tête; son rabat se pouvait appeler un honnête peignoir, et ses canons semblaient n'être

faits que pour servir de caches aux enfants qui jouent à cligne-
musette. . . . Un brandon de glands lui sortait de sa poche
comme d'une corne d'abondance. . . .

Or elle ne parle pas de son visage, pour la bonne raison que
Molière jouait masqué, aspect de son jeu lors de ses débuts à
Paris après 1658 qu'on assimile de façon abusive aux tradi-
tions de la *commedia dell'arte.*

C'est une confusion fâcheuse qu'on rencontre souvent, et
notamment dans l'excellent *Molière, a New Criticism* (1949)
de notre maître disparu, Will G. Moore:

> Lanson—dit Moore—showed how important for a real
> understanding of Molière's plays was the fact that he was
> trained to act in a mask, that Mascarille was by nomenclature
> a masked character, and that much of the fixity imposed by
> the mask clings to such creations as Alceste and Tartuffe
> (p. 16).

Toutefois le rôle de Tartuffe n'était pas joué par Molière,
qui jouait plutôt Orgon, dont le revirement au cinquième
acte—quelle que soit la raideur psychologique de ses
excès—constitue un élément essentiel du dénouement. Et
l'on peut mieux voir les dangers de cette approche un peu
plus loin:

> The farce and the *commedia dell'arte* clearly had much in
> common and it is not now, I think, possible to determine
> what Molière owed to each. Both were played in masks
> (p. 32).

Moore semble avoir oublié ici le frontispice de son livre, qui
reproduit celui d'*Elomire hypocondre* dont il a déjà été question: ni Scaramouche ni Molière n'est masqué, et Molière
tient à la main un petit mirror qui ne reflète que son visage—et la grimace qu'il apprend du comédien italien. Depuis *Il Teatro comico* de Goldoni on exagère la fixité de la
commedia dell'arte. Il importe de préciser ici l'originalité de
Fiorilli dans la tradition de la *commedia dell'arte.* Son
originalité consistait surtout à faire valoir la mobilité de son
visage. Rien ne dégage mieux son jeu de celui de Jodelet.
Aucun document que nous connaissons ne justifie pour les
années qui nous intéressent l'assertion de René Bray au
sujet de Scaramouche: "Jouant sous le masque, il développa

Molière as Sganarelle

la mimique" (p. 189). Il développa la mimique, mais non pas sous le masque. Son habit noir dégageait son visage.

"*Scaramucchia non parla, e dice gran cose:* Scaramouche ne parle point, et dit les plus belles choses du monde," a dit un prince italien après une représentation à Rome. C'est Gherardi qui le rappelle.[7] Et d'indiquer souvent des *grimaces* aussi bien que des *postures:* dans la *Matrone d'Ephèse,* par exemple: "*Après beaucoup de grimaces et de postures, Scaramouche tout tremblant s'enfuit d'un côté . . .*" Dans *Colombine avocat pour et contre,* Pierrot importune Scaramouche dans un rôle travesti. Ce dernier "*lève les coiffes, et fait une grimace horrible, qui épouvante tellement Pierrot, qu'il s'enfuit en criant: Le Diable! Le Diable!*" (III, 4). Ailleurs dans ce même scénario (II, 7) Pascariel entre chez Arlequin, où il trouve Scaramouche assis tout seul qui joue à la guitare. Sans faire connaître sa présence, Pascariel commence à battre la mesure au-dessus des épaules de Scaramouche, que cette action mystérieuse terrifie. "C'est ici," observe Gherardi (c'est nous qui soulignons):

> où cet incomparable Scaramouche, qui a été l'ornement du théâtre, et le modèle des plus illustres acteurs de son temps, qui avaient appris de lui cet art si difficile, et si nécessaire aux personnes de leur caractère, de remuer les passions, et de les savoir *bien peindre sur le visage;* c'est ici, dis-je, où il faisait pâmer de rire pendant un gros quart d'heure, dans une scène d'épouvantes, où il ne proférait pas un seul mot.

Et Scaramouche possédait aussi, poursuit Gherardi, la capacité de faire croire que cet art si difficile fût naturel. Car il touchait

> plus les coeurs par les seules simplicités d'une pure nature, que n'en touchent d'ordinaire les orateurs les plus habiles par les charmes de la rhétorique la plus persuasive.

Un jugement connu de Tralage vers la fin du siècle confirmerait l'impression que Molière s'intéressait à l'illusion du naturel dans l'art de Scaramouche: "Molière estimait fort Scaramouche pour ses manières naturelles; il le voyait fort souvent et il lui a servi pour former les meilleurs acteurs de sa troupe" (cit. Moore, p. 32).

Mais cet aspect de la dette de Molière, à la fois si connu et si difficile à préciser davantage, nous intéresse ici moins que son art de bien peindre les passions sur le visage. Moore, Bray, Duvignaud et d'autres érudits, qui ont bien connu les mêmes documents que nous, n'ignorent certes pas cet élément du jeu de Molière; et l'apport nouveau de ce qui suit serait surtout de dégager ce qu'ont de positif leurs analyses souvent si riches et si suggestives en les séparant de la fausse conception d'un Scaramouche masqué et en les associant à un théâtre où l'on pouvait voir les visages. Pour "se rendre parfait dans l'art de faire rire," affirme *Elomire hypocondre* (c'est nous qui soulignons):

> Chez le grand Scaramouche il va soir et matin,
> Là le miroir en main et ce grand homme en face,
> Il n'est contorsion, posture ni *grimace*
> Que ce grand écolier du plus grand des bouffons
> Ne fasse et ne refasse en cent et cent façons.
> Tantôt pour exprimer les soucis d'un ménage,
> *De mille et mille plis il fronce son visage;*
> Puis, *joignant la pâleur à ces rides qu'il fait,*
> D'un mari malheureux il est le vrai portrait.

Déjà en 1663 Donneau de Visé, dans *Zélinde*, accuse Molière d'avoir pillé à droite et à gauche ses idées et son jeu. C'est Zélinde qui parle à la scène 8 (et nous qui soulignons):

> Si vous vouliez [. . .] jouer Elomire, il faudrait dépeindre un homme qui eût dans son habillement quelque chose d'Arlequin, de Scaramouche, du Docteur, et de Trivelin, que Scaramouche vînt lui redemander ses démarches, *sa barbe et ses grimaces;* et que les autres vînssent en même temps demander ce qu'il prend d'eux, dans son jeu, et dans ses habits.[8]

Et de suggérer aussi qu'ils viennent tous ensemble demander "ce qu'il a pris dans leurs comédies," alors que dans une autre scène "l'on pourrait faire venir tous les auteurs et tous les vieux bouquins, où il a pris ce qu'il y a de plus beau dans ses pièces." C'est une manière polémique de mettre en valeur la "contamination" comme méthode de Molière, qui s'assimilait volontiers les idées littéraires et théâtrales qui lui convenaient. Elle a le mérite aussi de préciser des dettes particulières à Scaramouche, dont la moustache que porteront notamment Orgon et Harpagon, et les grimaces d'Arnolphe que signale *Zélinde* à la scène 3.[9] Une observation de Villiers de la même année confirme la transformation du jeu de Molière vers ce moment et sa nature: "Il contrefaisait d'abord les Marquis avec le masque de Mascarille; il n'osait les jouer autrement; mais à la fin il nous a fait voir qu'il avait le visage assez plaisant pour représenter sans masque un personnage ridicule" (cit. Moore, p. 33).

A la différence de Moore, nous citons ce témoignage, non pas pour démontrer que Molière avait joué Mascarille sous le masque (ce qui n'est plus douteux), mais pour constater chez ce contemporain la conscience qu'un visage plaisant était devenu un élément important du jeu de Molière.

Il est probable que Molière débuta dans ce nouveau style dans le rôle de Sganarelle du *Cocu imaginaire*, créé le 28 mai 1660. C'est le témoignage de La Neufvillenaine dans son édition clandestine de cette comédie publiée la même année qui atteste pour la première fois à notre connaissance le nouveau jeu de Molière. Les arguments publiés par La Neufvillenaine des scènes 6 et 12 surtout montrent l'importance du visage de Molière acteur. En citant ces textes très connus, nous soulignons les phrases qui concernent le visage plutôt que les postures et les gestes, lesquels un acteur masqué eût pu mimer:

> Il ne s'est jamais rien vu de si agréable que les postures de Sganarelle quand il est derrière sa femme: *son visage* et ses gestes expriment si bien la jalousie, qu'il ne serait pas nécessaire qu'il parlât pour paraître le plus jaloux de tous les hommes [scène 6, où Sganarelle observe sa femme qui admire le portrait de Lélie] . . .
> Il faudrait avoir le pinceau de Poussin, Le Brun ou Mignard pour vous représenter avec quelle posture Sganarelle se fait admirer dans cette scène où il paraît avec un parent de sa femme [scène 12]. L'on n'a jamais vu tenir de discours si naïfs, ni paraître avec *un visage si niais* et l'on ne doit pas moins admirer l'auteur pour avoir fait cette pièce que pour la manière dont il la représente. *Jamais personne ne sut si bien démonter son visage et l'on peut dire que dans cette scène, il en change plus de vingt fois.*

Jean Duvignaud a bien entrevu l'intérêt de cette dernière phrase, qu'il cite en commentant les pages que Bray consacre aux observations de La Neufvillenaine. Mais sous l'influence de Bray, apparemment, il détourne la question des grimaces de Molière pour mettre en valeur les aspects gestuels de son jeu: "Molière emprunte à Tiberio Fiorilli," dit-il, "l'usage que ce dernier fait de son corps comme support de conduites communicatives."[10] Les documents confirment que Molière lui a pris certaines démarches, des postures et des contorsions, mais aussi qu'il se servait déjà de son corps "comme support de conduites communicatives" avant de modeler son jeu sur celui de Scaramouche, qui lui a appris un nouveau style de se comporter sur la scène et surtout de démonter son visage. Pour artificiel qu'il fût, ce jeu a pu paraître naturel à d'excellents esprits, ce qui explique sans doute les derniers vers que La Fontaine consacre à la première représentation des *Fâcheux:*

> Jodelet n'est plus à la mode,
> Et maintenant il ne faut pas
> Quitter la nature d'un pas.

La relation de La Fontaine soulève d'autres problèmes sur lesquels nous reviendrons ailleurs. Cependant nous concluons que "la nature" dont parle le poète est l'illusion du naturel que suggérait le jeu que la troupe de Molière venait d'apprendre de Scaramouche, jeu qui rendait démodé celui du grande maître disparu qu'était Jodelet.[11]

La relation de La Fontaine a le mérite aussi de rappeler que l'activité de Molière n'était jamais liée à un seul théâtre, et qu'en particulier les visites—où il était souvent question d'un théâtre plus ou moins improvisé—ont toujours été d'une importance capitale pour sa troupe, qui savait fort bien s'y adapter. Il n'en est pas moins tentant de lier le jeu et Scaramouche et de Molière au théâtre qu'ils partageaient.

Les documents essentiels sont, avec le *Registre* de La Grange, le devis et marché du 18 novembre et le marché du 24 novembre 1660 (Minutier Central, LIII, 35) numérotés CXXIX et CXXX par Mmes Jurgens et Maxfield-Miller dans *Cent ans de recherches sur Molière.* Le roi ayant gratifié la troupe de Monsieur de la grande salle du Palais-Royal, qui avait, dit La Grange, "trois poutres de la charpente pourries

et étayées et la moitié de la salle découverte et en ruine"
(p. 26). Ratabon, surintendant des bâtiments du roi, reçut
l'ordre d'effectuer les grosses réparations; les aménagements
intérieurs incombaient aux comédiens, qui demandèrent au
roi, dit encore La Grange, "le don et la permission de faire
emporter les loges du Bourbon, et autres choses nécessaires
pour leur nouvel établissement. Ce qui fut accordé" (p. 26),
bien que Vigarani fît brûler les décorations. Nous avons
déjà suggéré en passant que les réparations n'ont pas du tout
rétabli la salle dans sa gloire originale, car elle n'était
"couverte que d'une grande toile bleue suspendue avec des
cordages" jusqu'au 15 mars 1671, date à laquelle on décida
"de faire un grand plaffond qui règne par toute la salle," "de
raccomoder toutes les loges et amphithéâtre bancs et balcons," et

> de faire peindre lesdits plaffonds, loges, amphithéâtre et
> généralement tout ce qui concerne la décoration de ladite (?)
> salle où l'on a augmenté du troisième rang de loges qui n'y
> était point ci-devant (pp. 124–5).

Mais le 18 novembre 1660 du Croisy avait conclu avec
Paul Charpentier un marché

> pour deux rangs de loges, l'un sur l'autre et un appui au-des-
> sus d'environ trois pieds de haut dont y aura dix-sept loges à
> chacun rang, lesquels auront six pieds de mitan en mitan des
> poteaux du devant desdites loges. . . . (p. 351).

Le projet du parterre a dû être modifié le 24 novembre.
Rappelons cependant que la salle était large de dix toises au
maximum, ce qui représente la longueur des énormes
poutres originales (Sauval, II, 163). Les deux rangs de loges
amenées du Petit-Bourbon avait une longueur totale de 17
toises: soit un peu plus de 33 m., chiffre qui vaut
évidemment pour la salle d'origine. Pourrait-on conclure
qu'elles devaient être rangées en courbe? Le parterre con-
venu le 24 novembre était un "plancher de quatre toises de
profondeur et six toises de largeur" (p. 355). C'est-à-dire un
parterre qui n'éloignait aucun spectateur de la scène, alors
que l'amphithéâtre dont il est question dans le *Registre* de La
Grange—ce qui reste des marches en pierre dont parle

Sauval?—eût pu se trouver entre le parterre et les loges en courbe derrière sans que ces dernières soient trop éloignées de la scène pour permettre aux spectateurs de bien voir les visages.

Roger Herzel n'accepte pas l'hypothèse d'une telle configuration des loges. Dans une lettre du 31 mars 1983 il s'explique ainsi:

> I disagree with you on the arrangement of the boxes: I don't think that the oval configuration was installed until 1674, when Lulli and Vigarani renovated the auditorium. During the Molière years I think that the boxes formed the standard rectangle: each tier of 17 had a row of six on each side, and a row of five facing the stage; the five toises at one end of the rectangle thus corresponds to the 30 pieds of the proscenium opening at the other end. Not all that different from the Hôtel de Bourgogne, up to this point. But what made Molière's theatre different and more "modern" and a better place for the spectator to see the play was the sloping floor: a *parterre* "en pente" much smaller than at the Hôtel de Bourgogne, and between the back of the *parterre* and the *loges du bout*, an amphithéâtre at ground level—the remnants of Sauval's 27 stone steps. In a modern theatre these would be the best seats in the house—and at new plays the amphithéâtre was just as expensive as the loges and the seats on stage.

Sans doute Herzel a-t-il raison, et l'on attend avec impatience les résultats définitifs de ses recherches à ce sujet. Cependant il est évident que Molière n'a pas utilisé la scène telle qu'elle avait été en 1641, car ce marché du 24 november précise qu'elle devait être recouverte d'un plancher "de huit toises et demie de largeur ou environ sur cinq toises de proffondeur," et que l'on devait "mettre des supports tant sous le théâtre qui est présentement dans ladite salle que sous le plancher ci-dessus exprimé, avec une cloison pour boucher le châssis du devant du théâtre de la hauteur de six pieds et de trente pieds de largeur . . ." (pp. 354-5). Sans doute y avait-il des places assises sur ce théâtre élevé, mais il suffit à notre propos d'avoir montré que la disposition matérielle du principal théâtre de Molière à Paris favorisait évidemment bien davantage que les tripots de ses débuts un jeu dont les grimaces frappaient les contemporains. Il est réconfortant que sur ce dernier point le grand spécialiste de la mise en scène qu'est Roger Herzel ait signalé son approbation:

> On the only really important point, of course, I agree with you absolutely: it was a very intimate theatre, and ideally suited for reading facial expressions.

Les grimaces formaient donc un élément essentiel du jeu de Molière acteur. C'est un jeu qu'il importe de séparer de l'idée des masques de la *commedia dell'arte* qui servaient à identifier certains personnages; et c'est un jeu qui n'a absolument rien à voir avec les principaux rôles moliéresques dont un masque métaphorique cache le vrai caractère—Tartuffe et Dom Juan—, rôles que Molière n'a jamais tenus. Faire d'une tradition de masques qui identifient une *persona* dramatique, la source des masques d'hypocrisie qui cachent les véritables intentions d'un personnage qui joue un rôle "métathéâtral" en contradiction avec son "vrai" rôle, a toujours été un contresens. Et ce contresens même est étranger aux dettes de Molière envers Scaramouche, qui lui a appris à jouer des personnages comiques sans masque. Si certains rôles que Molière a écrits pour lui-même font penser à Pantalone—Arnolphe de *L'Ecole des femmes*, Orgon de *Tartuffe*, Harpagon de *L'Avare*, M. Jourdain du *Bourgeois Gentilhomme*, et Argan du *Malade imaginaire*, par exemple—il est évident que Molière les interprétait lui-même d'une manière toute nouvelle. L'originalité de ces personnages dépend en partie de l'imitation d'une innovation déjà effectuée par le grand Scaramouche qu'était Tiberio Fiorilli. Rien n'est mieux établie que l'innovation apportée par ce dernier aux traditions de la *commedia dell'arte*. Rien ne saute mieux aux yeux que l'originalité de l'imitation de Molière, dont les rôles comportent d'importantes dimensions littéraires, voire poétiques et moralistes, à peu près étrangères au jeu de Scaramouche et peu développées dans les rôles de Pantalone. Si ces personnages moliéresques continuent la tradition de Pantalone, ils le font renaître avec des traits expressifs, changeants, originaux dus à Scaramouche. Qu'on pense à cette dette et à la conception des rôles qu'elle implique chaque fois qu'Arnolphe apprend d'Horace une fâcheuse nouvelle, chaque fois que Sganarelle se scandalise devant Dom Juan (ou s'étonne du refus du Pauvre), qu'Orgon s'impatiente, qu'Alceste s'indigne, ou qu'Harpagon se défie de son entourage. . . . Ces grands rôles sont écrits pour un acteur qui sait mettre en valeur l'expressivité et le comique de son visage.

4
Ponctuation et Dramaturgie

La pontuation des éditions originales de Molière reflète des éléments non négligeables de sa dramaturgie que la prétendue modernisation des éditions courantes fait souvent disparaître. La thèse que j'énonce n'est pas nouvelle. C'est l'idée qui a guidé les éditions que j'ai procurées du *Bourgeois Gentilhomme* et des *Femmes Savantes*.[1] C'est une approche que j'ai pu esquisser aussi dans un état présent des études moliéresques paru en 1975.[2] Cette thèse est acceptée, je crois, par quelques autres moliéristes, dont Mme Micheline Cuénin et M.J.T. Stoker.[3] Mais je saisis d'autant plus volontiers l'occasion qui m'est offerte de la développer ici qu'elle n'a pas convaincu tout le monde. On a l'habitude de se fier, de près ou de loin, au texte des *Oeuvres* de Molière établi à la fin du siècle dernier par Eugène Despois et Paul Mesnard pour la collection des Grands Ecrivains de la France. Le texte de cette édition remarquable reste à quelques dètails près la base de la plupart des éditions courantes : celles notamment des Classiques Garnier, des Nouveaux Classiques Larousse, des différentes collections Hachette, etc. Les variantes parfois considérables entre les différentes éditions modernes ne nous concernent guère ici. Les exemples que j'ai choisis sont destinés à mettre en valeur le décalage entre l'allure théâtrale des originales et les textes tels qu'ils sont modifiés à partir de l'édition Despois et Mesnard.

D'excellents critiques semblent ignorer à quel point Despois et Mesnard sont intervenus pour modifier la ponctuation des originales de Molière.[4] D'autres érudits nient plutôt aux originales toute autorité en fait de ponctuation, tel mon ami—j'espère qu'il restera mon ami, car j'ai la plus haute estime pour son érudition—M. Georges Couton dans sa présentation des *Oeuvres complètes* de Molière parues en 1971 dans la Bibliothèque de la Pléiade. Le problème de la ponctuation se poserait, dit-il, dans les mêmes termes que pour l'orthographe; et celle des originales

> semble correspondre aux usages des divers ateliers d'imprimerie et non pas aux habitudes personnelles de Molière dont, au reste, nous n'avons aucun manuscrit autographe et dont nous doutons qu'il ait revu lui-même les épreuves de ses pièces (I, XI).

M. Couton a donc adopté ce qu'il appelle "les usages modernes"—usages qui correspondent à peu de chose près dans les cas où je les ai vérifiés à ceux adoptés auparavant par Despois et Mesnard, qui avaient d'ailleurs gardé de nombreuses modifications déjà apportées aux textes de Molière par la somptueuse édition de M.-A. Joly illustrée par Boucher (1734). Bon nombre des points d'exclamation (!) des éditions courantes remontent ainsi à une modernisation de la ponctuation effectuée à l'époque de Marivaux et de Nivelle de La Chaussée, et je regrette de ne pas disposer d'assez de pages pour présenter les exemples que j'ai rencontrés en publiant *Le Bourgeois Gentilhomme*.

Despois et Mesnard remplacent volontiers les points d'interrogation (?) par des points d'exclamation (!), et vice versa. Ils manient à leur gré points (.) et points-virgules (;). Ils ajoutent à gogo des points de suspension (...). Mais la spécialité de la maison, c'est sans aucun doute les virgules (,), qui entre leurs mains paraissent, disparaissent et se déplacent avec une désinvolture qui ne saurait être sans conséquence pour le souffle des acteurs, le rythme des vers, les tons de voix indiqués, etc. Car les virgules représentent des pauses, de petites hésitations parfois, une manière de dégager un mot et même des gestes implicites, détails dont la présence théâtrale—réelle ou imaginaire—peut être considérable. L'intérêt individuel de ces détails est souvent assez limité. Mais leur effet est cumulatif. Dans les grandes pièces, les modifications se comptent pas centaines, mettons dix ou douze par page pour les éditions courantes, parfois davantage : soit plusieurs modifications d'intonation ou de rythme par minute de représentation. L'incidence précise de ces modifications, assez irrégulière, ne me concerne pas. Je n'apporte ni graphiques, ni statistiques exactes, car il suffit de constater que les modifications sont fréquentes— toutes les vingt secondes environ pour s'assurer qu'elles doivent altérer le caractère d'une représentation, même idéale.

Je ne parle évidemment pas ici des modifications qui sont apportées à toute représentation théâtrale par les acteurs, le metteur-en-scène et d'autres membres d'une troupe, mais de leur point de départ, qui n'est autre que celui d'un lecteur : le livre qu'on a devant les yeux et qui présente un texte dont la ponctuation propose déjà une première interprétation. La modernisation de la ponctuation change de façon significative ce point de départ. En général elle substitue à une ponctuation apparemment destinée à guider, puis je crois à rappeler, ou bien à remplacer une représentation théâtrale, une ponctuation plus conforme aux habitudes de lecture silencieuse diffusée surtout depuis la fin du dix-huitième siècle. On modernise en effet pour faciliter la lecture d'une pièce de théâtre comme s'il s'agissait d'un roman ou d'un essai. On éloigne d'autant le lecteur de l'imagination théâtrale de Molière.

Le terme MODERNISER se rapporte à un concept assez flou. On garde, nous l'avons vu, des leçons substituées à celles des originales par l'éditeur de 1734. Et l'on supprime des styles qu'on trouve encore dans des publications récentes. Car MODERNISER répond à plus d'une seule intention éditoriale. Ecartons celle de corriger. L'incorrection de certaines originales—celle de *Sganarelle*, non autorisée, et celle d'*Amphitryon*, retirée apparemment du commerce—justifient la préférence d'autres éditions. Mais la volonté de corriger une réplique mal imprimée peut amener un éditeur à modifier des éléments de ponctuation qui étaient probablement intentionnels de la part de Molière. C'est un processus qui se remarque déjà dans l'édition Vivot-La Grange de 1682. Voici une réplique du *Médecin malgré-luy* telle qu'elle paraît dans l'originale peu correcte (Ribou, 1667) (Acte I, scène 2):

Sganarelle

Tu es vne Folle, de prendre garde à cela. Ce sont petites
choses qui sont, de temps, en temps, necessaires dans
l'Amitié: & cinq ou six coups de baston, entre Gens qui s'aiment, ne font que ragaillardir l'Affection. Va ie m'en vais au
Bois : & ie te promets, auiourd'huy, plus d'vn cent de Fagots
(p. 19).

Dès 1682 une graphie nouvelle s'ajoute à une ponctuation
en partie corrigée, en partie modernisée:

Tu es une Folle de prendre garde à cela ; Ce sont petites
choses qui sont de temps en temps necessaires dans l'amitié,
& cinq ou six coups de bâton entre gens qui s'aiment, ne font
que ragaillardir l'affection. Va, je m'en vais au Bois, & je te
promets aujourd'huy plus d'un cent de Fagots (III, 217).

Sans doute a-t-on raison de biffer la virgule après *de temps* et
d'en ajouter une, je crois, après *Va*. Mais il me semble qu'en
faisant disparaître trois paires de virgules on ôte comme des
indications scéniques qui minimisent *(de temps en temps)*,
mettent au point *(entre gens qui s'aiment)* ou soulignent *(aujourd'huy)* de manière théâtrale les phrases qu'elles
dégagent. Et il est curieux de noter que Despois et Mesnard
rétablissent une paire de virgules là où ils ont reconnu une
intention burlesque, la traduction plaisante d'un vers de
Térence bien connu de Molière: "Amantium irae, amoris
integratio" :

Tu es une folle de prendre garde à cela : ce sont petites choses
qui sont de temps en temps nécessaires dans l'amitié ; et cinq
ou six coups de bâton, entre gens qui s'aiment, ne font que
ragaillardir l'affection. Va, je m'en vais au bois, et je te promets aujourd'hui plus d'un cent de fagots (VI, 46–47).

Il existe une subjectivité glissante qui va de l'intention de
corriger à celle d'améliorer, ou de simplifier, ou
d'interpréter, et surtout de normaliser.

Ce qui frappe dans l'exemple cité du *Médecin malgré lui*,
c'est que la "déthéâtralisation" de la ponctuation des pièces
de Molière remonte parfois même à l'édition Vivot-La
Grange. Molière homme de théâtre commence déjà à se
muer en Molière écrivain, phénomène dont l'iconographie

moliéresque offre une image suggestive : les portraits de l'acteur peints par ses amis peintres font place au dix-huitième siècle à des portraits idéaux d'un écrivain qui médite une grosse plume à la main. La modernisation de la ponctuation fait partie d'une consécration littéraire. Elle entraîne souvent la banalisation d'une ponctuation dont le caractère théâtral est sacrifié à la mode littéraire du moment. Je montrerai tout à l'heure comment, à mon avis, la modernisation des éditions courantes appauvrit l'imagination théâtrale de telle scène, affaiblit le comique de telle réplique, estompe les différences entre des rôles qui sont mieux contrastés avec la ponctuation de l'originale.

Répondons cependant à M. Couton, pour lequel la ponctuation des originales de Molière correspond "aux usages des divers ateliers d'imprimerie et non pas aux habitudes personnelles de Molière." Il s'agit évidemment d'un problème qui, en l'absence de manuscrits autographes, n'est pas susceptible d'une solution définitive; et les opinions peuvent légitimement différer les unes des autres. J'accepte volontiers que certains éléments de la ponctuation des originales de Molière reflètent vraisemblablement les usages des ateliers où elles furent imprimées. Nous n'en savons pas grand'chose, par comparaison avec les originales de Shakespeare, par exemple. On sait pourtant que les maisons d'édition ont souvent l'habitude d'imposer certaines conventions, et elles semblent en avoir imposé quelques-unes aux éditions de Molière. Mais là n'est pas la question. Il suffit qu'une édition soit correcte, cohérente, et faite selon les usages de son temps pour qu'elle mérite d'être respectée.

C'est du moins la conclusion de M. Fredson Bowers, d'après lequel il faudrait éviter, en publiant une édition sérieuse d'un texte ancien, d'en modifier les "accidents"— orthographe, ponctuation, emploi des majuscules, division des mots, etc.—non seulement quand on connaît les intentions de l'auteur, ou bien celles d'un intermédiaire autorisé et identifié, mais aussi quand les accidents sont conformes aux habitudes contemporaines de l'auteur.[5] C'est une conclusion qui me semble tout à fait pertinente au cas Molière. Car les originales de Molière se présentent en général très bien selon les usages des années en question, de 1660 à 1672. L'intention semble avoir été de ponctuer, et de virguler surtout, pour la voix et pour l'oreille autant que pour les yeux. Ce sont des usages qui ne se limitent nullement aux oeuvres dramatiques. On les recontre aussi par exemple dans les préfaces de Molière. Mais ces usages ont une importance particulière pour les oeuvres dramatiques, car ils préservent une manière contemporaine de les dire et de les imaginer. On peut trouver même dans les meilleures originales quelques fautes, mais leur ponctuation est loin d'être arbitraire. Là où elle semble fantaisiste, elle vient à l'appui d'éléments comiques du jeu qu'elle suppose à la représentation. La ponctuation la plus fantaisiste des originales est sans aucun doute personnelle à Molière, comme l'exemple suivant le fera voir.

Car il est certain que la ponctuation du rôle de M. Macroton dans *L'Amour médecin* ne reflète pas les usages de chez Girard. C'est donc Molière qui a su imposer cette ponctuation théâtrale au rôle, dont voici la première réplique (Acte II, scène 5) :

M. Macroton

Il parle en allongeant ses mots.
Mon-si-eur. Dans. ces. ma-ti-e-res. la. il. faut. pro-ce-der.
auec-que. cir-cons-pec-tion. &. ne. ri-en. fai-re, com.me.
on. dit, a. la. vo-lé-e. Dau-tant. que. les. fau-tes. qu'on. y.
peut. fai-re. sont. se-lon. nos-tre. mais-tre. Hip-po-cra-te. d'v-
ne. dan-ge-reu-se. con-se-quen-ce. (Girard, 1666, pp. 49–50)

Les éditions courantes restent fidèles à l'esprit de cette ponctuation fantaisiste, car il est évident qu'elle caractérise un rôle qui contraste notamment avec celui de M. Bahys, qui "parle tousiours en bredouillant."

Plus systématiques, Despois et Mesnard corrigent ce qui peut être une inadvertance de l'imprimeur original qui ne dégage pas la première syllabe d'*auecque* ; et ils remplacent des virgules par des points, comme s'il n'y avait pas une distinction évidente entre ces deux signes tels qu'ils se rencontrent dans ce rôle. Par contre, le point à l'intérieur de *com. me* est probablement une faute bien corrigée dans leur édition :

Mon-si-eur. dans. ces. ma-ti-è-res-là. il. faut. pro-cé-der. a-
vec-que. cir-con-spec-tion. et. ne. ri-en. fai-re. com-me. on.
dit. à. la. vo-lé-e. d'au-tant. que. les. fau-tes. qu'on. y. peut.
fai-re. sont. se-lon. no-tre. maî-tre. Hip-po-cra-te. d'u-ne.
dan-ge-reu-se. con-sé-quen-ce. (V, 327–28)

Ce ne sont pas les modifications apportées à ce passage
qui intéressent à présent, mais le fait que tous les éditeurs
acceptent que cette ponctuation étrange indique le jeu de
l'acteur. A la fin de cette même scène, la ponctuation est
d'ailleurs le seul indice de la mimique de Sganarelle, qui fait
le comique de son jeu :

Sganarelle

A Monsieur Macroton.
Ie. vous. rends. tres-hum-bles. gra-ces.
A Monsieur Bahys.
Et vous suis infiniment obligé de lá peine que vous auez prise.

La ponctuation de cette réplique est personnelle, théâtrale
et significative. Elle suggère à quel point il est hasardeux de
conjecturer que la ponctuation des originales de Molière ne
se conforme pas à ses habitudes personnelles. Les répliques
de M. Macroton comportent de nombreuses virgules avec
les points et les traits-d'union qui séparent les mots et les
syllabes ; c'est qu'on voulait indiquer un débit qui contraste
avec celui de M. Bahys, dont les répliques sont beaucoup
moins virgulées ;

M. Bahys

Apres nous en viendrons à la purgation & à la saignée, que
nous reïtererons s'il en est besoin (pp. 53–54).

Un aspect du contraste est donné dans les indications
scéniques déjà citées: M. Macroton parle "en allongeant ses
mots" ; M. Bahys, "tousiours en bredouillant." Mais la
rapidité du débit de M. Bahys est indiquée par la ponctuation de ses répliques, confirmée en ce cas par une observation de Sganarelle : "L'vn va en tortuë, & l'autre court la
poste" (p. 51). En ajoutant deux virgules à la réplique citée
de M. Bahys (après *purgation* et *reïtererons*), Despois et Mesnard, et M. Couton, font disparaître cet indice.
Despois et Mesnard acceptent aussi l'esprit de la ponctua-

tion de cette réplique du *Sicilien* où Adraste place Isidore pour la peindre : "Suis-je bien ainsy ?", demande-t-elle. Et Adraste de répondre :

> Oüy. Leuez-vous vn peu, s'il vous plaist ; vn peu plus de ce costé-là ; le corps tourné ainsy ; la teste vn peu leuée, afin que la beauté du cou paroisse. Cecy vn peu plus découuert. *Il parle de sa gorge* ; Bon. Là, vn peu dauantage ; encore tant soit peu (Ribou, 1668, pp. 51–52).

L'orthographe à part, je ne vois que deux modifications. L'indication scénique est mise entre parenthèses ( ). Et un point remplace le point-virgule après *plaist*, détail peu important. Car il suffit à ces éditeurs de reconnaître le caractère théâtral d'une réplique pour qu'ils en respectent la ponctuation.

C'est ainsi que les éditeurs modernes respectent l'allure de la répétition que se donne Sosie dans la première scène d'*Amphitryon*, que je cite d'après la deuxième édition originale (Ribou, 1668) ;

> Figurez-vous donc que Telebe,
>   Madame, est de ce costé :
> C'est vne Ville, en vérité,
> Aussi grande quasi que Thebe.
>   La Riuiere est comme là.
> Icy nos Gens se camperent :
> Et l'espace que voila,
> Nos Ennemis l'occuperent :
> Sur vn haut, vers cet endroit,
> Estoit leur Infanterie ;
> Et plus bas, du costé droit,
> Estoit la Caualerie (p. 12).

Il marque les lieux sur sa main, ou à terre.

Les quelques modifications souvent apportées en fin de vers ne frappent pas les virgules qui détachent, par exemple, *vers cet endroit* et *du costé droit*, expressions qui correspondent à des gestes, dont le style général est indiqué en marge. Ici encore l'écriture de Molière est évidemment assez théâtrale pour que le rythme de sa scène soit respecté.

Il n'en est rien, cependant, s'agissant d'un des vers les mieux connus de *Tartuffe*, où Dorine répond aux questions d'Orgon lors de sa première entrée en scène (Acte I, scène 4) :

> Tartuffe ? Il se porte à merveille,
> Gros et gras, le teint frais, et la bouche vermeille.

Pour expliquer un vers dont ils admirent "l'aisance du tour," Despois et Mesnard citent, d'après les frères Parfaict, un contemporain de Molière selon lequel du Croisy, qui créa le rôle de Tartuffe, "étoit gras, bel homme" (IV, 412). Mais dans l'originale ce vers n'a pas exactement cette allure classique, car il y a une virgule après *Gros* :

> Gros, et gras, le teint frais, & la bouche vermeille.

La pause après *Gros*, accompagnée peut-être d'un geste, met bien en valeur cet adjectif. La même pause dégage aussi les mots qui suivent : *et gras*, rythme qui suggère un personnage plus grossier que "gros et gras" dit sans hésitation. C'est un détail, dira-t-on. Mais c'est une suppression typique qui a pu favoriser, d'une part, l'idée pédagogique de l'alexandrin classique, idée assez fausse, je crois, car le rythme des alexandrins est plus varié dans les originales que dans les éditions modernisées, et, d'autre part, les interprétations historiques de Tartuffe dont la tendance a été de négliger dans ce rôle la grosse corpulence indiquée : les Tartuffes amoureux et élégants, par exemple, ainsi que les Tartuffes maigres, sinistres, tels qu'ils sont décrits dans le beau livre de M. Maurice Descotes[6].

Je ne pense pas que la virgule après *Gros* représente une faute, quoiqu'elle disparaisse dès l'édition de 1682. Elle ne reflète pas non plus une convention, car Ribou ne virgule pas toujours avant *et*. Elle doit correspondre à une pause indiquée, puis oubliée. En ce cas particulier, nous disposons d'ailleurs d'un autre indice, la source probable de ce vers que j'ai découverte au début d'un sonnet de Saint-Amant. Ce sont des vers que je cite d'après les *Oeuvres* de Saint-Amant publiées par Loyson en 1661, trois ans avant la première représentation de *Tartuffe* :

> ME voyant plus frisé qu'on (sic) gros Comte Allemant,
> Le teint frais, les yeux doux, & la bouche vermeille (p. 190).

"L'aisance du tour" du vers admiré chez Molière est déjà dans le vers de Saint-Amant. "Les yeux doux," Molière les déplace, et Tartuffe fera ailleurs des yeux doux à Elmire. Le mot *gros*, détaché au début du vers dans l'originale de *Tartuffe*, semble avoir été introduit dans le vers qui sert de modèle après avoir été enlevé au vers qui le précède dans le sonnet de Saint-Amant. Molière aura trouvé "et gras" pour compléter l'alexandrin, dont la ponctuation originale suggère une pensée qui se cherche plutôt qu'une formule qui se récite. Ce qui rend, à mon sens, la réplique de Dorine plus énergique et plus comique. A noter aussi que le vers de Saint-Amant est virgulé en 1661 exactement comme les éditions courantes virgulent le vers de Molière. C'est donc un style que Molière eût pu choisir s'il l'avait voulu, un style qui n'a rien de particulièrement moderne. En effet, l'intervention de l'édition Vivot-La Grange ne modernise pas ; elle banalise. Et c'est leur version banalisée de ce vers qu'on retrouve partout.

Sait-on que Molière détache, à la fin de cette même comédie de *L'Imposteur*, la formule "et sincère" ? Despois et Mesnard font imprimer sans virgules les deux derniers vers, qui en ont trois dans l'originale. C'est Orgon qui parle ;

> Et par vn doux hymen, couronner en Valere,
> La flame d'vn Amant genereux, & sincere.

Chaucune de ces virgules met en valeur le mot qui la précède, et la dernière permet en plus au dernier mot de la comédie de trouver sa valeur thématique. Ajoutons qu'on ne virgulait pas avant *et* chez Ribou quand une pause n'est pas indiquée. Témoin ces vers de Cléante (Acte I, scène 5) :

> Les bons & vrais Deuots qu'on doit suiure à la trace, (p. 15)
> [. . . .]
> De qui la sacrilege & trompeuse grimace
> Abuse impunément, & se joüé à leur gré,
> De ce qu'ont les Mortels de plus saint, & sacré (p. 16).

Ce qui représente une pure convention, c'est la suppression des virgules avant *et*, telle que l'ont effectuée Despois et Mesnard dans ces deux derniers vers et très souvent ailleurs.

Voici un dernier exemple, extrait de la grande scène où Tartuffe essaie de séduire Elmire alors qu'Orgon se cache sous la table (Acte IV, scène 5) ;

> Elmire
> C'est vn rhume obstiné, sans doute, & je voy bien
> Que tous les jus du monde, icy, ne feront rien.
> Tartuffe
> Cela, certe, est fâcheux.
>
>   Elmire
>   Oüy, plus qu'on ne peut dire.
> Tartuffe
> Enfin vostre scrupule est facile à détruire,
> Vous estes assurée icy d'vn plein secret,
> Et le mal n'est jamais que dans l'éclat qu'on fait (p. 74).

La distinction entre le mot *icy* tel qu'il est dit par Elmire, virgulé, et tel qu'il est attribué quelques vers plus tard à Tartuffe, sans virgules, pourrait répondre chez Elmire à des pauses destinées à gagner du temps, ou bien à une emphase par laquelle elle ironise à l'égard de son mari caché, alors que le même mot dit sans hésitation par Tartuffe correspondrait à sa hâte. Mais les éditions courantes font disparaître cette distinction avec les virgules d'Elmire. Ce qui frappe dans la suppression n'est pas la modernité, car je retrouve *ici* virgulé comme dans la réplique d'Elmire dans *Le Monde* daté d'aujourd'hui 18 mai 1979, à la page 2, rubrique "Langues." On trouve *ici* avec ou sans virgules dans les originales de Molière selon ce qui semble bien être l'intention de souligner ou de dégager ce mot, ou le contraire. Aussi Despois et Mesnard respectent-ils le caractère emphatique du mot *ici* virgulé quand ils en reconnaissent la valeur, comme dans le premier des exemples suivants du *Sicilien*. Dans la scène déjà citée, Adraste dit au sujet d'Isidore qui pose : "mais le Sujet, icy, ne fournit que trop de luy mesme . . ." (p. 49). Et Isidore qui pose dans une situation équivoque affirme : "Ce sont, icy, des choses toutes neufues pour moy . . ." (p. 52). Un peu plus loin au début de la scène XII Hali dit en entrant : "I'entre, icy, librement . . ." (p. 58). En supprimant les virgules d'Isidore on fait disparaître son hésitation devant l'ambiguïté des choses toutes nouvelles pour elle, qui font partie de l'idéalisation d'une jeune première amoureuse d'un homme qu'elle ne connaît pas encore très bien. En supprimant celles de Hali, on minimise un mot dont l'importance correspond à la présence en ce lieu précis d'un personnage qui y vient d'entrer sans s'être fait annoncer. L'emphase en chaque cas est "métathéâtrale."[7]

Le Bourgeois Gentilhomme fournit des exemples encore plus clairs. Au début du troisième acte, M. Jourdain se prépare à sortir pour montrer son nouveau habit par la ville. Nicole s'en esclaffe. Et Mme Jourdain s'en scandalise. "Vous moquez-vous du monde, demande-t-elle, de vous être fait enharnacher de la sorte ? et avez-vous envie qu'on se raille partout de vous ?" Dans les éditions courantes M. Jourdain répond : "Il n'y a que des sots et des sottes, ma femme, qui se railleront de moi". La réponse de M. Jourdain, présentée ainsi, peut paraître pléonastique. Mais dans l'originale il y a après *Sots* une virgule—c'est-à-dire, une pause—qui dégage toute la valeur dramatique des mots qui suivent : *et des Sottes :*

Monsieur Jourdain
Il n'y a que des Sots, & des Sottes, ma Femme, qui se railleront de moy.

Ainsi dégagés, ces mots visent, soit Madame Jourdain, qui gronde son mari, soit Nicole, toujours présente et qui s'était raillée de son maître pendant toute la scène précédente, soit les deux femmes ensemble. La bonne ponctuation théâtrale de l'originale invite à un geste, un coup d'oeil accusateur. La virgule, partout supprimée, n'est pas arbitraire. Ceux qui la suppriment sacrifient à la convention relativement récente d'ôter une virgule avant *et*, convention arbitraire qui fait disparaître ce qui peut être le seul indice que Nicole doit attirer en ce moment précis la colère de son maître avec un dernier rire mal étouffé. Le rythme de la réplique, telle qu'elle paraît dans l'originale, correspond à un jeu animé, quel qu'il soit, et non pas à une lecture purement logique. En ôtant au lecteur cette virgule, on lui ôte en même temps l'effet qu'elle peut produire.

Cette virgule me semble d'autant plus intentionnelle de la part de Molière, homme de théâtre, que dans l'originale les répliques du Maître de Philosophie sont virgulées d'une

manière pesante, différente du style des autres personnages, et notamment de celui du Maître à danser. C'est une
différenciation estompée dans les éditions courantes,
comme les exemples suivants le feront voir. A gauche, deux
répliques telles que les donne M. J. Thoraval en 1963 ; et à
droite, ces mêmes répliques citées d'après l'originale (Le
Monnier, 1671). Elles sont de la troisième scène de l'Acte
II :

Petits Classiques Bordas :	Le Monnier :
Maître à danser.—Comment !	*Maistre à dancer.*
Monsieur, il vient nous dire	Comment, Monsieur, il vient
des injures à tous deux, en	nous dire des injures à tous
méprisant la danse, que j'exerce,	deux, en méprisant la Dance
et la musique, dont il fait	que j'exerce, & la Musique
profession . . .	dont il fait profession? . . .
Maître de philosophie.—. . .	*Maistre de philosophie* . . .
Ce n'est pas de vaine gloire	Ce n'est pas de vaine gloire,
et de condition que les hommes	& de condition, que les Hommes
doivent disputer entre eux ;	doivent disputer entre'eux ; &
ce qui nous distingue parfaite-	ce qui nous distingue parfaite-
ment les uns des autres,	ment les uns des autres, c'est
c'est la sagesse et la vertu (p. 46)	la Sagesse, & la Vertu (p. 3–31).

La ponctuation originale suggère de la part du Maître à
danser un débit rapide, même impétueux, alors que le
Maître de Philosophie doit parler avec emphase, avec des
pauses pour dégager les grands mots abstraits qu'il affecte :
à noter les virgules après *gloire, condition* et *Sagesse.* Je ne vois
pas comment les différents styles de ces deux maîtres corre-
spondraient aux usages de l'éditeur Le Monnier, tellement
ils contrastent. Et que l'on ne dise pas qu'il était conven-
tionnel de virguler avant *et*, et qu'une telle convention expliquerait le phénomène que je présente. Car le Maître
d'armes dira peu après :

> Et moy, je leur soûtiens à tous deux, que la Science de tirer
> des Armes, est la plus belle & la plus necessaire de toutes les
> Sciences (p. 31).

Et le Maître de musique avait parlé dès la première scène de
"ce Monsieur Jourdain, avec les visions de Noblesse & de
Galanterie qu'il est allé se mettre en teste" (p. 3).

Il est donc raisonnable de supposer, soit que Molière a bien imposé une ponctuation différenciée pour distinguer des jeux différents, soit que son imprimeur suivait avec plus ou moins de fidélité un manuscrit qui comportait une telle différenciation. S'autoriser du défaut d'autographes pour modifier les accidents des originales me semble, en ce cas comme ailleurs, un raisonnement bien étrange. Car les imprimeurs originaux avaient devant eux les manuscrits qui nous manquent. Même s'ils s'efforçaient toujours d'imposer sur la ponctuation de ces manuscrits les conventions de leur atelier, ce qui n'est pas du tout certain, ils n'auraient guère su éliminer toutes les caractéristiques personnelles de l'auteur. Dans la réplique du Maître de Philosophie citée, je ne vois guère par quelle convention l'imprimeur eût imposé *gloire* et *condition* avec minuscules, et puis *Sagesse* et *Vertu* avec majuscules. Ce sont des différences que la normalisation fait disparaître, comme dans toutes les éditions modernes que j'ai pu voir. Mais ces minuscules et ces majuscules s'expliquent très bien par rapport au jeu d'un acteur qui minimise la *gloire*, et la *condition*, avant de souligner prétentieusement la valeur morale de *la Sagesse*, et de *la Vertu*. La normalisation prive le lecteur de signes très probablement destinés à l'aider à imaginer ce jeu.[8]

Dans *Le Misanthrope*, le rôle de Célimène en particulier perd une partie de son éclat avec la ponctuation supprimée dans les éditions courantes. Bornons-nous au portrait de Timante, qui perd entre les mains de Despois et Mesnard huit virgules en neuf vers—soit huit pauses destinées, me semble-t-il, à faire valoir la mimique dans le jeu de Célimène. Voici le portrait d'après Despois et Mesnard (Acte II, scène 4);

> C'est de la tête aux pieds un homme tout mystère,
> Qui vous jette en passant un coup d'oeil égaré,
> Et, sans aucune affaire, est toujours affairé.
> Tout ce qu'il vous débite en grimaces abonde;
> A force de façons, il assomme le monde;
> Sans cesse il a, tout bas, pour rompre l'entretien,
> Un secret à vous dire, et ce secret n'est rien;
> De la moindre vétille il fait une merveille,
> Et jusques au bonjour, il dit tout à l'oreille (V, 481).

Et le voici avec la ponctuation de l'originale, ponctuation qui en détachant des mots et des phrases, invite des gestes et des tons moqueurs, une mimique caricaturale beaucoup moins apparente sans cette aide précieuse:

> C'est, de la Teste aux Pieds, vn Hôme tout Mystere,
> Qui vous jette, en passant, vn coup d'oeil égaré,
> Et, sans aucune Affaire, est toûjours affairé.
> Tout ce qu'il vous débite, en grimaces, abonde;
> A force de façons, il assomme le Monde;
> Sans cesse il a, tout bas, pour rompre l'Entretien,
> Vn Secret à vous dire, & ce Secret n'est rien;
> De la moindre Vetille, il fait vne Merveille,
> Et, jusques au Bonjour, il dit tout à l'oreille (Ribou, 1667,
> p.31).

D'après M. Guibert, même les nombreuses majuscules de cette originale ne seraient probablement pas à attribuer à l'imprimeur.[9] Et je ne vois pas pourquoi on voudrait attribuer la ponctuation à l'imprimeur plutôt qu'à l'auteur-metteur-en-scène. Car les différentes paires de virgules aideraient l'actrice qui parle à dégager ses traits satiriques. La ponctuation théâtrale de ce portrait représente un aspect tout à fait caractéristique de son adaptation de l'épigramme de Martial qui en est la source. Aucune des versions contemporaines de cette épigramme que j'ai publiées n'est munie d'une ponctuation qui prête aussi bien à la mimique que celle de l'originale de Molière, invitant l'actrice à détacher des phrases susceptibles d'être accompagnées d'une imitation : *en passant, en grimaces, tout bas* . . .[10] Les virgules après les deux *Et* au début des vers serviraient à lancer en chaque cas la phrase qui suit, ponctuation qui contraste notamment avec celle de la réplique d'Acaste après ce portrait : "Et Geralde, Madame" ? L'intention théâtrale n'étant plus la même, *Et* n'est plus suivi d'une virgule.

Ce portrait de Timante n'est pas exceptionnel au point de vue de la ponctuation. La modernisation cache bonne partie de l'invitation à l'imitation, à la mimique qui me paraît si évidente dans l'originale. Elle estompe le ton moqueur de ce rôle si théâtral de Célimène. L'originale invite surtout à jouer un peu le personnage de chaque fâcheux dont Célimène offre le portrait satirique.

Par contre, c'est à peu près l'effet contraire que produit la modernisation du rôle d'Henriette dans *Les Femmes savantes*—là par exemple où dans la première scène elle demande à Armande :

> Et qu'est-ce qu'à mon âge on a de mieux à faire,
> Que d'attacher à soi, par le titre d'époux,
> Un homme qui vous aime et soit aimé de vous,
> Et de cette union, de tendresse suivie,
> Se faire les douceurs d'une innocente vie ?
> Ce noeud, bien assorti, n'a-t-il pas des appas ? (vv. 20–25).

C'est le texte tel qu'il est publié par Despois et Mesnard, M. Couton et d'autres. Dans l'originale, la ponctuation est assez différente. Je cite d'après mon édition, basée sur celle de Promé, 1673/2 :

> Et qu'est-ce qu'à mon âge on a de mieux à faire,
> Que d'attacher à soi, par le titre d'époux,
> Un homme qui vous aime, et soit aimé de vous;
> Et de cette union de tendresse suivie,
> Se faire les douceurs d'une innocente vie ?
> Ce noeud bien assorti n'a-t-il pas des appas ? (p. 78).

Le rythme, et par conséquent l'intonation, le style et le caractère indiqué par cette réplique dans l'originale, n'est plus du tout le même dans les versions dites modernisées. On ne saurait séparer ici le son et le sens théâtral de tels voeux. L'originale marque d'une virgule nécessaire à la prosodie même de l'alexandrin le vers :

> Un homme qui vous aime, et soit aimé de vous.

C'est un vers dont la forme antithétique semble destinée à mettre en valeur la réciprocité d'un amour idéal. Le point-virgule à la fin de ce vers marquerait une pause relativement longue, pour que l'actrice puisse jouer le personnage d'une fiancée qui se laisse aller à ce rêve romanesque. Au vers suivant, on modernise en ajoutant une virgule après *union*, alors que dans l'originale Henriette parle sans hésitation aucune d'une "union de tendresse suivie." Il y a, au théâtre, toute la différence entre une fiancée qui parle sans hésitation de tendresse et celle qui hésite. Aucune hésitation non plus au dernier vers de la réplique, où l'on modernise en détachant de virgules les mots *bien assorti*, ce qui donne à la réplique un ton plus calculateur. Encore une fois, la convention dont il est question ici n'est pas une habitude de chez Promé de virguler avant *et*, car cinquante vers plus loin dans la même scène on voit ces vers d'Armande:

> Et ce n'est point du tout la prendre pour modèle,
> Ma soeur, que de tousser et de cracher comme elle.
>
> (vv. 75–76, éd. Hall, p. 80)

Bien au contraire, on voit des distinctions d'un ordre tout à fait comparable dans, par exemple, *L'Ambigu comique* de Montfleury, publié par Promé en 1673. C'est apparemment selon le débit des vers indiqués que l'on lit dans la première scène de la tragédie :

> Achate . . .
> Je ne voy qu'à regret, que dans ce long sejour,
> La Gloire a moins de part que Didon, & l'Amour ; (p. 1)
> Aenée . . .
> Et que malgré nos soins sans elle nos Vaisseaux
> Cedoient à la fureur de l'orage & des eaux . . .
> Verrois-je sans amour, qu'en elle tous les Dieux,
> Prodigues des vertus de son Sexe & du nostre,
> Joignant l'orgueil de l'un à la douceur de l'autre,
> Semblent autoriser ma flamme & mon sejour ?
> Prince, & vous le sçavez, la Nature & l'Amour
> Ont joint dans cet Objet . . . (pp. 2–3).

La ponctuation de cette réplique d'Aenée, qui n'hésite pas encore entre son amour et son destin, contraste avec l'emphase majestueuse de Didon quelques minutes après (Acte I, scène 3) :

> Et que de mes Sujets le respect, & la foi,
> Reconnoissent en vous mon Epoux, & leur Roy : (p. 6).

Dans la pièce de Montfleury aussi l'imprimeur semble suivre une ponctuation non conventionnelle, mais théâtrale, d'un acteur-auteur.

Les exemples pourraient continuer. Je ne sais pas si ceux que j'ai choisis sont les meilleurs. Certains—ceux du *Bourgeois Gentilhomme*, par exemple—me semblent particulièrement favorables à ma thèse. C'est pourquoi je les reprends ici. D'autres sont choisis un peu au hasard, pour ne pas trop généraliser à partir d'exemples peu représentatifs. Je crois en avoir fourni assez en tout cas pour montrer que la ponctuation des originales de Molière est plus cohérente, plus correcte et surtout plus suggestive qu'on ne l'admet communément. J'aurais pu commencer là où Molière a plus ou moins fini, en attirant l'attention sur un organe d'une grande importance pour le théâtre : le poumon. Les acteurs en connaissent l'importance théâtrale mieux que certains éditeurs de comédies. Mais il vaudrait mieux finir là où Molière a commencé, au début de sa première publication : *Les Précieuses ridicules,* dont voici en regard les premières lignes telles qu'elles figurent dans l'édition des Grands Ecrivains et dans l'originale, d'après l'édition Cuénin :

Despois et Mesnard, etc.:	Ed. Cuénin, d'après G. de Luyne 1660
Du Croisy	Dv Croisi
Seigneur la Grange . . .	Seigneur la Grange.
La Grange.	La Grange
Quoi?	Quoy?
Du Croisy	Dv Croisi
Regardez-moi un peu sans rire.	Regardez moy vn peu sans rire.
La Grange.	La Grange
Eh bien ?	Et bien !

On voit déjà deux différences. Despois substitue des points de suspension (. . .) au point (.) de la première réplique de Du Croisy, et puis un point d'interrogation au point d'exclamation de la seconde réplique de La Grange. Or les points de suspensions sont souvent utilisés dans les originales de Molière, pour montrer qu'une réplique est interrompue, soit par l'interlocuteur, soit par une hésitation de la part de celui qui parle, tel Orgon qui cherche le mot juste pour décrire Tartuffe sans le trouver :

C'est vn Hôme . . . qui . . . ha. . . vn Home . . . vn Hôme

enfin.
(Acte I, scène 5, p. 13)

On aurait pu les utiliser ici si l'on avait voulu indiquer l'un ou l'autre de ces jeux. Il vaut donc mieux supposer que la réplique de Du Croisy n'est pas interrompue. Là n'est pas la signification de l'indication scénique implicite dans la seconde réplique de Du Croisy. Elle s'explique plutôt par la réponse de La Grange telle qu'elle est imprimée dans l'originale : "Et bien !" (avec point d'exclamation). Son jeu consisterait à jouer l'homme qui s'empêche de rire—sans doute de manière caricaturale et comique. D'où le point d'exclamation. En substituant un point d'interrogation, Despois propose plutôt le jeu d'un homme qui pose une question, qui attendrait les volontés de son compagnon, jeu très différent de celui d'un acteur qui dramatise l'acte de suivre l'ordre qu'on lui donne, en jouant de façon exagérée le rôle qu'on exige de lui. La prétendue modernisation fait disparaître ce jeu "métathéâtral" si comique où La Grange serait censé jouer le rôle d'un homme qui s'empêche de rire. Je ne vois pas que les signes substitués par Despois soient plus modernes que ceux qu'il supprime. C'est le type des substitutions arbitraires—beaucoup plus nombreuses que les fautes des originales—qui banalisent bien plus qu'elles ne modernisent. C'est une banalisation qui dépare à peu près chaque page de l'oeuvre moliéresque dans les éditions courantes.

Molière semble s'être particulièrement intéressé à deux aspects de la publication qui seraient extrêmement pertinents pour conclure cet exposé : la correction (l'exactitude) de l'édition et l'idée qu'elle pourrait donner de la représentation. Dans la préface des *Précieuses ridicules* il affirme qu'il publie sa comédie malgré lui, pour devancer une édition non autorisée, et qu'une grande partie de ses grâces "dependent de l'action, & du ton de voix." On ne peut évidemment pas savoir aujourd'hui quels étaient du vivant de Molière ces tons de voix et ces actions. Mais on pourrait s'en approcher de plus près si l'on ne se servait pas d'éditions qui faussent d'utiles indices : la ponctuation des originales. C'est Molière lui-même qui nous invite à deviner le jeu des acteurs derrière les mots imprimés. Dans l'avis *Au lecteur* de *L'Amour médecin* il répète qui'il y a

> beaucoup de choses qui dépendent de l'action ; On sçait bien que les Comedies ne sont faites que pour estre jouées, & ie ne conseille de lire celle-cy qu'aux personnes qui ont des yeux pour découurir dans la lecture tout le jeu du Theatre . . .

Ce jeu, Molière nous aide à le découvrir, je crois, avec la ponctuation des éditions originales, basées au moins en partie sur ses manuscrits disparus et les seules qu'il ait pu voir. A ceux qui voudraient insister sur la difficulté de démontrer un lien entre l'intention de l'auteur et la ponctuation des originales de ses pièces, je répondrais par une autre question. N'est-il pas encore plus difficile de supposer que des éditeurs des dix-huitième, dix-neuvième et vingtième siècles aient pu mieux saisir l'intention avec toutes leurs modifications arbitraires ? Molière répète qu'il voudrait que le lecteur pût retrouver dans le texte imprimé de ses comédies le jeu du théâtre. Il a su imposer à *L'Amour médecin* une ponctuation personnelle dont l'aspect le plus fantaisiste est incontesté, alors qu'on néglige d'autres aspects extrêmement suggestifs du système de ponctuation de cette comédie. Ce sont des indices de la rapidité, de l'intonation, du rythme des répliques et des rôles—tous détails à partir desquels on se constitue une interprétation des personnages et de leur caractère, de l'équilibre et de la signification d'une pièce. C'est un système cohérent et théâtral dont on retrouve les éléments essentiels dans toutes les originales soignées à partir de celle des *Précieuses ridicules*. La ponctuation des originales de Moilère—le point et le point d'exclamation au début des *Précieuses ridicules*, par exemple, les virgules de MM. Macroton et Bahys, de Célimène et d'Henriette—représente un système de faits de bibliographie matérielle qui seraient moins modifiés s'ils étaient mieux compris. Il n'est pas question de limiter les représentations et les "lectures" possibles à l'avenir, mais d'assurer un point de départ basé sur ces faits et non pas sur des interventions postérieures à la mort du dramaturge. On peut douter qu'il ait voulu tel ou tel signe d'une originale ; mais l'idée qu'il ne suivait pas l'impression de ses pièces est—à quelques exceptions près—tout à fait conjecturale. Ce dont on peut être sûr, par contre, c'est que Molière n'a pas choisi les très nombreuses modifications introduites dans les éditions courantes de son oeuvre.

5
Wordplay

Wordplay is such a usual element of comedy that it is surprising to find it minimized by critics and producers of Molière's comedies.[1] Language that means more than it says (as so often in Racine), or says more than it means to say (as in "Freudian" slips), is part of any good writing for the theatre. It may constitute dramatic irony, tragic or comic according to context; and Molière's comedies often exploit the latter. Or it may constitute some other form of wordplay, or simply puns, which often are more interesting, linguistically and theatrically, than commonly allowed. Certain notorious *équivoques* or puns were, of course, noticed at once by Molière's contemporaries: "mais ce *le*, où elle s'arrête," complains Climène in *La Critique de l'Ecole des femmes* (scene 3) with reference to the ambiguity of Agnès's hesitation in describing the progress of Horace's visit, "n'est pas mis pour des prunes. Il vient sur ce *le* d'étranges pensées." And how right Climène is about this aspect of Molière's stagecraft.

The language of Molière's comedies has been submitted to the most exhaustive linguistic analysis, but I hope to be forgiven for writing about puns and other wordplay without resort to the specialized vocabulary of synchronic semantics. In fact the term *pun* designates a variety of related concepts, as reference to *The Concise Oxford Dictionary* will confirm: "humorous use of word to suggest different meanings, or words of same sound with different meanings, play on words." In other words a pun may be, in the simplest form, either of two distinct linguistic phenomena; and the word may also refer more generally to any witty use of language, such as the paradox or the conceit. When in *L'Ecole des femmes* Agnès reports to Arnolphe, "Le petit chat est mort," there is a pun of the first sort, since in context

(Act II, scene 5) the word *chat* evokes not only the deceased pet, but also Arnolphe's fears for Agnès's *pudendum*—a slang meaning for *chat* in Molière's time (cf. "pussy"). Scarron supplies a useful example of the second sort of pun in *Le Virgile travesti*, where he refers to Mercury as "le Dieu qui vole / Moins des ailes que de la main"—playing on the words *voler*, one of which means "to fly" and another "to rob or to steal." No more than "Le petit chat est mort" is this an idle pun. Scarron brings together Mercury's functions as winged messenger of Jupiter and as god of brigands, hinting at the god's tendency to gratuitous evil: a humorous elaboration of a central problem in Vergil's *Aeneid*, the presence of evil in a world ruled by the gods. Scarron's burlesque treatment of the pagan gods devalues the ancient world in favor of the modern, foreshadowing Molière's characterization of Mercure in *Amphitryon* as a god "A la malice un peu porté" (Act III, scene 2). It is hoped that, without mercurial wit, an adequate number of examples of the third meaning of *pun*, "play on words," may be found in the following words on plays.

It may be thought that the current tendency is to exaggerate innuendo in the language of the stage. The Royal Shakespeare Company rarely misses an opportunity to bring out bawdy wordplay in scenes like Katerine's English lesson in *Henry V* (Act III, scene 5) or William's Latin lesson in *The Merry Wives of Windsor* (Act IV, scene 1), where so much depends upon the anglicized pronunciation "huge-ous" of "genitivo, hujus." Certain speeches in Molière's comedies invite a similar treatment: this *réplique* of Le Docteur, for instance, when he is provoked by Angélique's mockery in *La Jalousie du Barbouillé* (scene 6):

> Tu es docteur quand tu veux, mais je pense que tu es un plaisant docteur. Tu as la mine de suivre fort ton caprice: des parties d'oraison, tu n'aimes que la conjonction; des genres, le masculin; des déclinaisons, le génitif; de la syntaxe, *mobile cum fixo*; et enfin de la quantité, tu n'aimes que le dactyle, *quia constat ex una longa et duabus brevibus*. . . .

Le Docteur's *équivoques* are certainly no worse than Katherine's bilingual puns in *Henry V:* "Le foot et le count.

O Seigneur Dieu! ils sont mots de son mauvais, corrupt- ible, gros, et impudique, et non pour les dames d'honneur d'user: je ne voudrais prononcer ces mots devant les seig- neurs de France pour tout le monde. Foh! le foot et le count! . . ." Or than Evans's question in *Merry Wives:* "What is the *focative* case, William?" They belong to a tradi- tion against which the pure in ear, if not heart, were react- ing in France by the mid-seventeenth century. Boileau's *Satire XII sur l'équivoque* is an important early eighteenth- century witness to that reaction. But Boileau's *Satire XII* for that very reason is also a good witness to the strength of the tradition, else his reaction might have been less sharp. I shall argue later, on the basis of numerous examples from later plays, that such puns are not limited to the early farces. In *La Comtesse d'Escarbagnas*, a *comédie-ballet* per- formed at Court 2 December 1671, a young Count is asked to recite his Latin lesson and begins: "Omne viro soli quod convenit esto virile. Omne viri. . . ." To which La Com- tesse rejoins: "Fi! Monsieur Bobinet, quelles sottises. . . . je vous prie de lui enseigner du latin plus honnête que celui- là" (Act I, scene 7). The pun is on *vit* (penis), a word which many modern dictionaries are too chaste to include, though the pun is expertly glossed in the Couton edition of Molière's *Oeuvres complètes.*[2] In the preceding scene of *La Comtesse d'Escarbagnas* there is a pun on Martial when La Comtesse mistakes a reference to the Latin epigrammatist for a mention of a fashionable maker of gloves. In Act I, scene 2, of the same comedy Andrée (a servant) may be said to walk a pun, by starting for the *lieu d'aisance* with her mistress's muff, mistaking *garde-robe* (*armoire,* wardrobe or dressing room) for *garde-robes* (an indoor privy).

Nor is such innuendo surprising in the context of French theatrical tradition. Consider *Les Ramonneurs*, a prose com- edy written around 1624, probably by Alexandre Hardy.[3] The world did not wait for Freud to suggest chimney sweeping as a sexual metaphor, and the title makes a bawdy pun. Diane's lover disguises himself as a sweep. Diane or- ders a valet to find a sweep for a dirty chimney, and the valet replies: "Je crois que le feu commence bien à se mettre

à la vôtre, et qu'un bon ramonneur n'y ferait point de mal"
(Act III, scene 4). "Impudent," she retorts, "oses-tu m'user
de ces vilaines paroles . . .?" But the words themselves are
not ugly, only their implications.

Avoiding on stage all "vilaines paroles"—words banned
from polite usage—while bringing the words (or an image
of what they mean) to the audience's mind, is a technique
perfected by French comic authors in the seventeenth century. Consider this pun on *tiers*—a "third person" or a
"third party"—in Corneille's first comedy, *Mélite*, performed in Paris around 1629. Tirsis surprises his sister
Cloris kissing his friend Philandre in Act I, scene 5, and
observes:

> Je pense ne pouvoir vous être qu'importun,
> Vous feriez mieux un tiers, que d'en accepter un.

In editions of *Mélite* after 1644 Corneille omits this pun, and
the kiss that prompts it, which seemed too bold for the new
proprieties. But by then Molière was already acting profes-
sionally; and though he does not revive such erotic kissing
on stage, he does continue such suggestive wordplay.

Not that wordplay needs to be suggestive in an erotic
way. Of the characters in his second comedy, *La Veuve*,
Corneille declares in the "Au lecteur": "Le plus beau de
leurs entretiens est en équivoques, et en propositions dont
ils te laissent les conséquences à tirer. . . ." Key words in
various speeches take on a second and even a third meaning,
related to different levels of awareness on the part of the
characters involved and an alerted audience. Briefly, Alcidon loves the widow Clarice, who is also loved by his friend
Philiste. In order to deceive Philiste about his intentions,
Alcidon pretends to love Philiste's sister, Doris, who knows
about Alcidon's pretense without letting him know that she
knows. Thus Alcidon speaks both truly and falsely in Act
II, scene 5, when he tells her:

> Doris, si tu pouvais lire dans ma pensée
> Et voir tous les ressorts de mon âme blessée,
> Que tu verrais un feu bien autre et bien plus grand
> Qu'en ces faibles devoirs que ma bouche te rend.

Like Doris, we can appreciate both levels of the hypocrite's meaning: on the one hand, the apparent declaration that he loves her more than he can say; on the other, the disguised declaration of his love for Clarice. We can also enjoy the ironic ambivalence that Alcidon fails to detect in Doris's rejoinder:

Si tu pouvais aussi pénétrer mon courage (i.e., 'heart')
Pour y voir comme quoi ma passion m'engage,
Ce que dans mes discours tu prends pour des ardeurs
Ne te semblerait plus que de tristes froideurs. . . .

By no means limited to comedy, this sort of irony—based entirely upon *équivoques,* extended punning—became enormously popular on the French stage in the seventeenth century, even in tragedy. In this example, the comic irony depends in large part upon the ambivalence of the language, the punning on the different meanings—in this context—of the words. Corneille and other dramatists perfected a technique of verbal ambiguity by which lies in a sense are true, and the truth is meant to mislead. Such language has an obvious affinity with the device of the misunderstood oracle, popular in baroque stagecraft. But it is particularly effective in any "theatre of masks"—plays in which the characters for whatever reason play roles within their roles, acting within the world of the play a part which is not perceived as belonging to the "true" fictional character.

Molière handles such *équivoques* with consummate skill, nowhere better perhaps than in *Tartuffe.* The impostor has been surprised by Damis in his first attempt to seduce Orgon's wife. When Tartuffe's benefactor enters, Tartuffe makes a confession of evil only too apparent to the audience and to the outraged Damis:

Oui, mon frère, je suis un méchant, un coupable,
Un malheureux pécheur, tout plein d'iniquité,
Le plus grand scélérat qui jamais ait été . . . (Act III, scene 6).

All very true, but these words serve to conceal Tartuffe's iniquity from Orgon. This much discussed scene is not perhaps the most obvious example of wordplay in the ordinary sense of the word, but there is punning on all the important words, understood in the sense of excessive scrupulosity by Orgon—and by the rest of us in the more literal and specific senses suggested by what has just been witnessed on stage in Orgon's absence. Thanks to careful preparation, the whole elaborate comic structure of double reference arises from the basic punning technique of words used humorously to suggest different meanings.

Nor is this the only scene in which *Tartuffe* can be seen as a play on words. In the great seduction scene in Act IV Tartuffe is persuaded to renew his advances to Elmire while Orgon crouches under a table. As Tartuffe presses home his attentions, Elmire repeatedly coughs to alert her husband, who remains silent. In this situation references to scandal and even to Elmire's cough take on a progressively richer comic ambivalence as Elmire grows more and more exasperated with Orgon's silence. His concealed presence lends comic irony to the impostor's assurances: "Vous êtes assurée ici d'un plein secret," and the more scandalous "Et ce n'est pas pécher que pécher en silence." Clearly, in the situation as known to the audience, the impact of such words is perceived differently as heard by Elmire and as overheard by Orgon. But I should hesitate to call such wordplay punning, because the ambivalence of these lines does not function like the ambiguity of Tartuffe's "confession" in Act III, scene 6. Tartuffe's unconscious irony is also distinctly different from the deliberate ambivalence of Elmire's reply to his advances, "aprés avoir encore toussé":

Enfin je vois qu'il faut se résoudre à céder,
Qui'il faut que je consente à vous tout accorder,
Et qu'à moins de cela je ne dois point prétendre
Qu'on puisse être content, et qu'on veuille se rendre.
Sans doute il est fâcheux d'en venir jusque-là,
Et c'est bien malgré moi que je franchis cela;
Mais puisque l'on s'obstine à m'y vouloir réduire,
Puisqu'on ne veut point croire à tout ce qu'on peut dire,
Et qu'on veut des témoins qui soient plus convaincants,
Il faut bien s'y résoudre, et contenter les gens (11. 1507–16).

We do not know exactly how Molière staged this scene, or whether Orgon—concealed from Tartuffe—was visible to the audience, as the scene is sometimes played. But subject to the actors' interpretation, the most obvious stylistic feature of these lines is the extended punning mainly on *on*, appealing to Orgon and warning him without alerting Tartuffe. The ambiguity of *on* allows Molière to play upon the different meanings in this situation of all the important vocabulary. Thus to Tartuffe's *céder* means "to yield" to his advances, while there is a hint to Orgon that she is obliged to yield because she has so far been forced to yield to Orgon's view of him. Three lines later, *se rendre* functions in a similar way; and there is no doubt that *être content* refers on different levels to Tartuffe's anticipated satisfaction in love, and to the satisfaction Orgon seems to require in terms of evidence. *Tout accorder, en venir jusque-là, je franchis cela*, and finally *s'y résoudre, et contenter les gens* all suggest to Tartuffe what he calls "dernières faveurs," but refer on another level to Elmire's argument with Orgon. The line "On veut des témoins qui soient plus convaincants" plays upon the whole conception of the scene as a test of Tartuffe's sincerity devised to disabuse Orgon, and Tartuffe's own parallel demand for tangible proof—"d'assurés témoignages"—of what he takes to be Elmire's attraction to him. This is not a loose cluster of more or less related puns, like Le Docteur's lines quoted above from *La Jalousie du Barbouillé*, but a sequence of interrelated wordplay structured like the *équivoques* cited from Corneille's *La Veuve*. The punning is compounded, but the puns are none the less puns for being presented in a complex, structured, organic sequence.

Molière exploits another distinct but not dissimilar punning technique in various scenes in which the metaphoric language of gallantry used by one character is taken in the literal sense by another. This comic device is analogous to a standard technique of low burlesque, exploited by such writers as D'Assoucy, Scarron, and Charles Sorel. In Sorel's burlesque novel, *Le Berger extravagant*, published in Molière's childhood, an engraving of the lady Charite is based on a literal rendering of the favorite metaphors of the Petrarchan poet lovers. Charite is depicted with branches of coral for lips, round pearls for teeth, Cupid's bows for eye-

brows, a picture of Cupid (Love, Amour) himself en-
throned in the middle of her forehead, with little suns for
eyes darting dangerous arrows ("traits"), while lilies and
roses are etched in either cheek. Her hair includes an ens-
naring net, set with protruding fishhooks, baited with little
hearts which doubtless represent her "appas"—literally
"bait," but in the language of gallantry "charms." The
globes of her breasts—revealed in the fashionable *décolleté*
similar to that which Dorine is evidently wearing when met
by Tartuffe upon his first entrance—are clearly marked
with lines of longitude and latitude. Pictorial puns, perhaps, in support of the burlesque text satirizing an over-
worked convention of poetizing. But this is the device
which Molière exploits at the most elementary level, say in
Mascarille's impromptu song in *Les Précieuses ridicules* (scene
9):

> Votre oeil en tapinois me dérobe mon coeur.
> Au voleur, au voleur, au voleur, au voleur!

In *L'Ecole des femmes*, however, there is a much more
sophisticated punning on the language of gallantry, notably
when Agnès, the *ingénue*, dutifully reports to Arnolphe, her
jealous gaurdian, how she met Horace, the lover of the
comedy, during Arnolphe's absence. After a first exchange
of greetings from her balcony, Agnès relates, Horace had
sent an old woman to tell her that she had wounded his
heart: "vous avez blessé / Un coeur . . ." she quotes. Arnolphe is frenzied, but allows her to continue:

> "Moi, j'ai blessé quelqu'un! fis-je toute étonnée.
> —Oui, dit-elle, blessé, mais blessé tout de bon;
> Et c'est l'homme qu'hier vous vîtes du balcon.
> —Hélas! qui pourrait, dis-je, en avoir été cause?
> Sur lui, sans y penser, fis-je choir quelque chose?
> —Non, dit-elle, vos yeux ont fait ce coup fatal,
> Et c'est de leurs regards qu'est venu tout son mal.
> —Hé! mon Dieu! ma surprise est, fis-je, sans seconde:
> Mes yeux ont-ils du mal, pour en donner au monde?
> —Oui, fit-elle, vos yeux, pour causer le trépas,
> Ma fille, ont un venin que vous ne savez pas.
> En un mot, il languit, le pauvre misérable;

Et s'il faut, poursuivit la vieille charitable,
Que votre cruauté lui refuse un secours,
C'est un homme à porter en terre dans deux jours (ll. 512–
26).

By naively asking whether she had caused something to
fall from the balcony, Agnès is made unconsciously to pun
on *blessé*. But *yeux, coup fatal, regards, venin, languit, misé-
rable, cruauté,* and *secours* all belong to the special vocabulary of gallantry, commonplace and by 1662 a little worn
and tired when used seriously. Here they are revitalized by
the double mediation of the *entremetteuse* who is quoted and
the *ingénue* who quotes, with further comedy doubtless
from Arnolphe's barely restrained reaction to this setback
in his plans to keep Agnès for himself. Thanks to the inter-
posed characters, and to Arnolphe's presence, this *récit* introduces three levels of meaning into Horace's declaration
of love: (1) Agnès's literal-minded interpretation of words
like *blessé*, (2) the implicit sexual connotations given words
like *secours* through the involvement of an *entremetteuse* and
by Arnolphe's mimed concern that he fears the worst, and
(3) Horace's original intention to assure Agnès by the recognized language of lovers that his courtship is courtly. For
secours—by which Horace must merely mean "le bien de
vous voir et de vous entretenir"— becomes an elaborate pun
suggesting "first aid" to Agnès and copulation to Arnolphe,
and the three levels at once to an alert audience.

It is a triumph of Molière's art that the romance associated with the role of Agnès survives her literal-
mindedness, in part possibly because her naïveté ensures
that she is not contaminated by what she says and does, in
part also because she is unwittingly amusing. Molière also
skillfully ensures that the romance of Horace's committed
courtship—which offers Agnès an idealized alternative to
enslavement by Arnolphe—survives the mediation of the
entremetteuse he employs, although the very thought of an
entremetteuse is enough to put rather different thoughts into
the mind of Arnolphe. By interposing and superposing
characters on the words reported in Agnès's *récit*, Molière

enriches language which would have been banal as a routine declaration of love, turning it to comedy with no loss of romance, romance put to the test by the obstacle met in Arnolphe's jealousy. This peculiar blend of comedy and romance can be played in different ways, but it must depend upon a basic, structured punning on the language of gallantry as misunderstood by Agnès and suggestively listened to by Arnolphe.

In the last act of *L'Avare*, when the miser's mistaken assumption that Valère has stolen his treasure chest induces Valère to divulge his secret love of Harpagon's daughter, the *quiproquo* also plays upon different senses of words used as the language of love by Valère, but understood in a literal sense by the miser obsessed with his "chère cassette." A full analysis of this great scene (Act V, scene 3) is not necessary, because even casual readers appreciate the sort of pun that, talking at cross purposes with Harpagon, Valère makes on *trésor* when he begs to be given "ce trésor plein de charmes." Nor is it difficult to see the unconscious sexual innuendo in Harpagon's question: "tu n'y a point touché?" But Valère's indignant rejection of Harpagon's misinterpreted question turns the bawdy to romance, because his reply reaffirms his role as a committed lover: "Moi, y toucher? Ah! vous lui faites tort, aussi bien qu'à moi; et c'est d'une ardeur toute pure et respectueuse que j'ai brûlé pour elle"—not feelings of a mere fortune hunter or an "homme à bonnes fortunes." Just as Agnès's literal understanding of Horace's use of *blessé* characterizes her as an *ingénue*, Valère's misapprehension of *trésor* as a term of gallantry or affection characterizes him—above and beyond the immediate joke—as a true lover. It is worth contrasting Harpagon's own strained punning on the language of gallantry, which does nothing of the sort. When he meets Mariane in Act III, scene 5, he enters with spectacles: "Ne vous offensez pas, ma belle, si je viens à vous avec des lunettes . . .," a great comic entrance the clue to which is not in any stage direction, but written into the line itself. The spectacles are an outward and perceptible sign that

Harpagon is ridiculous in the role of lover and an unsuitable rival to his son; and his pun on *astre*— which means a "heavenly body" in either the language of astronomy or that of gallantry—shows he understands nothing of the spirit of the language he attempts to employ, beginning with a pun on *lunettes* ("spectacles," "telescopes"):

> mais enfin c'est avec des lunettes qu'on observe les astres; et je maintiens et garantis que vous êtes un astre, mais un astre le plus bel astre qui soit dans le pays des astres.

It might be argued that Harpagon's failure to amplify the conceit he simply repeats suggests he lacks true wit and that the phrase *maintiens et garantis* characterizes the man of money behind the role of lover which Harpagon attempts and comically misplays.

There are probably more ordinary puns—like the one above on *lunettes*— in Molière's comedies than critics often allow. In the opening scene of *Le Médecin malgré lui* there is a clever series, none extended or developed. Martine asks rhetorically whether she is fortunate to have as her husband "un homme qui me réduit à l'hôpital, un débauché, un traître, qui me mange tout ce que j'ai?" "Tu as menti," answers Sganarelle, "j'en bois une partie"! But the pun is quite complex, playing first on two meanings of *manger* ("to eat" and "to squander"), and then on two meanings of *boire:* the general sense "to drink" as opposed to the literal sense of *manger* which it emphasises, comically crossing Martine's moralist meaning with a physical notion, and the restricted sense "to drink intoxicants," anticipating Martine's epithets "ivrogne," "sac à vin," and the famous drinking song in Act I, scene 5. Sganarelle's next pun is simpler. Martine protests: "J'ai quatre pauvres petits enfants sur les bras!" Sganarelle replies: "Mets-les à terre," again crossing the moral intention with a comic intrusion of the physical act implicit in the literal misinterpretation of Martine's metaphor. Such punning in series anticipates a favorite routine of music-hall comedy to which a number of successful mid-twentieth-century comic playwrights have had recourse, and no doubt it belonged to show business before Molière. But in *Le Médecin malgré lui* this routine also characterizes Sganarelle and sets the tone of the farce.

Like other comic writers, Molière puns on proper names, sometimes improperly. In *Le Malade imaginaire* the doctors' names play on words with medical associations which are also themes of the comedy: M. Purgon on *purger*, "to purge, to clear the bowels"; M. Diafoirus, doubtless on *foireux*, "suffering from diarrhoea, from looseness of the bowels," with the Latinized name in *-us* suggesting academic pedantry, like the name Vadius in *Les Femmes savantes*. But the name of the other pedant in *Les Femmes savantes* is more interesting. That impostor was first called Tricotin, which is the title by which Madame de Sévigné first refers to the comedy in which he appears: an allusion to the Academician Charles Cotin, two of whose poems are read to the learned ladies in Act III, scene 2, where it was probably Molière's intention for the performance to suggest sexual *équivoques* in such words as *fièvre* in the sonnet, though Cotin had clearly intended none. But in the published text Molière softens the personal allusion by substituting *Trissotin* for *Tricotin*, implying something like "trois fois sot" or "thrice a fool." Possibly the new name is no less offensive to Cotin, but it is more abstract, more farcical, nearer the medieval convention of allegorical names in drama, and certainly related to such lines as Clitandre's assertion: "Qu'un sot savant est sot plus qu'un sot ignorant" (Act IV, scene 3). *M. Purgon*, the abandoned *Tricotin*, may only allude, generally or personally as the case may be; *Trissotin* puns in a meaningful way.

The word *sot* in French means "cuckold" as well as "fool," and this ambiguity is the basis of a neat pun in *L'Ecole des femmes* when Arnolphe declares: "Epouser une sotte est pour n'être point sot" (Act I, scene 1). Rhetorically reminiscent of the *sententiae* (the moral aphorisms) of baroque tragedy, Arnolphe's line has a certain hubristic quality; but if the form of the line suggests a stance of misguided heroism, the pun on *sot* introduces a note of burlesque travesty. Because this line is so suggestive of both the theme

and style of *L'Ecole des femmes*, it seems worthwhile to explore its background in Dorimond's *L'Ecole des cocus*, which
may have prompted Molière's comedy based on the same
tale of Scarron. Le Capitan (who corresponds to Arnolphe)
declares in scene 4:

> Je veux me marier, mais je veux épouser
> Une innocente, afin de la mieux maîtriser . . . ;

and Philis amplifies that declaration:

> Vous voulez épouser une sotte, un oyson,
> Une beauté stupide, une pauvre ignorante,
> Pour n'être point trompé. . . .[4]

Thus Dorimond's mainly provincial audiences got all the
help they needed with full elaboration of the theme, but no
mock-heroic *sententia*, and no pun on *sot* to encapsulate the
theme and give it comic point.

Not only the names of characters, but the titles of comedies may make allusions not immediately recognizable by
twentieth-century audiences. *L'Ecole des femmes* probably alludes—more directly than the first two *L'Ecole de* . . . plays
in French published in 1661—to a little book called *L'Ecole
des filles*, written possibly by Scarron, secretly published in
1655, but soon condemned in a special trial, and the located
copies confiscated and burned. *L'Ecole des filles*, an extremely
rare copy of which can be read in the *Enfer* collection of the
Bibliothèque Nationale, is the first wholly erotic book
printed in French and the first practical sex manual in that
language. Possibly its title was already a little ironic, since
its form is that of Chevreau's *L'Ecole du sage* (1646), a moralist work which in chapter 7 I shall argue to be an important
source of Molière's comedies. *L'Ecole des filles* is mentioned
by a character in Wycherley's *The Country Wife*, adapted in
some substantial part from *L'Ecole des maris* and *L'Ecole des
femmes;* and it is not implausible that the second of Molière's
titles alludes ironically to *L'Ecole des filles*, whence perhaps
part of the indignation the comedy aroused. Insofar as
L'Ecole des filles has a story, it is that of a youth introduced
into the bed of an *ingénue* quick to learn new tricks, not

dissimilar in outline (adultery apart) from the plot of Scarron's *La Précaution inutile* and of Dorimond's *L'Ecole des cocus*. As a *fille*, and not a *femme* ("wife"), Agnès in some respects is closer to the Fanchette of *L'Ecole des filles* than to the wives in the established sources. Obviously Arnolphe fears some such scenario, the background of which makes possible the highly comic *équivoques* already analyzed in Agnès's lines. Arnolphe's fear of a scenario like that of *L'Ecole des filles* only makes true *équivoques* possible, however, because the plot of *L'Ecole des femmes* is different. The special quality of Molière's comedy does not depend here, or in *L'Avare* and other comedies which exploit this sort of *équivoques*, on the bawdy alone, but on the concomitant suggestion of innocence and idealism which—beyond the laughter—evoke romance and the successful pursuit of happiness.

The name Arnolphe and the name he assumes for his role within his role, M. de la Souche, may bring us back to puns and allusions in proper names. A legendary Saint Arnolphe was, humorously, the patron saint of cuckolds, which suggests that the name Arnolphe is ironic. So probably is that of the misanthrope, Alceste, the Greek root of which suggests something like "strong man." But the title by which the bourgeois Arnolphe lays claim to nobility is perhaps more complex as well as more obviously comic. The word *la souche* means "stump," and by extension "blockhead"— suggesting the fool Arnolphe makes of himself in his effort to avoid cuckoldry. But *la souche* also means "stock," which seems appropriate to Arnolphe's effort to disguise his ancestry by a change of name. Phallic connotations have also been suggested for the name M. de la Souche; and while these are certainly compatible with the character of Arnolphe and with other aspects of Molière's wordplay, the primary metaphoric level of *souche* was (and is) a suggestion of hardheaded or wooden stupidity. The newly assumed name characterizes. So does the new name of George Dandin, who to his cost assumes the title M. de la Dandinière: *dandin* means "simpleton," and *dandiner* to move with an awkward, oscillating gait. The provincial noble family into which Dandin marries is ironically named Sotenville: say the Foolsintowns.

Country bumpkins were a frequent source of comedy for Molière after his return to Paris, from the "pecques provinciales" satirized in *Les Précieuses ridicules* to the pretentious title role of his last play but two, *La Comtesse d'Escarbagnas*. He was not of course alone in the satirical use of ridiculously allusive names in comedy. Raymond Poisson, the comic actor-author who was Molière's chief rival at the Hôtel de Bourgogne, gives us an amusing comic hero whose name is mud: Le Baron de la Crasse, a character of crass stupidity. Thomas Corneille gives us *La Comtesse d'Orgueil*, together with *Le Baron d'Albikrac*, a name sufficiently outlandish without allegory, like d'Escarbagnas. In Racine's *Les Plaideurs* a major role is played by la Comtesse de Pimbêche, whose title is based on the word for "vixen" or "harridan." But Molière's wit combines the outlandish with quasi allegorical allusion in M. de Pourceaugnac, a title role characterized by both the porcine qualities associated with the word *pourceau* and the unfashionable manners of any of those towns in the south or west of France whose names end in *-ac*.

The title role of *Tartuffe* has a number of established literary sources and various models in contemporary French society have been proposed, but the name alludes primarily to the female hypocrite La Tartufe portrayed in Lagniet's illustrated *Proverbes*, widely circulated in the mid-seventeenth century.[5] The name of the sanctimonious *sergent* who extends the portrait of the hypocrite in *Tartuffe*, M. Loyal, characterizes by *antiphrase*, as Dorine is quick to observe: "Ce Monsieur Loyal porte un air bien déloyal!" (Act V, scene 4). But Mme Pernelle makes the most notorious pun in *Tartuffe* when protesting in the opening scene against "Ces visites, ces bals, ces conversations" and the associated gossip:

Et comme l'autre jour un docteur dit fort bien,
C'est véritablement la tour de Babylone,
Car chacun y babille, et tout du long de l'aune. . . .

The pun is not on the "tour de Babylone" itself, because seventeenth-century French made no distinction between the city of Babylon and the Tower of Babel, which have the same name in Hebrew—interpreted in Genesis XI as meaning the confusion of tongues. Associated wordplay on *babiller*, "to babble" or "to chatter," is attested by a number of texts earlier than *Tartuffe*. But it has only recently been shown that the "docteur" in the passage must go back to François de Sales and the report of one of his sermons in Paris made by the novelist Jean-Pierre Camus, Bishop of Belley.[6] After the sermon a number of women wished to speak with Sales, and all at the same time, writes Camus: "Si ce n'était la tour de Babel, au moins c'était celle de Babil, ou de Babylone; car elles babilloient tout au long de l'aune." Probably Molière included this pun as an example of the humour actually current in certain pious circles, to characterize. But the probable source allows us to see the difference in attitude between Mme Pernelle and the Salesian mainstream of Christian humanism in seventeenth-century France. Camus presents Sales's pun as an "argutie de bonne grâce" destined to assist the ladies in their conversation with him, while Mme Pernelle uses it to attack neighbors she despises. In his *Introduction à la vie dévote* Sales does not attack such activities as visits, balls, and social gatherings in themselves, but in Part III, chapter 33, discusses balls and dancing as types of activities indifferent in themselves, though presenting real dangers to those in search of God. In Part III, chapter 29, he does attack slander, however, beginning with "le jugement téméraire" which produces "le mépris du prochain, l'orgueil et complaisance de soi-même et cent autres effets pernicieux. . . ." In context Mme Pernelle's pun earmarks an abuse of religious authority characteristic of bigots in Molière's comedies.

Not all of Molière's puns are so explicit; and *Dom Juan*, whose subtitle, *Le Festin de Pierre*, perpetuates a pun on *pierre* = "stone"/*Pierre* = "Peter" which arose from a mistranslation of the Italian title *Il Convitato di pietra*, contains a good example of what might be called the implied or implicit pun, which works in conjunction with an idiom, proverb, or familiar phrase not actually spoken. In the "scène du Pauvre" Dom Juan offers the mendicant a *louis d'or*, first if he will blaspheme, and then when the mendicant refuses to blaspheme, "pour l'amour de l'humanité"—a blasphemous play on words substituting *humanité* for *Dieu* in the phrase—too familiar in Molière's time to be glossed, or misunderstood—used for asking alms in the name of God. In context it shows no humanitarian outlook, but a contempt for the mendicant's feelings and values, contempt characteristic of virtually all of Dom Juan's dealings with other human beings in the comedy.

The *équivoque* cited at the beginning of this chapter may be considered another sort of implied pun, though the word feared by Arnolphe is never intended or spoken by Agnès. In Act II, scene 5, of *L'Ecole des femmes* Arnolphe is attempting to discover just what he may have taken from her in his absence, and learns about the kisses. "Ne vous a-t-il pris, Agnès, quelque autre chose?," he enquires. Hesitantly Agnès begins: "Hé! il m'a pris . . . Pris . . . Le . . . ," holding Arnolphe in excruciating suspense, the mime of which must have been meant as an integral part of the comedy. Finally she blurts out: "Il m'a pris le ruban que vous m'aviez donné." But the ribbon is given no symbolic importance, like the handkerchief Othello gives Desdemona. Everything is in the *équivoque* on the unspoken word *pucelage* and Arnolphe's uneasiness over its implications. The play on words is a suggestive silence, elaborately prepared. We have noted that Arnolphe fears a scenario like that of *L'Ecole des cocus* or *L'Ecole des filles* in which the heroine is seduced. But Molière does not rely on such specific knowledge. He does introduce Agnès very briefly in Act I in a scene which might be thought an unnecessary fragmentation of her appearances on stage. In fact it serves to establish Agnès in the anticipated role of *ingénue* earlier described by Arnolphe by disclosing a simple girl, sewing in hand (Act I, scene 3). At the same time, Moliere keeps alive the audience's awareness of Arnolphe's suspicions, partly though a pun on the headwear with which she is occupied: "Je me fais des cornettes," headdress suggestive of the little horns feared by Arnolphe. But observe how he introduces a salacious idea entirely compatible with the character of the *ingénue*, whose first news is that she is well, "Hors les puces, qui m'ont la nuit inquiétée." "Ah!" replies Arnolphe, "vous aurez dans peu quelqu'un pour les chasser," preparing by the vagueness of *quelqu'un* the *quiproquo* on Agnès's husband-to-be in Act II, scene 5, and more pointedly the unspoken *équivoque* on *Le . . .* in the same scene. In the first place the flea has been associated with sexual desire, and sexual humour, at least since Rabelais. Specifically, *Le Parnasse satyrique* contains a bawdy poem called "La Puce," attributed to Fornier, but also published as "La Chasse de la puce sur la belle Uranie" and attributed to Motin. The diverse sources suggest it must have been much passed about. The poetic speaker begins with a desire to crush "cette importune puce, / Qui . . . / Vous pique, et vous mord, et vous suce . . ." and ends with a pun that suggests why the flea in Act I, scene 3, helps prepare the *équivoque* in Act II, scene 5, of *L'Ecole des femmes:*

> Je disais bien, ma grande amie,
> Qu'à la fin de la maladie
> Vous imploreriez mon secours:
> Ça donc! mon coeur, ça! ma rebelle,
> Ça, mon âme, ça! mes amours,
> Qu'à ce coup je vous dépucelle.

The flea suggestive of Agnès's attraction to Horace is at once associated by Arnolphe with her *pucelage*.

Thus the implied pun of Agnès's *Le . . .* is also innuendo, some examples of which in *La Jalousie du Barbouillé* and other comedies have already attracted comment. It would be a mistake to assume that such *équivoques* belong only to Molière's early farces and to *L'Ecole des femmes.* I have commented on those in *La Comtesse d'Escarbagnas*, a late *comédie-ballet*. They are also a feature of his most polished literary comedies, especially *Les Femmes savantes.* It is not difficult to see that Martine's lines about marriage in Act V, scene 3, invite innuendo in the words I italicize:

> Ce n'est point à la femme à prescrire, et je sommes,
> Pour céder le dessus *en toute chose* aux hommes,

lines which echo an epigram of Martial's which couples male superiority with the superior position in love-making. Similarly, when Bélise declares in Act III, scene 2:

> Je m'accommode assez pour moi des petits corps;
> Mais le vide à souffrir me semble difficile,
> Et je goûte bien mieux la matière subtile.

she displays a nonsensical eclecticism purporting to synthesize the materialist atomism of followers of Gassendi (*petits corps* = "atoms," the smallest units of matter in Gassendi's materialist philosophy) with Descartes's rejection of Pascal's demonstration of the existence of vacuums in nature, preferring to suppose a "matière subtile" between the vortices of his cosmos. Or perhaps it is better to say that her words may be coherently, if nonsensically, related to contemporary philosophic controversies. But the comedy of these lines depends in large measure upon the sexual innuendo of words like *petits corps*, *vide*, and *matière subtile*, which all suggest unconscious sexual deprivation and are fully consistent with the characterization of Bélise as a maiden aunt whose fixed idea is that all the men she meets passionately love her. Reference to Descartes's rigorous separation of mind and body provides one background for Bélise's conception of love in the penultimate scene of the comedy, but it is not difficult to see another meaning:

> La substance qui pense y peut être reçue,
> Mais nous en bannissons la substance étendue.

It is, I suggest, a special irony of *Les Femmes savantes* that in Act III, scene 2, Philaminte proposes to abolish

> . . . ces syllabes sales,
> Qui dans les plus beaux mots produisent des scandales,
> Ces jouets éternels des sots de tous les temps,
> Ces fades lieux communs de nos méchants plaisants,
> Ces sources d'un amas d'équivoques infâmes,
> Dont on vient faire insulte à la pudeur des femmes.

The reference is to words like *confesse* and *concupiscence*, the syllables of which can be made to do the things to which Philaminte objects and provoked quite a lot of discussion and satire in the seventeenth century. But here her proposal must alert the audience to the possibility of such *équivoques* and others more generally in this and other comedies, as indeed does the reaction of the Comtesse d'Escarbagnas against syllables in *vi-*.

Philaminte also suggests the basic tension under which Molière must have developed this aspect of his stagecraft, which exploits a freedom dependent upon restraint. Where anything can be said, there is no scandal in speech and no point in *équivoques*. Where everything is proper, there is no comedy. Racine boasted in the preface to his sole comedy, *Les Plaideurs*, that it contains none of those "sales équivoques" or "malhonnêtes plaisanteries" which "coûtent maintenant si peu à la plupart de nos écrivains, et qui font retomber le théâtre dans la turpitude d'où quelques auteurs plus modestes l'avaient tiré" (1669). In 1690 the French and Italian players were forbidden to "dire un seul mot à double entente, sous peine d'être chassés," probably because the innuendo had come to swamp the polite meaning. It is fundamental to Molière's art of the *équivoque* that, at its best and in his mature comedies, it really does work on two or more levels and does not merely function as a pretext for the bawdy, opposition to which was very strong in the circles in which he moved.

So many of the examples discussed above illustrate the successful duality of Molière's *équivoques*, that I shall cite only one more, a much discussed line in *Le Misanthrope*. Pressed by Oronte to give his sincere opinion of a new sonnet in Act I, scene 2, Alceste asserts: "Franchement, il est bon à mettre au cabinet." For three centuries critics have argued whether *cabinet* means "study"—as e.g. when the poet Gabrielle de Coignard apostrophizes her own sonnet 14 of her *Oeuvres chrétiennes* (1595) "Mes vers demeurez cois dedans mon cabinet"—or "lavatory," which is the sense to illustrate which Antoine Furetière misquotes this line in his *Dictionnaire* (1690):

CABINET, se prend quelquefois pour une garderobe, ou le lieu secret où on va aux nécessités de nature. Ainsi Molière a dit dans le Misanthrope en parlant d'un méchant sonnet, Franchement il n'est bon qu'à mettre au *cabinet*.

The "study" sense still exists; and Furetière was a well informed contemporary whose *Roman bourgeois* was published in the same year that *Le Misanthrope* was first performed. It therefore seems reasonable to conclude that *cabinet* is an *équivoque*, a pun that plays on the limits of the decently sayable, proper in one sense, crude in another, but outrageously comic. The so-called ambiguity of Alceste's character, and the divergent historical interpretations of the role, spring in part from the different interpretation of lines like this one, whose ambivalence is, I think, intentional and intentionally comic. It is like the pun on *garderobe* in *La Comtesse d'Escarbagnas*.

Oronte's sonnet offers the best example of the *précieux* conceit in Molière's theatre, the *pointe* or *chute* that Philinte calls "jolie, amoureuse, admirable" and the first audience—according to the letter-preface to the first edition (1667)—applauded until Alceste made known his disfavor:

> Belle Philis, on désespère,
> Alors qu'on espère toujours.

The conceit plays on the two meanings of *espérer*, "to wait" and "to hope," in opposition to *désespérer:* a neat example of the genre, of which there are a number of other plays, mainly for the comic effect of a public reading. The dramatic point of Oronte's sonnet—beyond the comic situation in which it places Philinte and Alceste—consists in the *chute*, which is (a) the first ultimatum intended for Célimène in the comedy and (b) a declaration of love which Oronte insists that his rival must approve. No wonder Alceste replies aside to Philinte's exclamations over it: "La peste soit de ta chute! . . . / En eusses-tu fait une à te casser le nez!" It is through a pun on *chute* that Molière characterizes the latent aggressiveness in the role of the Misanthrope, with the valuation of the role very much dependent on the extent to which one assumes such violence to have been deliberately (or innocently) provoked by his rival.

Another well-known line of Alceste's may be considered a paradox, the last type of wordplay I shall consider. At the beginning of Act V, scene 1, the disappointed Misanthrope declares: "J'ai pour moi la justice, et je perds mon procès!" In chapter 2 I argued that this paradox makes a "comic image," so richly does it satirize the gap between "justice" and "law," between selfrighteousness and impartiality, etc. But there is clearly a pun on *justice* to which we may compare Harpagon's threat in *L'Avare*, Act V, scene 1: "et si l'on ne me fait retrouver mon argent, je demanderai justice de la justice." For Harpagon, "justice" entails no punishment too great for the crime of stealing his 10,000 *écus*, and he wants Le Commissaire to arrest "la ville et les faubourgs."

From *George Daudin* we may take our final paradox, another "comic image." At the beginning of the play he learns from Lubin that Clitandre is courting his wife, but can do nothing in the face of their denials to prove to his overbearing parents-in-law that he is wronged, and not simply making trouble. Warned in Act I, scene 6, not to repeat his misbehavior, Dandin responds: "J'enrage de bon coeur d'avoir tort, lorsque j'ai raison." To be in the wrong when one is right is clearly paradoxical, and once more the paradox turns on the ambivalence of an expression: *avoir tort*, "to be wrong" or "to be in the wrong." M. de Sotenville has just said, " . . . votre procédé met tout le monde contre vous"; and in Act II, scene 6, Dandin hopes that discovery of Clitandre in his house will help him "avoir raison aux yeux du père et de la mère." Dandin's paradox voices the situation of a number of Molière's characters, such as Mme Pernelle in the first scene of *Tartuffe*, or better: Damis in that play, when asked (like Dandin) to apologize to the hypocrite he has attempted to expose (Act III, scene 6). It expresses the Misanthrope's situation almost better than his own paradox. When satirized by Célimène in her portrait scene (Act II, scene 5), "Les rieurs sont pour vous, Madame. . . ," he notes; but "l'on a tort" he adds a little later. In the great letter scene, she also turns the tables on an accusing Alceste, who complains (Act IV, scene 3):

Quoi? d'un juste courroux je suis ému contre elle,
C'est moi qui me viens plaindre, et c'est moi qu'on querelle!

It is Molière's triumph to have made an ambivalence of language in paradoxes turning on words like *justice* and *avoir tort* express a duality of vision which (1) comically dramatizes the gap between our perception of ourselves and the appearance we present to others, and (2) the gap between what we observe in the world about us and sometimes feel things ought to be.

Such gaps may be greatest, however, when least expected, as Molière hints at the end of *Le Bourgeois Gentilhomme*. M. Jourdain has been made a Mamamouchi, and he is persuaded that his daughter may marry the son of the Sultan of Turkey: that is, the lover Cléonte in disguise. After initial hesitation dramatizing her fidelity to Cléonte, Lucile recognizes him. All are now party to the ruse but Mme Jourdain, who obstinately refuses to countenance the match until she too understands the disguise. "Ah!," exclaims M. Jourdain, "voilà tout le monde raisonnable." The wordplay on *raisonnable* is part of a larger irony by which M. Jourdain measures the reasonable in terms of his own extravagant illusions: on one level, *raisonnable* must work by *antiphrase*, because everyone else is aware of the illusory nature of the situation. But beyond M. Jourdain's unreason, *raisonnable* is also valid at face value as a judgment of conduct designed to deal with an individual so much subject to his own imagination that he cannot be reached by reason. At a higher level, the other characters are all reasonable because they recognize the limits of rationality and deal effectively with an extravagant visionary in the only way his obsession permits, through that obsession and in terms of his fantasy.

In conclusion, the wordplay in Molière's stagecraft shows a greater awareness of the differences that may exist between words and concepts, words and things, words as spoken and words as understood, than the French seventeenth century is often supposed to have possessed—an awareness shared by such masters of irony and paradox as Corneille, La Fontaine, and La Rochefoucauld. The discrepancies, the ambiguities to which Molière invites attention are a weakness of verbal language. Molière's stagecraft exploits the comic potential of words destined for use on stage in conjunction with well-chosen aids to non-verbal communication, such as disguise and mime. But the puns, conceits, ironies, and paradoxes of Molière's comedies are evidence also of the sort of "lateral" thinking by which the individual human mind—unlike the system of a computer—can declare itself independent of any program of information put to it. The mind can interpose a new order of thought and answer on an unprogrammed plane. This is why bad puns are abhorred in good conversation: they divert it into unstructured futility. But the pun that prunes a topic may start a more vigorous side shoot. More than any other form of humor, wordplay exemplifies the mind's capacity to pattern its own program, whatever the program that may be put to it, be its response silly or insightful. Perhaps this is why certain systematic thinkers—builders of philosophic systems, like Kant—deny all meaning to wordplay and to humor generally. But is this not rather the significant sense in which "le rire est le propre de l'homme"? Computers and cats do not play with words. High priests, tyrants, and terrorists pun sparingly. For wordplay is not only basically human, and humane; wit may spark new approaches to problems, new systems of thought, an independent way to reassess the world and its values.

6
Satire of Medicine: Fact and Fantasy

Historically, Molière's comedies have been both an incentive and an obstacle to the understanding of medical practice in France in the mid-seventeenth century. An incentive, because the notoriety of Molière's medical satire has inspired much of the research on the medical practice of that period: the first detailed investigation was undertaken by Maurice Raynaud (1862) for a doctorate in the history of literature; and this perspective is still evident a century later in François Millepierres's book (1964) and the beautifully illustrated *Molière et la médecine de son temps* (*Marseille* 1973).[1] An obstacle, because a serious historian of medicine like R. H. Shryock (1947) could begin his book by mentioning Molière between the origins of the Royal Society and the work of Thomas Sydenham, but discuss none of the actual French doctors of this period; though French historians took them more seriously.[2] What the theatre historian needs for assessing the fairness and the significance of Molière's satire is accurate knowledge from independent sources of contemporary French medical practice. Historians of medicine, not to say literary critics, may need reminding of the special nature of dialogue, characterization, and costume in theatrical performances when the printed texts of comedies are used as historical evidence.

So much of the original evidence contained in early performances has been lost, with all it could tell us about nuance and tone. We know that pulse-taking was an important ritual, especially among doctors who did not accept Harvey's discovery of the circulation of blood: the pulse-taking in *Le Malade imaginaire* (Act V, scene 6) is therefore fair caricature. Thomas Diafoirus's diagnosis that it is "duriuscule, pour ne pas dire dur" mocks carefully shaded,

Latinized rhetoric (cf. Latin *duriusculus*) based entirely upon wrong theory. But we do not know when the tradition began by which Thomas Diafoirus at this moment holds the arm of Argan's chair, which certainly belongs to comic fantasy and not to fact. More generally, almost any feature of a comedy may be grounded more in the traditions of theatre than in observation of contemporary society. Some aspects of Molière's comedies containing caricatures of medical practice derive from Italian and Spanish theatre, while other features may relate in the first instance to other imaginative writings. In some respects Molière's attitudes are reminiscent of Montaigne's *Essais*; and it is important to recognize the extent to which we are faced with literary as well as medical continuities.

I have sought a balance between broad issues and detailed analysis of the wit that gives life to Molière's comedies. Since I know less about medicine than about Molière, I have woven into my essay a brief review of his career with a view to situating the eight comedies in which medicine is parodied or satirized. Apart from Jean Riolan's *Manuel anatomique et pathologique* (1682) and Guy Patin's letters (Reveillé-Parise 1846), I have done little primary research on medical sources.[3] But I have taken note of various papers recently published in out-of-the-way places on seventeenth-century French doctors and case histories: a more sympathetic assessment of Patin's career, among the doctors; and among patients, the two kings of France during Molière's lifetime, Louis XIII and Louis XIV, who must be among the most documented, if not actually the most medicated, cases in history.

While we need to be careful in generalizing from such exceptional cases, which could distract us by the very abundance of information, the medical *Journal* kept by various *premiers médecins* on each of these two royal patients is rivaled in minuteness only by the other. They are to that extent atmospheric; and whatever might be argued about the quality of an individual appointment, Héroard's *Journal* suggests the state of medicine in France as a whole around the time when Molière was born.[4] It shows that incisions

were made on the future Louis XIII's tongue the day after
he was born, that he was regularly purged with suppositories from the age of ten days, that suppositories were
replaced by laxatives at age two years when suppositories
ceased to be effective, and countless other apparently gratuitous interventions. Such medication, argues an American scholar, turned "an infant of robust constitution, of
outstandingly favorable intellectual and physical endow-
ment, and of abundant material and affectional resources"
into "a neurotic, unhappy, and handicapped adult" (Marvick 1974, p 364). The reply to a Paris thesis question of
1625, "An speciosa sanitas suspecta?," was "yes"; and there
is still fair satire as well as bawdy innuendo in *Le Médecin
malgré lui* (Act II, scene 4) when Sganarelle tells a buxom
nurse in robust health: "Cette grande santé est à craindre, et
il ne sera mauvais de vous faire quelque petite saignée ami-
able, de vous donner quelque petit clystère dulcifiant."
Medicine, Molière makes Béralde say to Argan in *Le Malade
imaginaire* (Act III, scene 5), is only for those fit enough to
survive treatment as well as their illness. I have always
pitied the young Marquis de Fors who, aged twenty, suc-
cumbed to wounds received in line combat at the siege of
Arras in August 1640—and the twelve bleedings administered by Cardinal Richelieu's personal physician, Citois.

The particular relevance of Louis XIV's medical history
will be illustrated later; but it does not of course include the
boost that Félix de Tassy's operation on the king's anal
fistula gave to surgery in 1686, thirteen years after Molière's
death.[5] Also, lest reference to kings seem inappropriate in
our age of demography if not democracy, these points seem
valid: (1) Molière was born into a household directly em-
ployed in the royal service. (2) Court fashion, even in
medicine, was influential throughout the kingdom, as illustrated by the enhanced status of emetic wine after its not
unsuccessful administration to Louis XIV in 1658.
(3) Court preference for Montpellier-trained *premiers
médecins* in an area under the control of the Paris Faculty led
to jurisdictional disputes echoed in Molière's comedies.
(4) Molière's *comédies-ballets* satirizing doctors were written

for performance at Court, and (5) the first of these, *L'Amour médecin*, almost certainly satirizes recognizable Court doctors, as Georges Couton sums up in his "Notice" on this play: "Les médecins étaient désignés par des noms qui laissaient transparaître des personnages notoires, dont les médecins du roi, de Monsieur, de Madame, de la reine. Des témoignages non négligeables établissent que Molière avait fait faire des masques à leur ressemblance."[6] Perhaps Couton is right to conclude that Molière's comedy thus became 'aristophanesque'— personally polemical in its satire of doctors. There is no doubt that Molière's satire was at times personal, and it was often polemical; but the theatrical inspiration of *L'Amour médecin*, even in the doctor scenes, is strong and inclines me to wonder whether the tone is as sharp as sometimes alleged. Just because the allusions seem so personal one could argue an analogy with the end-of-term review, destined to "take off" but not necessarily to disgrace the butts of satire. Tone is hard to assess in retrospect.

Certain generalizations are possible, however: that the medicine Molière knew throughout his life was more authoritarian than empirical; that it could be formalistic, even ritualistic, to the detriment of a patient's health; and that its orientation was rhetorical rather than clinical, are attitudes to which Molière's satire points accurately time and again, but more insistently in his last great medical *comédies-ballets*, *Monsieur de Pourceaugnac* and *Le Malade imaginaire*. Ignorance masked by pretentious jargon and unhelpful Latin is mocked from beginning to end of his comedies, and nowhere perhaps better than in *Le Médecin malgré lui*, Act 2, scene 4. But Molière's mockery of jargon is not limited to doctors: lawyers, notaries, scholars, *précieuses* and *femmes savantes*, hyprocrites, even the fencing master in *Le Bourgeois Gentilhomme* and the actors of the rival Hôtel de Bourgogne theatre are mocked for the abuse of jargon and other forms of rhetoric that seek to blind with science.

Born in 1622, Molière lived for fifty-one years, like Shakespeare. Like Shakespeare, he was an actor; and he left almost the same number of plays, about three dozen. Early in the Regency of Anne of Austria he joined a company of actors which failed in 1645 after a bold beginning under the patronage of the Lieutenant de France, Gaston d'Orléans. Released from debtor's prison, Molière and a few survivors of that first troupe joined forces with a troupe in the service of the duc d'Epernon. For thirteen years it operated mainly in the west and south of France before returning via Rouen to Paris in October 1658 by which time Molière was leader of the troupe. He had adapted two high comedies from Italian originals and composed a number of one-act farces, now mainly lost, but at the age of thirty-six had published nothing. Mid-century portraits show him mostly as a tragic actor, in roles like that of Julius Caesar in Pierre Corneille's tragedy *La Mort de Pompée*. However, Molière had known the burlesque poet d'Assoucy rather well in the provinces and on his return to Paris promptly associated the great burlesque actor Jodelet with his troupe, through Jodelet soon afterwards died. Molière seems to have sensed the potential of his farces, partly because Parisians appear to have found him less acceptable as a tragic hero than provincials had done, partly perhaps because he was no longer the ideal age for the *jeune premier* expected in tragic roles.

Of the early farces, two or possibly three survive: three, if *Le Docteur amoureux* recovered and published by A. J. Guibert in 1960 really is, as I believe, the "petite comédie" Molière performed for Louis XIV and the Court on 24 October 1658.[7] Couton and some other French specialists doubt this, but it does allow me to make the point that the "doctor" in French farce at this time is not normally a medical doctor, but some sort of pedant, in some degree related to the Dottore mask of *commedia dell'arte*: a graduate as a rule in philosophy or in law, associated by Allardyce Nicoll (1963) with jargon-bashing bureaucrats.[8] It is all the more remarkable that another of the early farces generally— though not universally—admitted to the *corpus moliericum* is indeed a farce involving the parody of medical practice, *Le Médecin volant*. Molière's first Sganarelle (which he acted himself) disguises himself as a doctor and travesties a house call, complete with a urinalysis by drinking the specimen.

There is no evidence that there is any allusion to the diagnosis of diabetes by tasting urine, first done apparently by Willis and well attested in the eighteenth century. Or perhaps on reflection it is better to say that any caricature of urine-tasting is not polemical, but lavatory humor related to the comic fantasy of one or more of the *commedia dell'arte* scenarios entitled *Il Medico volante:* in one of these scenarios the specimen, apparently swallowed, is spewed over Pantalone's face. Though there is no agreement on the exact nature of the relation of Molière's farce to the Italian ones, it is right, I think, to conclude that his *lazzi* too involves more buffoonery than satire.

Suddenly, a year after his return to Paris, Molière delighted and shocked the capital by making his first new play, a one-act farce called *Les Précieuses ridicules* which was also his first publication, the vehicle for very pointed satire of *préciosité:* that is, as travestied in this prose farce, exaggerated feminism with affected speech, novelistic daydreams, and silly fashions both in verse and in dress. Two years later with *L'Ecole des maris* Molière created what I have called elsewhere the comedy of ideas, by blending a debate on conflicting ideologies into an ironical obstacle comedy—a formula perfected in masterpieces like *L'Ecole des femmes, Tartuffe, Le Misanthrope* (with the obstacle to marriage interiorized), and *Les Femmes savantes.* In that same summer of 1661 Molière also created another complex new dramatic genre with *Les Fâcheux*, the first French *comédie-ballet*—a collaborative effort in which satirical comedy is fused with the sort of music, dance, lavish costumes and stage-sets used in Court ballets, mixing courtiers skilled as amateur dancers with professional theatre people and musicians. The success of this formula led to a new production in some variant of this form in more or less every season until Molière's death in 1673, usually in collaboration with the great, neglected Italian-born musician Jean-Baptiste Lully. Eventually, Lully broke with Molière after their *tragédie-ballet Psyché*, which is practically an opera, and in that same year 1672 founded the Paris Opéra. Lully's franchise caused Molière a great deal of trouble, because it severely restricted the role of music in Molière's last play, *Le Malade imaginaire*. The planned premiere at Court had to be abandoned. For the music, Molière fell back upon Marc-Antoine Charpentier, who also composed new incidental music for *Le Médecin malgré lui*.[9]

The point here is that these highly imaginative *comédies-ballets* constitute a third of Molière's total output of plays, including three of the four mature plays in which the satire of medicine is central: *L'Amour médecin* (1665), *Monsieur de Pourceaugnac* (1669), and *Le Malade imaginaire* (1673). The fourth play in which medical satire is central is *Le Médecin malgré lui* (1666), a three-act farce in prose in which a Sganarelle is beaten into "admitting" he is a doctor and then in a stage-doctor's gown imposes upon the credulity of a Géronte.

There as in *Le Médecin volant* and *L'Amour médecin*, and later in *Le Malade imaginaire*, the doctor disguise favors a love story. Molière's other satirical references to doctors occur in machine-plays—plays in which scene-shifting machinery is used for spectacular effects based on illusion, the supernatural, and surprise: *Dom Juan* (1665) and *Amphitryon* (1668). To *Dom Juan* we shall return, because Molière's satire of medicine really begins with a farcical disguise of Sganarelle as a doctor unprecedented in any earlier version of the Don Juan legend. It will suffice to say here that in *Amphitryon* the medical satire is also introduced into a dramatic subject in which it previously had no part, and so is clearly deliberate. In Act II, scene 3, Cléanthis attacks the suggestion that babies conceived in intoxicated copulation might be born unfit to live. It seems unlikely that the pretext her husband Sosie had found to put off her reproaches of neglect is pure fantasy, or that Cléanthis's vehemence is fully explained by reference to Quillet's *Callipédie* of 1655. We could perhaps better appreciate the satirical reference of these lines (which of course work comically on stage without any such precise indexing) if we knew to which medical treatise an apparently polemical reference is made. At the same time, it is noteworthy that all of Molière's medical satire occurs in plays belonging to genres in which the element of fantasy is high: farce, *comédie-ballet*, and machine-plays; and this fact is not altered by the current vogue for *Dom Juan* which neglects both its farcical and its supernatural elements.[10]

If now we return to Molière's first satirical comedies, we meet a number of satirical themes: fashion, education, sex, feminism, *préciosité*, the pharisaical abuse of religious authority, and so on. *L'Ecole des femmes* and especially *Tartuffe* provoked an outcry partly because these comedies link sex with religion, and *Tartuffe* was banned until 1669. Yet in none of the new plays produced between 1659 and 1664 does Molière ever satirize medicine. On the contrary, in *Tartuffe* we meet the only favorable reference to doctors in Molière's theatre: returning home in Act 1, scene 4, Orgon discovers that his wife had been suffering from nausea, headache, and fever, at last relieved by a bleeding. This is the famous scene in which the servant tries to inform Orgon of his wife's indisposition, only to be interrupted with his repeated questions: "Et Tartuffe?," followed by "Le pauvre homme!" Here are Dorine's lines:

> A la fin, par nos raisons gagnée,
> Elle se résolut à souffrir la saignée,
> Et le soulagement suivit tout aussitôt.

In the dramatic context these lines might be thought to have more to do with preparing the comic contrast between El-mire's indisposition and the indifference to it shown by the two men in her life who affect piety. Or they may be admired as a little slice of daily life conferring "realism" on a mannered theatrical scene. But nothing in the handling of Elmire's illness betrays the slightest scepticism about either the practice of medicine in general or about bleeding in particular. This scene is assumed to belong to the first *Tartuffe*, of May 1664.

There could be no clearer contrast with Molière's next comedy, *Dom Juan*, first produced in February 1665: the first of the seven mature plays in which Molière satirizes doctors right up until his death eight years later. The most striking feature of the scene of medical satire introduced by

Molière into his handling of a popular dramatic subject is the reference to emetic wine and to the fashion for its use in the Paris region that had developed since Louis XIV had survived repeated doses of it when ill, probably with typhus, in 1658: his recovery was attributed to the emetic wine, and not to the innumerable bleedings and purgings also duly administered at the time. Guy Patin's letters are full of references to this remedy, based on antimony, and to the deaths he links with its use. The status of antimony in the Paris Faculty's jurisdiction had been an issue for decades, but was especially controversial when *Dom Juan* was produced because the debate in the Paris Faculty which led to its acceptance the following year had just reached an acute stage. Molière's interest in the question may have been aroused by one in a series of three deaths close to him late in 1664; that is, in the last months before the contract for the stage decorations for *Dom Juan* was signed on 3 December 1664. The circumstances of the deaths in November of the actor Du Parc and of Molière's ten-day-old son Louis are not clear enough to help in this context. Infant mortality in any case was high, and it is only in the past five years that we have learned that Molière also lost a new-born daughter, in 1668.[11] But Guy Patin writing on 26 September 1664 of the death of Molière's friend, the younger La Mothe Le Vayer, the philosopher's son, says:

> M. de la Mothe le Vayer avoit un fils unique d'environ 35 ans, qui est tombé malade d'une fièvre continue, à qui Messieurs Esprit, Brayer et Bodineau ont donné trois fois le vin émétique et l'ont envoyé au païs d'où personne ne revient.

Sganarelle's medical disguise at the beginning of Act 3 of *Dom Juan* is a comic *coup de théâtre*, because the plan had been for him merely to exchange clothes with his master: ". . . je ne sais où tu as été déterrer cet attirail ridicule," remarks Dom Juan. They then engage in repartee in which Dom Juan makes the point amplified in later comedies that contemporary medicine is based on wrong theory ("pure grimace") and irrelevant to recoveries attributable to nature or good fortune. Sganarelle is scandalized that Dom Juan does not believe "au séné, ni à la casse, ni au vin émétique," continuing:

> Cependant vous voyez, depuis un temps, que le vin émétique fait bruire ses fuseaux. Ses miracles ont converti les plus incrédules esprits, et il n'y a pas trois semaines que j'en ai vu, moi qui vous parle, un effet merveilleux.
> DOM JUAN: Et quel?
> SGANARELLE: Il y avait un homme qui, depuis six jours, était à l'agonie; on ne savait plus que lui ordonner, et tous les remèdes ne faisaient rien; on s'avisa à la fin de lui donner de l'émétique.
> DOM JUAN: Il réchappa, n'est-ce pas?
> SGANARELLE: Non, il mourut.
> DOM JUAN: L'effet est admirable.
> SGANARELLE: Comment? il y avait six jours entiers qu'il ne pouvait mourir, et cela le fit mourir tout d'un coup. Voulez-vous rien de plus efficace?
> DOM JUAN: Tu as raison.

The satire could hardly be closer to personal bereavement, given Molière's friendship with La Mothe Le Vayer *fils*. It also touches upon a controversial topic of public interest during the Faculty debates. The ironic tone is very close to repeated protests in Guy Patin's letters: "En moins d'un mois le vin émétique, donné de la main de M. Guenaut, a tué ici quatre personnes illustres. . . ." (4 May 1663). M. de Longueville died, Patin writes on 18 May 1663, "febre tertianâ et duabus dosibus vini antimonialis emetici. . . . Avoir Guenaut pour ami par lâcheté, dire quelque mot grec et avoir 300,000 écus de beau bien, et être le plus avaricieux du monde, cela fait venir de la pratique, à Paris" (18 May 1663). Or later in the same letter:

> Je vis en consulte une femme mordue d'un chien enragé. . . . On . . . amena un charletan qui lui fit avaler du vin émétique, et, après, lui donna une pillule, dont elle mourut trois heures après. Les charlatans tuent plus de monde que les bons médecins n'en guérissent.

Though delivered by a superstitious servant disguised as a doctor of farce, Molière's satire in *Dom Juan*—and to some extent the attitudes in *L'Amour médecin* and *Le Médecin malgré lui* performed in the next eighteen months—reflects the conservatism of Guy Patin and his hostility to the chemical medicine dispensed by the Montpellier Faculty and its graduates in Paris and at Court. Sganarelle's disguise is largely stage fantasy—Parisian doctors dressed as sober bourgeois except on ceremonial occasions when gowns were used; and the farcical presentation may have served to gild the satirical pill. It is interesting, however, that *Dom Juan* was never performed at Court during Molière's lifetime. Guy Patin remained hostile to emetic wine even after its acceptance by the Paris Faculty; Molière seems to have lost interest in it. The severe illness he suffered himself late in 1665 may have altered his views on medicine; it is too late to account for the sudden irruption of medical satire in his comedies, though there are good grounds for assuming that in later years his deteriorating health influenced the way in which he conceived the roles he wrote for himself. We have noted in passing that his last comedy, *Le Malade imaginaire*, contains references to his health. In fact there is a clear reference—"Le poumon" repeated in Act III, scene 10, by Toinette disguised as a doctor—to the tubercular condition from which Molière died shortly after being stricken on stage in the fourth performance of that comedy.

Probably around early 1667 Molière became the patient of a Montpellier-trained doctor named Mauvillain, then a professor of botany in Paris and a champion of chemical medicine. Mauvillain also had a very un-Cartesian interest in what we now call psychosomatic afflictions. It seems fair comment that Mauvillain would have accepted the implications of Molière's title, *L'Amour médecin*, as symbolic beyond the metatheatrical role-playing within roles in that comedy. For he directed theses in honor of Venus. In any case Molière seems to have been aware as early as 1665–66 of this current of thought, whether or not linked specifically with Faculty theses. Various traditional manuals recommend *emplâtres* (e.g. Guybert 1645, pp 302 ff). Molière makes Jacqueline observe, in *Le Médecin malgré lui*, Act 2, scene 1: ". . . votre fille a besoin d'autre chose que de ribarbe et de séné, et . . . un mari est une emplâtre qui guarit tous les maux des filles."

I am not sure whether a peasant's reference to the killing power of emetic wine in Act III, scene 2, of the same comedy is more satirical of antimonialists than it is of peasants. But it does suggest caution in assimilating Molière's view too closely with Mauvillain's, certainly in 1666, because Mauvillain had led the campaign to establish antimony which triumphed that year. The fact remains that Molière abandons satire of chemical medicine as such after *Le Médecin malgré lui*, while psychosomatic implications culminate in *Le Malade imaginaire*, taken very seriously by J-M Pelous (*Marseille* 1973, pp 179–187).

In *Monsieur de Pourceaugnac*, which might be considered "le malade malgré lui" or "the patient in spite of himself," rhetoric, ritualism, and formalism are brilliantly satirized both in *médecins* and in *apothicaires;* and a new fashionableness of clysters and giant syringes designed to administer them is reflected especially in burlesque ballet *entrées* during which M. de Pourceaugnac is pursued by dancers wielding such instruments. Satire on formalism and wrong theory is continued in *Le Malade imaginaire;* but the satirical lash in Molière's last comedy falls on opponents of Harvey's discovery of the circulation of blood, then fighting a last-ditch battle against Harvey's supporters in the Paris Faculty, as Dr. Peter Nurse makes clear in his edition of *Le Malade imaginaire* (1965).[12] Some elements of Molière's satire are constant; but here he seems to have come full circle, satirizing not the Montpellier-based innovators but the Parisian conservatives. The burlesque ceremonial by which Argan is made his own doctor shows striking resemblance to the Montpellier graduation exercise described by John Locke in his *Journal*, 18 March 1676; and Molière might well have seen the ceremonial when playing for the Estates of Languedoc in Montpellier in the 1640s. But an early version of the ceremonial ballet in *Le Malade imaginaire* clearly states that the new doctor is licensed to kill in Paris and throughout the world. The thesis that the foolish young doctor

Thomas Diafoirus has just defended against "Circulators" can also best be understood against a background in which such theses had recently been defended in the Paris Faculty. In the third *Intermède* the Praeses gives the Bachelierus "Virtutem et puissanciam, Medicandi, Purgandis, Seignandi, Perçandi, Taillandi, Coupandi, Et occidendi Impune per totam terram."

It is an excellent illustration of Molière's satirical mixture of fact and fantasy: he conflates the medical reliance on medicines, purging, and bleeding, with the arts of the surgeon, which must have scandalized a doctor like Guy Patin, a devoted enemy of any form of manual work. But the meaningful fantasy in "occidendi" picks up the serious point made by Patin and others that aspects of medical practice involved a license as it were to kill.

There are many pages of brilliant medical satire in Molière's comedies to which I have pointed, but inadequately to convey their full force and flavor. It is tempting to suggests links between the "mélancolie hypocondriaque" wrongly diagnosed in a great virtuoso comic tirade in *Monsieur de Pourceaugnac*, Act 1, scene 8, and the gallery of melancholics in Molière's theatre, all roles he wrote for himself; and all of them hoarders or misers in one way or another: Arnolphe in *L'Ecole des femmes*, who hoards a virgin; Orgon in *Tartuffe*, who tries to hoard salvation; Alceste, the Misanthropist, who hoards goodwill and thus has never really been appreciated as comic by the left-wing of any generation; Harpagon, the Miser, who hoards gold and— like the Hypochondriac, who tries to hoard his health— mimes death when he fears the hoard is lost. Molière was so good at acting such characters that he was himself satirized in 1670 as *Elomire hypocondre*. But not the least interesting feature of Molière's late comedies is diagnosis of self-pity and fear of death as a source of hypochondria, itself in turn a source of the irrational power of doctors over credulous patients.

But let me leave the last word to Béralde, who articulates better perhaps than any other character the link betwen formalism and opportunism in medical practice. In Act III, scene 3, of *Le Malade imaginaire* Béralde makes two distinctions of great importance. The second is perhaps the most fundamental and follows a round denunciation of the rhetorical "roman de la médecine," a practice built less on fact than on fantasy: "Dans les discours et dans les choses, ce sont deux sortes de personnes que vos grands médecins. Entendez-les parler: les plus habiles gens du monde; voyez-les faire: les plus ignorants de tous les hommes."

Popularization of this recognition that medical ritual was based on wrong theory seems to me of the greatest significance, not merely in the history of medicine or the history of the theatre, but in the whole intellectual development of modern France. This is partly because it is linked by Béralde's earlier distinction, with which I shall conclude. There are, he declares, two sorts of doctors: "C'est qu'il y en a parmi eux qui sont eux-mêmes dans l'erreur populaire, dont ils profitent, et d'autres qui en profitent sans y être." This is the distinction between doctors like M. Purgon in the play, "un homme tout médecin, depuis la tête jusqu'aux pieds; un homme qui croit à ses règles plus qu'à toutes les démonstrations des mathématiques. . . ," and doctors like M. Diafoirus, who consciously exploit a ritual they find advantageous. In Act II, scene 5, M. Diafoirus indeed declares to Toinette that he prefers general practice to practice at Court, where the patients insist on being cured:

> Le public est commode. Vous n'avez à répondre de vos actions à personne; et pourvu que l'on suive le courant des règles de l'art, on ne se met point en peine de tout ce qui peut arriver. Mais ce qu'il y a de fâcheux auprès des grands, c'est que, quand ils viennent à être malades, ils veulent absolument que leurs médecins les guérissent.

Toinette replies ironically:

> Cela est plaisant, et ils sont bien impertinents de vouloir que vous autres messieurs vous les guérissiez: vous n'êtes point auprès d'eux pour cela; vous n'y êtes que pour recevoir vos pensions, et leur ordonner des remèdes; c'est à eux à guérir s'ils peuvent.

M Diafoirus agrees wholeheartedly: "Cela est vrai. On n'est

obligé qu'à traiter les gens dans les formes."

Béralde's distinction between convinced believers and conscious profiteers in medicine has close counterparts in other comedies: the self-satisfaction of the *femmes savantes* exploited by the hypocritical Trissotin, for example. But the best analogy is with the contrast in *Tartuffe* between conscious and unconscious religious hypocrites. This analogy appears to be no accident. The Paris Faculty was so theologically oriented that theses were still written on Biblical subjects and problems. The apparent allusion in Act III, scene 10, to Matthew 5:29–30 is probably intentional satire; and it is, I think, fair satire that in Act III, scene 6, M. Purgon excommunicates his doubting patient Argan from medicine.

7
Characterism of Vices

It is unusual to argue either an English or an ecclesiastical inspiration for Molière's comedies. This essay proposes both. Not that Molière had direct access to the first English collection of "Characters" published in 1608 by Joseph Hall, later Bishop of Exeter and afterwards of Norwich. Within two years Tourval had published *Caractères des vertus et des vices. Tiré de l'anglois de Joseph Halles . . .* (Paris, 1610, 12mo). Nearer to Molière, however, a new French translation was published by Urbain Chevreau (an active playwright in Molière's youth) as part of *L'École du sage* (Paris, 1646, 12mo). The book had some success, since it was followed by the revised edition from which I quote: *L'Escole du Sage. Reueuë, corrigée, & augmentée par l'Autheur—Dédiée à Madame la Comtesse de la Suze* (Paris, 1652, 12mo), by a *Suite de l'école du sage* (Paris, 1660), and by Chevreau's *Considérations fortuites, traduites de l'anglois de Joseph Hall* (Paris, 1659).[1] *L'École du sage* anticipates the vogue of literary portraits that developed particularly in the circle of the Grande Mademoiselle in the 1650s. Its title may also be the point of departure for a form of title made famous in the theatre by Molière after intermediate use for the first fully erotic book in the French language, *L'École des filles* (1655), and ironic use in Dorimond's *L'École des cocus, ou la précaution inutile*, which (as noted in chapters 3 and 5) probably preceded *L'École des maris* on a Paris stage by several months.

Of J. Hall's *Characters of Vertues, & Vices. Two Bookes*—which I quote from the folio edition, London, 1620, in *A Recollection of such Treatises as have been heretofore severally published. . .* , London, 1621—only the second book, *Characterismes of Vices*, is of real interest for Molière studies. It begins with the "Character of the Hypocrite," ". . .the worst kinde of Plaier, by so much as hee acts the better part. . ." (p. 175).[2] The Hypocrite is followed by the Busie body, the Superstitious, the Profane, the Male-content, the Vnconstant, the Flatterer, the Slothfull, the Couetous, the Vaine-glorious, the Presumptuous, the Distrustfull, the Ambitious, the Vnthrift, and the Enuious. In *L'École du sage*, in the "Advertissement" to which Chevreau acknowledges that "le premier Liure des Caracteres des Vertus & des Vices, est tiré de Joseph Hall, Euesque d'Exceter . . . traduit en certains endroits, & paraphrasé en d'autres . . .," these characters form chapters 10 to 24: L'Hypocrite, Le Curieux, Le Superstitieux, Le Profane, Le Mal-content, L'Inconstant, Le Flatteur, Le Paresseux, L'Auaricieux, Le Glorieux, Le Presomptueux, Le Deffiant, L'Ambitieux, Le Prodigue, and L'Enuieux. Not even all of these "caractères des vices" seem especially relevant to Molière; but some are most suggestive, and together they provide important insights into the moralist background of some of his most celebrated characters.

It is a commonplace of Molière criticism since La Bruyère's *De la mode* to observe that Onuphre plays the hypocrite's part better than Tartuffe because he plays the part less obviously.[3] But obvious display has been an aspect of hypocrisy as defined in the Christian tradition since the Sermon on the Mount:

> Moreover, when ye fast, be not, as the hypocrites, of a sad countenance: for they disfigure their faces, that they may appear unto men to fast (Matthew 6: 16).

Such is the evangelical message to which J. Hall gives form—in imitation of Theophrastus—in his "Character of The Hypocrite," which I quote from Chevreau's translation in *L'École du sage*:

> Il a toûjours deux visages & souuent deux coeurs, & dans la piece qu'il jouë, il est d'autant plus meschant acteur, qu'il enjoüe le plus beau rolle. Il semble qu'il tienne à gage la tristesse & la grauité: Toutes deux paroissent en mesme temps sur son visage, cependant que la galanterie & la joye occupent toute sa pensée; & dans cet estat il rit en luy-mesme, lorsqu'il songe, qu'il a l'art de tromper de si bonne grace . . .(p.47).

Poor player of the finest part, with counterfeit gravity and

inward "galanterie" ("wanton and carelesse within,"
J. Hall, p. 175), such precisely is Tartuffe, who also shares
with the character of the Hypocrite a tendency to show
exaggerated piety in Church when under observation (Act
I, scene 5). According to Orgon in the same speech, "Il
s'impute à péché la moindre bagatelle" (l. 306), while J.
Hall's Hypocrite "turneth all Gnats into Camels" (p. 175).
In comic portraits, remarks Dorante in *La Critique de l'École
des femmes*, "vous n'avez rien fait, si vous n'y faites
reconnaître les gens de votre siècle" (scene 6). But to make
any of them recognizable, say, as hypocrites, intelligible
clues to that character are required; and some of these
Molière appears to have found in *L'École du sage.*[4] It follows
that we should be careful not to label as "libertine," satire of
hypocrisy in Molière's play whose inspiration is traceably
evangelical and indeed Anglican.

Lest this last observation be exaggerated or miscon-
strued, I would add—in contradiction to the widespread
misconception of *Tartuffe* that sees Orgon as "sincerely devout" or as a "good man victimized"[5]—that it is a play about
two sorts of hypocrisy: deliberate and obvious in Tartuffe,
insidious and self-deceptive in Orgon, a Pharisee quite as
subtle in his hypocrisy as La Bruyère's Onuphre. Biblical
authority for this interpretation would include Matthew 23,
where Christ repeats: "Woe unto you, scribes and
Pharisees, hypocrites!," observing: "Even so ye also out-
wardly appear righteous unto men, but within ye are full of
hypocrisy and iniquity" (23:28). It would also include the
Pharisee who prays: "God, I thank thee, that I am not as
other men are . . ." (Luke 18:11). But the evidence on which
this interpretation mainly rests is a book mentioned in the
first scene of *Sganarelle: La Guide des pécheurs*, by the Spanish
Dominican Luís de Grenada, doubtless the new translation
of this well-known author published in Paris in 1658 by
Guillaume Girard, secretary to the duc d'Épernon and
"Conseiller du Roy en ses Conseils." Grenada's analysis of
the "fausse assurance" and the "fausse justice" of the presumptuous leads to this important distinction of two hypo-
crisies:

Il arrive de là, que ceux qui sont justes de cette sorte, tombent

dans vne tres-dangereuse espece d'hypocrisie. Pour bien entendre cecy, il faut sçavoir qu'il y en a de deux sortes; l'vne
basse & grossiere, qui est de ceux qui voyent clairement qu'ils
sont méchans, & qui veulent neanmoins paroistre bons, afin
de tromper le peuple; l'autre est plus fine & plus subtile, par
laquelle l'homme ne trompe pas seulement les autres, mais se
trompe aussi luy-mesme, comme estoit celle du Pharisien: Car
sous cette ombre de justice il avoit non seulement trompé les
autres, mais il s'étoit trompé luy-mesme; puisqu'estant verita-
blement mauvais, il pensoit neanmoins estre homme de bien.[6]

Surely these are the two sorts of hypocrisy dramatized in
Tartuffe and Orgon, "l'vne basse & grossiere," the other,
"plus fine & plus subtile." Not a "libertine" analysis of
hypocrisy, but one whose inspiration is Biblical and
Dominican.

If Orgon be accepted as the worse hypocrite, because a
Pharisee more subtle and self-deceptive, an illuminating
perspective is opened on other comic characters, beginning
with the Gorgibus of *Sganarelle* who would use *La Guide des
pécheurs* as a pretext to tyrannize his daughter. In *L'École des
femmes* Arnolphe seems distinctly pharisaical at times. But
the most striking—though to many the least obvious—
analogy is with the misanthrope Alceste: in his insistence
"qu'on me distingue" (l. 63), in his claim "J'ai pour moi la
justice . . ." (l. 1492), in the way he exempts himself from
"l'iniquité de la nature humaine" (l. 1549). That some of the
attitudes of this champion of sincerity could be seen as
hypocritical, witness this observation (1668) by Saint-
Evremond: "Je ne suis point la dupe de ces hypocrites de
Cour qui preschent les autres sur la retraite, qui ne peuvent
se persuader qu'elle soit un bien. . . ."[7] Like Orgon,
moreover, Alceste seems fully prepared to sacrifice anyone
close by to a distant ideal: "le Ciel" for Orgon; and for
Alceste either the "vertus des vieux âges" (l. 153) or "la
postérité" (l. 1544), but nothing here and now. These mil-
lennial conceptions allow Orgon to regard people as dung
(ll. 273ff.) and provide the theoretical justification for Alceste's rudeness to the "hommes de notre âge" (l. 1546) and
desire to dominate Célimène. Though there are obvious
and important differences between Orgon and Alceste, I

suggest that the Pharisee is an important point of departure for Molière's satire of contemporary abuse of what Mircea Eliade calls one of the great eschatological myths of the Asiano-Mediterranean world:

> le rôle rédempteur du Juste (l'"elu," l'"oint," l'"innocent," le "messager"; de nos jours, le prolétariat), dont les souffrances sont appelées à changer le statut ontologique du monde.[8]

It is Alceste's claim to be such a *Juste* that has attracted utopian idealists, notably J.-J. Rousseau; and doubtless Alceste's denunciation of the present in the name of a mythical past or for posterity explains his attraction for Marxist critics who tend to ignore his insistence on class privileges (ll. 129, 1074) and absence of any workable plan of reform. For as Eliade continues:

> la société sans classes de Marx et la disparition conséquente des tensions historiques trouvent leur plus exact précédent dans le mythe de l'Age d'Or qui, suivant des traditions multiples, caractérise le commencement et la fin de l'Histoire (p. 175).

But Molière seems less concerned with embodying an ancient aspiration, which undoubtedly infuses Alceste with some of his mythical resonance, than with satirizing the abuse of such aspiration in the urge—under sufficient doctrinal cover—to humiliate and dominate here and now. Hence the psychological affinity of Alceste and Orgon— even to the underlying tendency toward violence everywhere written into the roles—with terrorists and tyrants who make good causes a cover for sadism or a means for getting their own way. Such, in part at least, is the vice denounced by Christ in Pharisees. In the plays both Orgon and Alceste behave unconsciously like Joseph Hall's Hypocrite: ". . . the strangers Saint, the neighbours disease . . . an Angell abroad, a Deuill at home; and worse when an Angell, than when a Deuill" (p. 176).

As far as Alceste is concerned, this reading finds support in *L'École du sage*, where Chevreau—as author, and not as far as I know as translator—observes in chapter 9 of the second book "De la corruption du siecle" that it is hard to tell where we are in

> la loy de Grace, ou dans la loy de nature; il semble que la vertu n'est plus qu'vne beauté imaginaire . . . pour treuuer de l'innocence & de la pureté parmy les hommes, il faudroit remonter iusques au premier âge du monde (pp. 279–80).

But the character of Le Mal-content is denounced for turning distant virtues into scorn of the present day:

> . . . de tous les temps, il n'en haït que le present, quoy que sa bouche soit toûjours ouverte aux plaintes. Celuy-là est l'object commun de son mépris & de sa haine: ce qui n'est plus, est la matiere de son admiration et de ses loüanges, & dans ses occupations il semble qu'il veüille plus faire que Dieu, qui ne peut rappeller les choses passées. Il ne considère pas ce qu'il a, pource qu'il s'attache trop à ce qu'il n'a pas; & son humeur est si estrange, qu'il ne se soucie pas de ce qui est, pource qu'il est toûjours en peine de ce qui n'est point (pp. 70–1).

Célimène might agree that Alceste does not sufficiently admire what she is in his concern for her to be something different.

There are further elements of Le Mal-content that suggest Alceste more obliquely. If we substitute Oronte's offer of friendship for the gift in the following lines, for example:

> Si quelqu'vn luy fait vn present, il témoigne que c'est l'auoir reconnu dignement, que de ne l'auoir refusé : Quand il est digne de son estime, il se persuade qu'on le flatte . . . (p. 71).

The analogy I suggest is not in the particular circumstances, or the dramatic symbolism used by Molière, but solely in the basic analysis of character. Nowhere is the analogy stronger than in Alceste's confusion of personal conviction with truth; Le Malcontent

> veut que ses paroles soient autant d'authoritez, & que ses opinions soient autant d'Arrests & de Loix. Sa fantaisie seule est la raison de sa haine, & par vne disposition, qui luy semble estre particuliere, il s'est fait une telle habitude de la médisance, que la vertu mesme n'est pas exempte de ses outrages . . . (p. 72).

Not the whole character of Alceste, but the side of him that shows deep latent affinity with Célimène, the "médisante" that Molière staged opposite his *misanthrope* in order to facilitate satire of "toute la terre," as Donneau de Visé puts it in the "Lettre sur la comédie du *Misanthrope*", "puisque l'un hait les hommes, et que l'autre se plaît à en dire tout le mal qu'elle en sait."[9] J. Hall goes on to stress cruelty and cowardice in the character of Le Mal-content, duly translated by Chevreau (p. 73). He also suggests an affinity with L'Inconstant, since both characters make change their sovereign good, even if "celuy-cy ne s'arreste qu'aux choses futures, & que celuy-là n'a d'amour que pour les choses passées" (p. 74).

L'Inconstant calls to mind Dom Juan, even though J. Hall does not discuss this character with any particular reference to the inconstant lover. Part of the analysis of L'Inconstant seems to fit Molière's Dom Juan:

> La justice & la prudence ne moderent point ses passions :
> Elles sont toutes precipitées auec ardeur : Ce qui luy plaist le
> rebute au mesme moment qu'il l'anime . . . (p. 75).

More striking, however, is the juxtaposition of Le Superstitieux (ch. 12) with Le Profane (ch. 13):

> Le Superstiteux a toûjours des Dieux en grand nombre, & le
> Prophane n'en peut conceuoir aucun, si peut-estre le monde
> n'est son Paradis, & s'il n'est luy-mesme son Dieu (p. 65).

This is precisely the contrast Molière offers between Dom Juan and Sganarelle, especially in Act III, scene I, where Sganarelle's Moine-Bourru is contrasted with Dom Juan's "deux et deux sont quatre." Not of course the whole complex relationship, which has other well-known literary sources and Molière's own more powerful imagination behind it; but a precedent—basically Anglican—for the doctrinal contrast between the major roles, which is perhaps the most significant alteration Molière made in adapting the other Dom Juan plays on which he is known to have worked.

On the one hand, witness Le Superstitieux:

> Sa croyance est fondée sur vne Religion malheureuse, & sur

vne impiété déuote. Il est ridicule dans ses observations; il est
esclaue dans sa crainte; il inuoque Dieu selon son caprice, &
luy donne plus qui [*sic*] ne faut, & toûjours autre chose qu'il
ne luy demande . . . Sa timidité treuue par tout des pretextes
& des excuses, & par vne metamorphose inconnuë à tous les
autres, il change les moindres apparences en des veritez in-
faillibles (pp. 59–60).

Compare Sganarelle *passim*, but for the last two points especially, his role in Act III, scene 5, when he first sees the
Statue.

On the other hand, consider the character of Le Profane:

Dans tout ce qui regarde la Religion, son cœur est vn morceau
de chair morte qui ne ressent ny les craintes, ny les soins, ny
les remords de sa conscience. Par vn vsage long & maudit, il
est devenue tellement stupide, qu'il semble auoir perdu tout
sentiment, & s'est fait vne telle habitude de ses crimes, qu'il
ne sçauroit plus faire autre chose (pp. 65–66).

Contemporary religious literature abounds in sermons on
the hardened heart and final impenitence; and it is Molière's
triumph in the play to cast Dom Juan not simply as
"stupid" in this ecclesiastical sense, but to endow him with
charm, wit, grace, and verve.[10] But the callousness beneath
the charm, the mockery of religion, the brilliant false logic,
immediate response to appetite (cf. "j'ai une pente naturelle
à me laisser aller à tout ce qui m'attire," Act III, scene 5),
and especially the hypocrisy of Dom Juan are all already a
part of the character of Le Profane:

Il pecha d'abord sans repentir, & peche maintenant sans connoissance. Il n'a point d'autre souuerain que son appetit; la
Raison est sa sujette, la Religion sa boufonne, le sens son
écriture, & la regle de sa creance: & quand la piété luy doit
estre heureuse, il peut tout ensemble la mépriser, & la con-
trefaire (p. 66).

Doubtless the religious hypocrisy that Molière writes into
the role of Dom Juan not only for his last meetings in Act V
with Dom Louis and with Dom Carlos, but in his first
encounter with Done Elvire, relates on one level to the
quarrel over *Tartuffe*. But it is already an element of the
character of the Profane, which Joseph Hall opposes to the

Superstitious: ". . . and if Pietie may be an aduantage, he can at once counterfet and deride it" (p. 178). This passage too seems more quotable in the original: "neither is any mirth so cordiall to him, as his sport with Gods fooles. Euery vertue hath his slander, and his iest to laugh it out of fashion . . ." (p. 178), as when Dom Juan explains to Sganarelle, "la constance n'est bonne que pour des ridicules" (Act I, scene 2). But above all Le Profane is a prisoner of self-love: "Il n'aime que luy-mesme. . . . Il ne regarde pas quelles personnes il peut fouler, pouru̇eu qu'il s'éleue: Sa conuersation n'est qu'vn outrage, sa vie n'est qu'vne licence de crimes . . ." (p. 69). Not exactly Molière's Dom Juan, but—*mutatis mutandis*—a useful reminder that Dom Juan's behavior in the play suggests neither "love of humanity" nor that he is Molière's spokesman.

Le Glorieux suggests attitudes and even a dramatic device exploited by Molière, especially in *Le Bourgeois Gentilhomme*. This detail for instance, behind the fun that Molière's art extracts from M. Jourdain's cry "Laquais! holà, mes deux laquais!" (Act I, scene 2): "Pour faire croire qu'il ne manque point de Valets," observes J. Hall through Chevreau, "il en appelle plusieurs, quoy qu'vn seul soit bien souuent son train & toute sa suite" (p. 97). More central to Molière's stagecraft, however, is the following passage, where it is said that Le Glorieux:

> représente toûjours le plus superbe personnage de la Comedie, cependant qu'il en joüe chez luy le plus infame; & quoy qu'il éclate en apparence, il découvre pourtant sa bassesse à mesure qu'il la déguise. C'est un Capitan Espagnol sur vn Theatre Italien; vn vaisseau remply de vent; vne chanson dont les tons sont faux, & dont les paroles sont belles; & pour tout dire, la merueille des foux, & le fou des sages (pp. 98–9).

Particularly arresting is the observation "il découvre pourtant sa bassesse à mesure qui'il la déguise" which I take to be the *moraliste* basis of Molière's comic stagecraft in *Le Bourgeois Gentilhomme*, where all of M. Jourdain's costumes—from "cette indienne-ci" in which he first appears to the Turkish ceremony in which he is made a Mamamouchi—are in effect disguises that do not hide, but reveal and emphasize his bourgeois identity, especially perhaps when he carefully counts out tips to the Garçons Tailleurs who dress him up at the end of Act II. It is not a case of choosing between Molière as a "moraliste" and Molière as an "homme de théâtre," but of grasping the significance of the fun his stagecraft provides—a moral significance already expressed in theatrical terms in a *moraliste* book.

Metaphorically at least, "vne chanson dont les tons sont faux, & dont les paroles sont belles" suggests a frequent technique—at once expansive and burlesque—of this *comédie-ballet*—the crude execution of a lovely minuet, for example. Full discussion—in terms of the dénouement—of "la merueille des foux, & le fou des sages" would take us beyond the scope of this paper into a domain explored by W. G. Moore.[11] But it is best to add that Molière seems to draw on Le Glorieux for other characters in his comedies, and that for M. Jourdain he may also draw on Le Prodigue. The sort of Glorieux who "ne compte que des Grands parmy ses amis, & ne parle que de la Cour, pour faire croire qu'il en a toute la connoissance, ou toute l'estime . . ." may suggest Dorante in *Le Bourgeois Gentilhomme* and—more strongly—Acaste and Clitandre of *Le Misantrope*. *Per contra*, Le Prodigue "ne partage pas sa fortune auec ceux qui l'aiment; il la donne mesme à ceux qui ne l'aiment pas; il distribuë ses richesses à ceux qui le trahissent de meilleure grâce . . ." (p. 116)—as Dorante elegantly betrays M. Jourdain.

Opposite the prodigal M. Jourdain in Molière's theatre we find the miser Harpagon. A commonplace affinity between these opposites is suggested in the character of L'Ambitieux, who seeks honor as the other, wealth: "son defaut peut estre appellé vne avarice superbe, vne perpetuelle soif d'honneur, vne maladie de la raison; & pour tout dire, vne folie galante & releuée" (p. 110). Similarly, just as Le Mal-content cannot bear to hear anyone else praised (p. 72), L'Avaricieux hates others to be well off, ". . . & peut-estre qu'il se pendroit, lorsque les autres remercient Dieu hautemēt d'vne heureuse année, s'il n'estoit point obligé d'en payer la corde" (p. 94). Clearly the comic hyperbole with which Molière characterizes Harpagon is already current in moralist writing, but the striking difference in Molière's comic character is the absence of envy in his avarice. Though greedy as well as miserly, Harpagon is cast as so little specifically envious of others that I find nothing at all quotable in connection with his role in the character of L'Enuieux. This, I would argue, is because Molière chose in satirizing both the acquisitive and the hoarding instincts associated with Harpagon to develop the more farcically stageable qualities associated with the character of Le Deffiant:

> Son cœur est toûjours dans ses yeux, ou dans sa main; & pour ne pas douter d'vne chose, il faut de necessité qu'il la voye, ou qu'il la touche. Il est tout à fait perfide, ou tout à fait simple; & c'est pour cette raison qu'il se deffie de tout le monde, pource qu'il sçait bien que tout le monde se deffie de luy . . . S'il enferme quelque argent dans son coffre, il regarde par le trou de la serrure s'il n'y a point enfermé quelque voleur . . . Il vit comme si tous les hommes estoient des larrons, & n'est pas asseuré luy-mesme, s'il ne l'est pas . . . Il n'est point charitable dans ses censures, il est confus dans ses craintes, miserable dans ses richesses, opiniastre dans sa folie, perfide dans sa prudence; & seroit heureux, s'il ne viuoit point auec luy-mesme comme auec son plus grand ennemy (pp. 105–09).

Could it not be plausibly argued that Molière comically dramatizes just this sort of moral analysis—in Harpagon's inspection of La Flèche (Act I, scene 3), in Harpagon's secrecy about his wealth and inspection of his money-box, in his burlesque bewilderment and self-pity in the soliloquy that ends Act IV, where he distrusts even the audience as thieves and captures himself as if he were one? Nor would this argument be weakened, on the contrary, if it could be shown that Joseph Hall based his polemical portrait of The Distrustfull in part upon the scene from Plautus's *Aulularia* reworked by Molière in Harpagon's soliloquy.

This reading finds support in a handsome emblem book which happens to have been dedicated to the young Louis XIV the same year that Chevreau published *L'École du sage:* Gomberville's *Doctrine des moeurs.*[12] Of the many images Gomberville presents of avarice, I shall quote from one in support of my interpretation of Molière's stagecraft in Harpagon's soliloquy: the line "C'en est fait, je n'en puis plus; je me meurs, je suis mort, je suis enterré," which Molière adds to his sources and which I have seen an actor of the Comédie-Française choose as the moment to stand up and walk around.[13] Not only does such a "serious" treatment of the line lose the opportunity Molière writes into the line for laughter in direct rapport with the audience if only the actor will mime dying and death before asking : "N'y a-t-il personne qui veuille me ressusciter, en me rendant mon cher argent. . . ?" It also misses the meaning that cries out to be mimed farcically, a meaning Gomberville expresses by his fifty-second emblem: the miser "meurt cent fois le jour de soupçons et de craintes." That is because, as the title of the fifty-fifth emblem puts it, "L'Avare est son bourreau"—a Self-Tormentor, *Heauton Timoroumenos*, as Terence entitled the famous comedy; a comic playwright not infrequently behind the *moralistes* behind Molière. It is hard to escape the conclusion that Molière would be better appreciated as a *comédien* if he were better understood as a *moraliste*, and vice versa.

To sum up, Molière probably knew *L'École du sage*, which has some part in the characterization and distribution of major roles in comedies from *Tartuffe* to *Le Bourgeois Gentilhomme* (1664–1670). But I should guess he did not know *L'École du sage* in 1661, since the "Caractères des vices" do not find what would have been a natural home in *Les Fâcheux*. Chevreau's version of J. Hall's *Characterismes of Vices*—along with other *moraliste* and literary works—suggests important latent affinities among Molière's characters, and in particular something of the way in which he selects, rejects, combines, and redistributes literary sources—as well no doubt as personal observation and imagination, arguably more vital, but far more difficult in retrospect to analyze except in connection with such hard evidence as surviving texts provide. I do not conclude that Molière was Anglican because he draws upon a Bishop of Exeter, or that he was a Dominican because he mentions a devotional book by a Spanish friar containing such an attractive definition of hypocrisy. I do conclude that he is too hastily judged libertine because he can also be shown to have read libertine books and to have had a few libertine friends. Molière should certainly not be considered libertine for satirizing characters like L'Hypocrite, Le Profane, and Le Superstitieux—in a theatre built by a great prince of the Church, Cardinal Richelieu, and provided by "le Roi très Chrétien"—since they are concurrrently satirized in the multifarious and now badly-known religious literature of the period, which formed such an important part of its context.

Above all I conclude a tight relationship between comic stagecraft and moral significance, which is not that of Molière's sources, but of Molière. Doubtless the precise nature of this relationship must always depend in part upon a very personal imaginative reconstruction of that stagecraft, but this should not prevent the pursuit of available evidence related to meaning. Molière has suffered too long from being read alternatively as ideas without comedy or comedy without ideas. I hope to have illustrated a few cases where the ideas invite the comedy and the comedy expresses the ideas. Not that Molière was no showman, or that he did not write to entertain, but that he is often most charged with meaning when most entertaining.

8
Parody in
L'Ecole des femmes

First performed in the Palais-Royal theatre 22 December 1662 and published the following February, *L'Ecole des femmes* is Molière's fourth five-act comedy in verse; and it is the five-act play of which the greatest number of performances are recorded in the *Registre* kept by Molière's colleague La Grange during Molière's lifetime (1662–73). In the play, Arnolphe—a Parisian bourgeois aged forty-two has brought up his ward Agnès, aged seventeen, in ignorance of the facts of life. He plans to marry her, as he confidently explains to Chrysalde in the opening scene, in hopes that an ignorant wife would never cuckold him, a fate he fears obsessively. But since Arnolphe is also a status-seeker, he has recently assumed the would-be noble title "de la Souche," a change of name that confuses the youthful Horace, the lover of the play. Shortly before the play opens Horace had arrived in Paris, noticed Agnès during a brief absence on the part of Arnolphe and fallen in love with her, without realizing that she is the ward of Arnolphe, the family connection from whom he accepts money and in whom he confides. Hence scenes—already evoked in chapter 5 on "Wordplay"—in which Agnès in her innocence and Horace under a misapprehension about the identity of M. de la Souche repeatedly inform Arnolphe about the progress of their attachment and plans for elopement, while Arnolphe does his best to feign joy at any signs of progress reported by his rival and distress at any setbacks, which of course delight him.

The role of Arnolphe, written by Molière for himself as an actor, is a virtuoso role which dominates the play, featuring in almost every scene. It is a role which appears to have developed out of Molière's own roles as Sganarelle in

Sganarelle, ou le cocu imaginaire and in *L'Ecole des maris*, the acting style of which is discussed in chapter 3. Since there is abundant scope for comic mime and grimace in *L'Ecole des femmes*, the continuity of his acting in these related roles seems especially pertinent. It is clear from the contemporary evidence emanating from the "querelle de *L'Ecole des femmes*" that Molière did indeed exploit the opportunities for comic acting everywhere written into the role.[1] In *La Critique de l'Ecole des femmes*, Dorante (a sympathetic spokesman) commends the comic and theatrical use of narrative in the scenes in which Horace unwittingly makes his rival a party to his plans. Those *récits* or reports, argues Dorante, are an integral part of the action,

> d'autant qu'ils sont faits innocemment, ces récits, à la personne intéressée, qui par là entre, à tout coup, dans une confusion à réjouir les spectateurs, et prend, à chaque nouvelle, toutes les mesures qu'il peut pour se parer du malheur qu'il craint (scene 6).

On Molière's stage the narrative parts of the play were almost more important for what they allow Arnolphe as listener to mime than they are for the verbal content which so dominates the printed page. Yet these *récits*—the scenes with *récits*—also focus major themes of the play: the theme of the lover as blunderer whose blunders confirm his sincerity, which runs from the early comedy *L'Etourdi* through Cléonte of *Le Bourgeois Gentilhomme* to Clitandre of *Les Femmes savantes;* and the theme of useless precaution, which Molière carries forward from his sources in Scarron's tale *La Précaution inutile* and Dorimond's one-act scenario, *L'Ecole des cocus, ou la précaution inutile*, a theme which the inadvertence of Horace underscores far more wittily than any of the sources. The *récit* scenes also represent a convergence of techniques related to the structure of the comedy. They make possible much of the comic irony and some of the *équivoques* discussed in chapter 5, the *revirements* or reversals which heighten suspense in relation to the progress of the lovers, and above all the scope for comic mime.

It may be that *L'Ecole des femmes*, as W. D. Howarth suggests in his excellent edition, is among the more straightforward examples of Molière's theatre.[2] But as the late Raymond Picard observes, readers have not been lacking for whom Arnolphe is a figure of pathos if not of tragedy.[3] This perception of the play takes particular note of the final reversal by which Arnolphe, who had reared Agnès as an object for his own convenience and in abhorrence of cuckoldry, falls in love with her and offers (if only she will marry him and let him love her as he would) to allow her to behave in any way she will:

> Sans cesse nuit et jour je te caresserai,
> Je te bouchonnerai, baiserai, mangerai.
> Tout comme tu voudras tu pourras te conduire;
> Je ne m'explique point, et cela c'est tout dire.
> *(A part)*
> Jusqu'où la passion peut-elle faire aller?
> Enfin à mon amour rien ne peut s'égaler.
> Quelle preuve veux-tu que je t'en donne, ingrate?
> Me veux-tu voir pleurer? veux-tu que je me batte?
> Veux-tu que je m'arrache un côté de cheveux?
> Veux-tu que je me tue? Oui, dis si tu le veux:
> Je suis prêt, cruelle, à te prouver ma flamme.
> (Act V, scene 4, ll. 1594–1604)

There is no doubt that at this point Arnolphe's scheme has collapsed; but it is a fundamental misreading to suggest that his world has collapsed, because he is not characterized like that. At this point in the plot the focus is more on Agnès's liberation than on Arnolphe's loss, which the play suggests is in any case necessary and deserved. Evidence from the "querelle de *L'Ecole des femmes*" suggests, moreover, that Arnolphe's declaration as played by Molière himself was farcical. In *La Critique de l'Ecole des femmes*, a hostile spokesman, Lycidas, wonders whether there is not some contradiction in that "ce Monsieur de La Souche. . . , qu'on nous fait un homme d'esprit, et qui paraît si sérieux en tant d'endroits," makes such a grotesque declaration of love:

> ne descend-il point dans quelque chose de trop comique et de trop outré au cinquième acte, lorsqu'il explique à Agnès la violence de son amour, avec ces roulements d'yeux extravagants, ces soupirs ridicules, et ces larmes niaises qui font rire tout le monde? (scene 6).

Through Lycidas Molière is giving detailed stage directions which really are already written into the lines of *L'Ecole des femmes* in the scene in question, where Arnolphe delivers these lines:

> Ecoute seulement ce soupir amoureux;
> Vois ce regard mourant, contemple ma personne . . .
> (ll. 1587–88).

It is fundamental to Molière's characterizations that, as Dorante explains in *La Critique de l'Ecole des femmes*,

> il n'est pas incompatible qu'une personne soit ridicule
> en de certaines choses et honnête homme en d'autres
> (scene 6).

But there can be no serious doubt that in his declaration of love Arnolphe as played by Molière was grotesquely comic. To the commentary in *La Critique* to that effect it is hardly necessary to add that, in context, "contemple ma personne" is an old, and very successful comic turn which Molière might have noticed in the role of the braggart soldier Matamore in Corneille's *L'Illusion comique:* "Contemple, mon ami, contemple ce visage" (l. 318). He makes a fool of himself and then calls attention to it. There can be no reasonable doubt that this scene was first acted in the burlesque tradition associated with the role of Sganarelle in *Le Cocu imaginaire*, with Scaramouche and the great Jodelet roles of comedies written for him by Corneille, Scarron and others in the 1640s and 1650s.

Such a scene as this must have had an element of "absolute comedy," or funning for the sake of fun in the burlesque tradition; but Dorante's commentary on it in *La Critique de l'Ecole des femmes* shows that, in the author's mind at least, the acting was also significant as satire of contemporary manners:

> Et quant au transport amoureux du cinquième acte, qu'on accuse d'être trop outré et trop comique, je voudrais bien savoir si ce n'est pas faire la satire des amants, et si les honnêtes gens même et les plus sérieux, en de pareilles occasions, ne font pas des choses. . . ? (scene 6).

The word *satire* must suggest some degree of ridicule and

scorn for folly if not for vice as manifested in Arnolphe's behavior but Dorante's tone is not fierce; and the passage as a whole would seem to carry also a gentler general implication of humorous enjoyment of social behavior judged to be both odd and yet typical of lovers. More importantly for the present argument, the phrases "trop outré et trop comique" and "satire des amants" confirm that the scene does involve parody, of the comportment of real-life lovers.

The particular forms of parody involved in this scene are often called burlesque, a term which applies to literary as well as to acting styles, convergent in the tradition which leads through Scarron's Jodelet roles and the Sganarelle of *Le Cocu imaginaire* to Arnolphe. However, it is to literary parody, including both low and high burlesque, that I invite attention as a feature of style and as a confirmation of the tone and interpretation of the comedy as a whole, because it can be clearly seen as complementary to the acting style attested by *La Critique de l'Ecole des femmes*.

A good deal of attention has been paid to the development of the burlesque in the mid-seventeenth century in France, for instance by Francis Bar in his thesis, *Le Genre burlesque en France au XVIIe siècle* (Paris, D'Artrey, 1960).[4] The word *burlesque*, according to Gilles Ménage (1613–92), was a neologism invented by Jean-François Sarasin (1603–54), the satirical poet who secured for the troupe of Molière the reluctant protection of the young Prince de Conti during their wagon days. It tended to replace such synonyms as *grotesque, narquois, familier, goguenard, enjoué, badin*, and *bouffon*, not all of which convey a dimension of travesty or parody particularly associated with the burlesque, especially with low burlesque. One could scarcely improve upon Eugène Géruzez's definition of low burlesque as

> la transformation des caractères et des sentiments nobles en figures et en passions vulgaires, opérées de telle sorte que la ressemblance subsiste sous le travestissement, et que le rapport soit sensible dans le contraste. . . .[5]

This sort of burlesque is exemplified in such works as Charles d'Assoucy's *L'Ovide en belle humeur* (1650), Charles

Beys's *Les Odes d'Horace en vers burlesques* (1652) and especially Scarron's unfinished *Virgile travesti* (books I to VII,
1648–53).

If now we look again at Arnolphe's "transport
amoureux," we find that the lines are scripted in literary
burlesque in support of the acting style evoked in *La Critique de l'Ecole des femmes*. In line 1595, for instance, "je te
bouchonnerai" introduces vocabulary typical by its familiarity of the literary low burlesque, but alien to tragedy as
written in Molière's time for the Paris stage. Stylistically,
bouchonnerai intensifies *caresserai* of the line before, while
behind the metaphor lurk the main general associations of
bouchonner with wringing out washing and rubbing down
horses. I venture to add that in this context the stem *bouchon*
also suggests, improperly, the sort of stopper imagined by
Alexander Pope in *The Rape of the Lock* (IV, 54): "And maids
turn'd bottles, call aloud for corks." Moreover, Arnolphe's
aside, "Jusqu'où la passion peut-elle faire aller?," parodies
an intervention by the poet Vergil in his narration of Dido's
death in *Aeneid*, book IV: "Improbe Amor, quid non mor-
talia pectora cogis!" Scarron had already put Vergil's apostrophe into the third person in rendering this line in his
Virgile travesti: "Et jusqu'où fut ta passion!" When allow-
ance is made for the shift from narrative to drama, and from
octosyllabic verse to alexandrine in *L'Ecole des femmes*, the
lines are as close as it is reasonable to expect any two such
lines to be.

With such preparation line 1599 must seem extravagant
(as in a similar situation Alceste also does in Act IV,
scene 3, of *Le Misanthrope*). "Quelle preuve veux-tu que je
t'en donne, ingrate?" (l. 1600) seems to use the language of
tragedy, but in context can only parody such language,
which in any case—and by Arnolphe's design!—must be a
foreign language for Agnès. The vocabulary of the following lines fully supports this reading. In French classical
tragedies characters weep, and their audiences might weep
with them; but in no tragedy to my knowledge does a serious character threaten to weep unless he gets his way with a
girl. "Veux-tu que je me batte?" is more evocative of the

beatings of farce than of the combat of heroic drama. Characters in great distress in tragedies have been known to pull out some of their hair, or the actors in the role pretend to; but to threaten to do so? This surely is a character who first postures and then climbs down, as the later lines show: like Sganarelle, like Orgon in *Tartuffe*, like Alceste, like Le Bourgeois gentilhomme himself and Chrysale in *Les Femmes savantes*. And so much for the suicide threat:

> Veux-tu que je me tue? Oui, dis si tu le veux:
> Je suis tout prêt, cruelle, à te prouver ma flamme (ll. 1603–04).

Indeed the whole speech has the apparent form of a great tragic outburst: note the anaphora of the repeated questions "Veux-tu. . . ?" culminating in its inversion in an insistent, affirmative form: "Oui, dis si tu le veux"; and note the themes of love, tears, and death. In particular the line "Je suis tout prêt, cruelle, à te prouver ma flamme" is flagged with the vocabulary of the *style galant* of contemporary tragedy: *cruelle, flamme*. . . . Such a line might occur in a tragedy. Perhaps this one did and researchers will be able to show where, as for the known sources of other lines in this comedy. In context it is burlesque, like Arnolphe's earlier outburst: "Eloignement fatal! Voyage malheureux!," a parody of tragic lamentation at the beginning of Act II. In Act IV Arnolphe's offer parodies a tragic stance, as Agnès's uncultivated dismissal of such high rhetoric confirms:

> Tenez, tous vos discours ne me touchent point l'âme.
> Horace avec deux mots en ferait plus que vous (ll. 1605–06).

The abruptness of Arnolphe's self-contradiction in response to Agnès's refusal has comic potential of its own if well timed. But the point here is that the posturing which we know from *La Critique de l'Ecole des femmes* formed part of Molière's acting style in the role is scripted with pompous clichés borrowed from heroic drama and grotesquely out of place in such a domestic scene: "Ah! c'est trop me braver, trop pousser mon courroux" (l. 1607). That such a line is scripted for parody rather than for pathos is confirmed by the low burlesque vocabulary of the lines which immediately follow, including "bête," "dénicherez," and "cul de couvent," expressions at home in *Le Virgile travesti*, but alien to the great tragic drama of Corneille and Racine.

Arguably this passage combines the techniques of low burlesque—the "transformation des caractères et des sentiments nobles en figures et en passions vulgaires," i.e. in contrast with an ideal tragic "transport amoureux"—with devices of high burlesque or mock heroic, in which the more ordinary events of everyday life are "written up" in heroic language, as in Boileau's *Le Lutrin* and Pope's *Rape of the Lock*. For any reader who remembers his Vergil, the aside "Jusqu'où la passion peut-elle faire aller?" represents low burlesque. But if the model burlesqued in the aside were unknown, it could be read as high burlesque, because it introduces some of the rhetoric of heroic poetry into a domestic scene. Unless Molière is taking off some scene of a once familiar and now forgotten tragedy, there would appear to be in the passage more elements of high burlesque than of low burlesque. But both forms of the literary burlesque converge in lines scripted for acting in a low burlesque stage style which contemporaries contrasted with other moments of the role. Elements of parody everywhere written into the lines were scripted for the parody on stage of a "transport amoureux."

The burlesque stagecraft argued for Act V, scene 4, is neither isolated nor untypical of comically heightened scenes in *L'Ecole des femmes*. It is no secret that at the end of Act II Arnolphe orders Agnès to go inside (to exit) with lines borrowed *verbatim* from Corneille's tragedy *Sertorius*, which Molière's troupe had produced in 1662 some months before *L'Ecole des femmes*: "C'est assez. / Je suis maître, je parle; allez, obéissez." Few I think would doubt that at this moment Molière derives comedy from the parody of a tragic stance, and doubtless it is no accident that the final line is a perfect syllogism, with a major premise ("je suis maître"), a minor premise ("je parle"), and the conclusion which follows ("allez, obéissez"). The authoritarian attitude which such a line expresses through its form as well as through its content becomes in Arnolphe's mouth a masquerade, a parody of the masterful and heroic to which the counterpoint is the groveling, permissive, but still possessive "transport amoureux" of Act V.

In Act I, scene 3, Arnolphe's soliloquy is a parody of the challenges of heroic drama:

> Héroïnes du temps, Mesdames les savantes,
> Pousseuses de tendresse et de beaux sentiments,
> Je défie à la fois tous vos vers, vos romans,
> Vos lettres, billets doux, toute votre science,
> De valoir cette honnête et pudique ignorance (ll. 244–48).

The apostrophe is a great trope of tragedy, and I can point to no specific source for this parody which introduces a theme of Molière's playwriting from *Les Précieuses ridicules* to *Les Femmes savantes*. But there can be little doubt that the form parodied is that of Rodrigue's challenge to absent warriors in Corneille's *Le Cid:*

> Est-il quelque ennemi qu'à présent je ne dompte?
> Paraissez, Navarrais, Mores, et Castillans,
> Et tout ce que l'Espagne a nourri de vaillants,
> Unissez-vous ensemble, et faites une armée . . . (Act V,
>   scene 1).

For Don Rodrigue chivalric love is a spur to chivalric valor, and the effect of his soliloquy challenge is heroic. Arnolphe merely uses an heroic form to express rejection of the feminist literature whose emancipatory ideals he challenges but (unlike Don Rodrigue) cannot defeat. There was a social distinction in Molière's time betwen the sword and the pen.

There is nothing unusual or impractical about a mature bridegroom offering moral guidance to a teenage wife, as Arnolphe does in Act III, scene 2, with "Les Maximes du mariage." In the early 1660s the poet Jean de La Fontaine, for instance, wrote moral advice to his teenage bride. A few years earlier the English diarist John Evelyn, who married in Paris the teenage daughter of the English resident, presented her with an edifying volume to prepare her for her new role as housewife. It is the emphasis and the absoluteness of Arnolphe's stance which make this scene a parody of such experience, flagged by a line reminiscent of

Corneille's tragedy *Horace*. It is line 745 which Arnolphe addresses to Agnès in presenting the "Maximes": "Et je veux que ce soit votre unique entretien." In Corneille's tragedy the legendary Roman here utters the lines parodied in an order to his somewhat less heroic sister that "mes trophées / . . . soient dorénavant ton unique entretien" (Act IV, scene 5). But that is only one element of a complex parody. It has been suggested that because Agnès reads out ten maxims, Molière intends to mock the Decalogue, though of course she begins an eleventh, which is interrupted. That, combined with Arnolphe's impatience with the boredom for him involved in his scheme even when it seems to be going well, implies more than ten "Maximes." I suggest that there is a more obvious parody—through utter contrast—with the once famous "Douze tables des loix d'amour" of Honoré d'Urfé's novel *L'Astrée*. These twelve tables begin "Qui veut estre parfaict amant," with the emphasis firmly on the obligations of the male lover. And so they continue, as in the seventh:

> Que son amour fasse en effet,
> Qu'il juge en elle tout parfait . . . ,

lines which make just as impressive a contrast with the attitudes of Alceste as a lover in *Le Misanthrope* as they do with the possessiveness of Arnolphe, which they closely resemble in content if not in literary style.[6]

A loose parody of the Ten Commandments is not excluded by implied parody of the "Douze tables des loix d'amour," and any such parody may coexist imaginatively with Molière's more direct travesty of the *Instruction to Olympia* by Saint Gregory of Nazianzus, the Church Father who wrote a tragedy of which Christ is the hero. More precisely the scene travesties a translation, the *Préceptes de mariage de Saint Grégoire de Nazianze* which Jean Desmarets, later Sieur de Saint-Sorlin, presented in 1640 to the king, Louis XIII. This translation appears in the *Œuvres poétiques du Sieur Desmarets* (Paris, 1641), partly a collected edition which was (and still is) the most convenient way of owning copies of most of Desmarets' plays, one of which—*Les Visionnaires*—was in Molière's repertory in 1662 and is a known source of features of *L'Ecole des femmes*. But the parody involves a significant distortion by which the original *Préceptes* become a pretext for domestic tyranny. The same may be said for the parody in lines 679 ff. of Boccaccio's story of Griselda, the last tale told in the *Decameron*, a tale traditionally interpreted—e.g. in French translations from Petrarch's Latin translation—as an allegory of the marriage of the soul to Christ:

> Je vous épouse, Agnès, et cent fois la journée
> Vous devez bénir l'heur de votre destinée,
> Contempler la bassesse où vous avez été,
> Et dans le même temps admirer ma bonté
> Qui,de ce vil état de pauvre villageoise,
> Vous fait monter au rang d'honorable bourgeoise.

From poor "villageoise" Griselda had become Marchioness of Saluzzo, etc. Nor is it far-fetched to suggest a parody of the Griselda story here. In the first place the attitude it embodies, like that of the *Instruction to Olympia*, is highly pertinent through the parody to the questions concerning marital relationships raised by *L'Ecole des femmes*. In the second place Molière must have known the *Decameron*, which is a source of the plots of *L'Ecole des maris* and *George Dandin*, both deeply concerned with marital values.[7]

Moreover it is well known that the scene as a whole parodies a conventual relationship. At the outset Arnolphe orders:

> Faites la révérence. Ainsi qu'une novice
> Par coeur dans le couvent doit savoir son office,
> Entrant au mariage, il en faut faire autant (ll. 739–41).

François Chauveau's frontispiece for the 1666 edition shows Angès standing before the seated Arnolphe before the actual reading begins, like a novice standing before her superior in a convent. Arnolphe's *tirade* on the authority of husbands is a complex verbal fantasy, with elements of the Catholic marriage ceremony, moralist implications of the

Griselda story, etc. But Molière is also parodying, in the "chaudières bouillantes" mentioned in line 727, a repressive form of religiosity directed particularly toward women.

Not the least comic aspect of *L'Ecole des femmes* is that, as Arnolphe boasts to Chrysalde in the exposition, he chose as his school for wives a "petit couvent, loin de toute pratique" (line 135), upon leaving which Agnès could still inquire, "Si les enfants qu'on fait se faisaient par l'oreille" (line 164). In *La Critique de l'Ecole des femmes*, Dorante suggests that these words "ne sont plaisants que par réflexion à Arnolphe," and that they are not intended so much as a joke in themselves, "mais seulement pour une chose qui caractérise l'homme, et peint . . . son extravagance . . ." (scene 6). In context they also characterize Agnès as ignorant, but not stupid. For Agnès's question—the report of which to Chrysalde gives the actor in Arnolphe's role the opportunity to mime "une joie inconcevable" (as I interpret Dorante's commentary on the line)—also discloses the content and the limits of her education and what she has been able logically to make of one aspect of it. For such a novice might have noticed in an account (or painting?) of the Annunciation that the Virgin Mary conceived through the ear. In the lovely "Hymn to the Blessed Virgin Mary," *Quem terra, pontus*, occur the following lines:

> Mirentur ergo saecula,
> quod angelus fert semina,
> quod aure virgo concipit
> et corde credens parturit.[8]

Auricular conception was fairly popular as a theme in baroque devotional poetry. It occurs in Racan's early hymn "O gloriosa Domina," written between 1603 and 1609:

> Ce qu'une femme avoit perdu,
> Une Vierge nous l'a rendu,
> Lors que la foy te fit concevoir par l'oreille.[9]

It is also found in Cardinal Du Perron's "Cantique de la vierge" published in 1622:

C'est celle dont la foi pour notre sauvement
Crut à la voix de l'Ange et conçut par l'oreille.[10]

There were doubtless many variations on this theme, of which Rabelais's joke about Gargantua's birth was one. However, Rabelais does not write that Gargantua was "conçu par l'oreille," but simply that he "nasquit en façon bien estrange" and that he "sortit par l'aureille" (*Livre* I, chapter 6). Perhaps Rabelais's joke involves *contaminatio* or blending of the Annunciation with other mythic and miraculous births, such as that of Minerva from Jupiter's forehead. Agnès's question is much more to the point, as it also characterizes an *ingénue*. Like Rabelais, but more directly, Molière parodies a living tradition of piety. But it is apparently one which by 1662 was falling into disrepute. Little girls like Agnès might have noticed in early-seventeenth-century breviaries the phrase "quae per aurem concepisti" in the *Officium parvum*. However, I could not find any such phrase in the *Office de la Vierge Marie*, the first translation into French verse, dedicated to the Queen Regent Anne of Austria in 1645 by Desmarets de Saint-Sorlin. The phrase also appears to have disappeared from my breviary published around 1700, perhaps in the revision authorized by the Holy Office in 1679—though I suspect it was earlier, as further research could show. Molière is unlikely to have imagined that the "petit couvent, loin de toute pratique" chosen for Agnès as a school for wives kept a stock of the most current editions, which may be part of the joke which caused contemporary offense.

For the background of Agnès's question is not one of general *naïveté* only. It is a pointed reference to a type of establishment where what was proper seems not to have been practical and which continued a style of piety wide open to parody by any witty and clear-sighted commentator. In *La Critique de l'Ecole des femmes* the hostile critics are not satisfied with Dorante's explanation that its words "ne sont plaisants que par réflexion à Arnolphe." Climène considers it "d'un goût détestable," because (I suggest) it exemplifies so well Dorante's point when he remarks elsewhere that in a comedy, "vous n'avez rien fait si vous n'y faites reconnaître les gens de votre siècle" (scene 6). The question which produces Arnolphe's infectious laughter in the comedy is also a comment on the education of a certain sort of seventeenth-century "jeune fille rangée."

Here again parody is an important constituent of satire. But not every intertextual reference in the comedy involves parody. In the opening scene, for example, Arnolphe cites Pantagruel's reply to Panurge in Rabelais's tale: "Pressez-moi de me joindre à femme autre que sotte . . ." (ll. 117 ff.). Arnolphe's allusion is self-characterizing. It further confirms a literary continuity, but not through parody. Or to take another example, Arnolphe congratulates himself after the "Maximes du mariage" scene in a quatrain which calls to mind the myth of Pygmalion, the sculptor who assumed he could possess the beautiful Galatea, because he had made her as the statue which came to life and with which he fell in love:

> Je ne puis faire mieux que d'en faire ma femme:
> Ainsi que je voudrai je tournerai cette âme.
> Comme un morceau de cire entre mes mains elle est,
> Et je lui puis donner la forme qui me plaît (ll. 808–11).

The Pygmalion archetype lends depth to Molière's characterization, but these lines in context are ironic, not a parody.

Let one more illustration suffice. In the opening scene Chrysalde criticizes Arnolphe for taking in mid life the new name "de la Souche," recalling:

> Je sais un paysan qu'on appellait Gros-Pierre,
> Qui, n'ayant pour tout bien qu'un seul quartier de terre,
> Y fit tout à l'entour faire un fossé bourbeux,
> Et de Monsieur de l'Isle en prit le nom pompeux (ll. 179–82).

It is commonly assumed that (despite denials of any personal satire voiced in *La Critique de l'Ecole des femmes*) this is a joke at the expense of the playwright Thomas Corneille, who had recently begun to style himself the Sieur de l'Isle. And so it may well be. But it is also a topos, a variant of which Molière might have found in Erasmus's colloquy *La*

Noblesse empruntée, as it appears in *Les Entretiens familiers d'Erasme*, translated for the first time into French prose by Samuel Chappuzeau and published in Paris in three volumes in 1662, a few months before the opening of *L'Ecole des femmes:* the basis of plays by Chappuzeau familiar to *Moliéristes* as sources of *Le Bourgeois Gentilhomme* and *Les Femmes savantes*. In *La Noblesse empruntée* Harpale has just admitted to his origins in the poorest village in the province. Nestor asks:

> . . . Mais ne se trouve-t-il point quelque éminence voisine de ce hameau?
> *Harpale:* Il s'en voit une.
> *Nestor:* Et accompagnée sans doute de quelque roche?
> *Harpale:* Vous pouvez ajoûter des plus escarpées.
> *Nestor:* Il faut donc vous faire appeler désormais, *Harpale de Come, Chevalier de la Roche d'or* (I, 27).

In Chrysalde's lines we have a new form of this old joke from a new version of a Renaissance moralist dialogue. Chrysalde's lines are no parody, but (I would argue) an adaptation to a new context. Molière's rephrasing poeticizes, polemicizes and perhaps personalizes Erasmus's ironic exchange. The change within an intertextual continuity yields satire without parody.

Elsewhere in *L'Ecole des femmes*, however, and widely throughout his other plays Molière has written into the lines elements of parody which, in context, constitute a clear guide to the original acting style of major roles, such as the first scene in *Tartuffe* in which Tartuffe courts Elmire and the last scene in *Le Misanthrope* in which Alceste courts Célimène.

9
Some Background
to *Tartuffe*

Much still remains to be discovered about Molière's *Tartuffe* after three centuries of investigation. Of course a great deal has come to light, especially concerning its social and religious background, the circumstances in which it was first performed, censored, and revised, and its relation to the satire of hypocrisy before Molière.[1] But enough texts have come to my attention in recent years to convince me that many more may be discovered to help situate *Tartuffe* and that meanwhile the following may be of interest, some merely as a likely source for favorite lines, others for the light they may shed on the general inspiration of the play.

Dorine's familiar description of Tartuffe as "Gros et gras, le teint frais, et la bouche vermeille" (l. 233) attracts the following gloss in the new Pléiade edition of Molière's *Œuvres complètes:* "Telle était la complexion de Du Croisy qui a créé le rôle (I, 1341)." Doubtless true, but there is a literary source in one of Saint-Amant's bawdy sonnets, as indicated in chapter 4:

> Me voyant plus frisé qu'un *gros* comte allemand,
> *Le teint frais*, les yeux doux, *et la bouche vermeille.* . . .[2]

Molière's memory, trained to retain thousands of lines in major roles in over a hundred plays, must have retained these lines, which in their way are as helpful in analyzing his style as a manuscript or a proof correction might be. He recasts the second line, bringing down "gros" and redoubling it in an initial "Gros, et gras"—I restore the original punctuation—to replace "les yeux doux," with advantage to his comic portrayal of a hypocrite gluttonous as well as lascivious.

Dorine's remarks on Orgon's infatuation with Tartuffe:

144

Ses moindres actions lui semblent des miracles.
Et tous les mots qu'il dit sont pour lui des oracles (ll. 197–8),

are anticipated by a passage in Jean de Lannel's *Roman
satirique* (Paris, 1624) informing us that Agiosanir, a famous
Sacrificateur,

> acquit en moins de quinze jours une si grande autorité, et une
> telle croyance auprès de l'Empereur que sa Majesté
> s'imaginait que toutes ses paroles étaient des oracles, et toutes
> ses actions des miracles (p. 1086).

Although the passage illustrates the view reflected also in
Molière that "le zèle indiscret, et la superstition ont une
grande puissance sur les faibles esprits" (pp. 1085–6), this
rapprochement must remain somewhat tentative, for it is not
uncommon to find *oracles* linked to *miracles*. Yet Lannel's
conception of the novel as a satirical portrayal of contemporary life is near enough in some ways to Molière's conception of comedy to suggest he may have known it, a
possibility of particular interest in the light of the
dénouement of *Tartuffe*, the king's intervention, which as
Jacques Guicharnaud observes completes the play's structure

> as contrast to the small family kingdom, described throughout
> the play in political terms. Orgon's entourage reacts to him
> rather like subjects toward a king [devoted] . . . to a bad
> minister.[3]

If indeed Molière did find inspiration for part of *Tartuffe* in
this part of *Le Roman satirique*, Guicharnaud's insight is
strikingly confirmed by the shift from imperial court to
bourgeois household.

No source by way of dramatic technique has been proposed for Tartuffe's famous entry in Act III, scene 2:

> Laurent, serrez ma haire avec ma discipline,
> Et priez que toujours le Ciel vous illumine (ll. 853–4)

Yet Emilie's second entry in Samuel Chappuzeau's *Le Cercle
des femmes. Entretien comique tiré des Dialogues d'Erasme* (Lyon,
1656) is quite similar:

EMILIE. Isabeau. *Elle parle derrière la toile.*

HORTENSE. Mais j'entends sa voix.

EMILIE. Remettez sur mes tablettes cet Hérodote que j'ai laissé sur la table, et que mon cabinet soit en ordre lorsque ces dames me viendront trouver. *Elle sort sur le théâtre.*

Since Molière readapted and pillaged plays by Chappuzeau, and was interested in feminism throughout his career, it appears likely that he was struck by this symbolic entry of a *femme savante* and that for the Herodotus and notebooks which symbolize her pedantry he substituted hairshirt and scourge as emblems of hypocrisy for the no less symbolic entry of Tartuffe.

That hairshirt and scourge do admirably symbolize the impostor is fully appreciated. The new Pléiade edition devotes a long note to these lines, their devotional background, the aphrodisiac quality of the exercises hypocritically evoked, and contemporary comment on the hypocrisy attending misuse of such equipment. But it may be worthwhile adding St. François de Sales's remarks in his *Introduction à la vie dévote*, since this was a perennial bestseller in seventeenth-century France and a good guide to the attitudes of those sincerely pious without fanaticism. In the chapter "Des exercices de la mortification extérieure" (III, xxiii) he writes:

La discipline a une merveilleuse vertu pour réveiller l'appétit de la dévotion, étant prise modérément. La haire mate puissamment le corps; mais son usage n'est pas pour l'ordinaire propre ni aux gens mariés, ni aux délicates complexions, ni à ceux qui ont à supporter d'autres grandes peines. Il est vrai qu'ès jours plus signalés de la pénitence, on la peut employer avec l'avis du discret confesseur.

Such words as *modérément* and *discret* confirm the extent to which Molière has not simply seized on conventional emblems of devoutness to mark Tartuffe's entry, but caused the impostor to invoke them in a manner clearly excessive in comparison with the most widely read devotional guide of the day.

Mme Pernelle's zeal obviously fails the same test. It has recently been shown that when, for example, she tells Elmire:

> Ces visites, ces bals, ces conversations
> Sont du malin esprit toutes inventions. (ll. 151–2),

Molière incorporates into her speech the vocabulary and imagery of the Jesuit Nicolas Caussin's *La Cour sainte*.[4] But the speech is more interesting in some ways for what it is not, for it flies in the face of the strong Christian humanist current which certainly warned against the dangers of such activities, but considered the distractions themselves indifferent. Witness again St. François de Sales, who begins the chapter "Des bals et passetemps loisibles mais dangereux" (III, xxxiii) of his *Introduction:* "Les danses et bals sont choses indifférentes de leur nature . . ." (p. 252). Of course this view was contested, but just how far Mme Pernelle is from the contemporary ideal of the *honnête femme* can be shown by contrasting her attitude with that of the Franciscan moralist Du Bosc, who takes up the question in the third volume of *L'Honnête Femme:*

> Je sais bien que Monsieur de Sales a laissé dans ses livres, que le bal et les jeux sont indifférents: et que même il a maintenu cette doctrine, quand elle a été choquée. J'avoue encore une fois, que je n'attaque ni les jeux ni les autres divertissements permis, mais seulement l'excès et le désordre qui s'y rencontrent.[5]

Since Mme Pernelle is manifestly not, in such a matter as this, at all representative of the devotional mainstream, it follows that Molière's satire is directed against an obviously extremist fringe.

There is an equally clear contrast between Mme Pernelle's strictures on visits and conversations and the chapter "De l'honnêteté des paroles et du respect que l'on doit aux personnes" in Sales's *Introduction* (III, xxvii). The saint evokes the pleasure to be found in the modest exchange of innocent wit, the

> [. . .] vertu nommée eutrapélie par les Grecs, que nous pouvons appeler bonne conversation; et par iceux on prend une honnête et aimable récréation sur les occasions frivoles que les imperfections humaines fournissent (p. 233).

Not only is the attitude toward recreation or entertainment

expressed by these moralists far more human and moderate than Mme Pernelle's, but Molière himself must be considered on this point clearly within the Salesian mainstream when in the preface to *Tartuffe* he advances the assumption that "les exercices de la piété souffrent des intervalles et que les hommes aient besoin de divertissement." In Gomberville's neo-Stoic *Doctrine des moeurs* (1646), the novelist turned moralist proposes to the young king Louis XIV figures with captions such as "L'esprit a besoin de repos" and "Le sage n'est pas toujours sérieux" (nos. 17 and 18), explaining "que l'homme est homme; et que ces continuelles contentions d'esprit, qui nous élèvent au-dessus de la matière, ne sont propres qu'à ces Intelligences bienheureuses, qui en sont entièrement séparées [i.e., angels]" (folio 79).

The relation of *Tartuffe* to François de Sales and other spiritual spokesmen for the mainstream of Christian humanism suggested here finds confirmation in the excellent article by Jacqueline Plantié cited in chapter 5, in elucidation of Mme Pernelle's pun on *Babylone* in the opening scene. The point here is that whereas François de Sales with the pun rebukes gently and humorously, as a prelude to charitable discussion, Mme Pernelle uses the same words harshly, to reject and to condemn. This is a point worth stressing because Roger Planchon, in his second production of *Tartuffe* (1973–74), used Salesian texts as if they were the straightforward context of the extravagant devoutness of Orgon and his mother. The play makes better sense in its historical context if instead such texts are understood as pretexts.[6]

It is also a misconception, I now consider, to suppose that in Orgon Molière seeks to satirize a man sincerely devout. As indicated in chapter 7, Granada's *Guide des pécheurs* translated into French by the secretary of the duc d'Epernon, Gillaume Girard, and published in Paris in 1658, proposes two sorts of hypocrisy: one gross and conscious, the other self-deceptive, Pharisaical and more serious. The book has a very good index, so the passage quoted at length in chapter 7 has always been easy to find simply by looking up *Hypocrisie* in the back of the book. And there is no doubt about its emphasis on the hypocrisy of self-deception. Such "hypocrites à eux-mêmes" are in a state so dangerous, the *Guide des pécheurs* continues, "qu'en vérité ce serait un moindre mal d'être méchant, et de se croire tel . . ." (p. 727).

La Guide des pécheurs is one of the few books mentioned by title in Molière's theatre, in *Sganarelle*, scene 1; but it is not necessary to suppose that he knew it thoroughly to see that in *Tartuffe* he has dramatized the dominant aspects of hypocrisy according to this complex definition: the two sorts of hypocrisy, their interaction, and the way each sort uses the other to forward its own evil ends. Orgon by the standards of *La Guide des pécheurs* is not sincerely devout, but a Pharisee, presumptive of his own motivation, scornful of others, one of those lost in "une fausse assurance que leur cause cette fausse justice, qui est le plus grand de tous les dangers . . ." (pp. 725–6). It is as a Pharisee that Orgon is guilty of what Sartre would come to call "mauvaise foi" and Merleau-Ponty unconscious or "metaphysical" hypocrisy, as opposed to the "psychological" hypocrisy of the sort practised deliberately by Tartuffe. My aim is not to quarrel with such modern vocabulary if it helps in analysis of the play, but simply to suggest that Molière is unlikely to have considered such a character as Orgon sincerely devout. The notion that the Pharisee is a hypocrite has interesting implications also for the character of Alceste in *Le Misanthrope*. Though certainly not the sort of religious hypocrite condemned by Cléante in his great speech in Act I, scene 5, for putting themselves forward through prayer, the basic contradiction in his attitude is neatly caught in Cléante's line 372: "Et prêchent la retraite au milieu de la cour."

I shall return to the religious and philosophical background of Cléante's speech. Meanwhile I would argue that the mention of *La Guide des pécheurs*, Pibrac's *Quatrains*, and other devotional texts by Gorgibus at the beginning of *Sganarelle* is not intended, in context, to suggest that he is a character steeped in and respecting such traditions. It

would be easier to argue the reverse, that like Arnolphe in
L'Ecole des femmes and Orgon in *Tartuffe*, he is using them as
a pretext for tyranny. Consider this one example, pertinent
because like Gorgibus, Orgon first promises his daughter's
hand to a suitable young man whom she wishes to marry,
and then withdraws his promise in order to suit himself.
Gorgibus invokes Pibrac's *Quatrains* as the sort of reading
that would make Célie strictly obedient, but they are not
quite like that. In fact Pibrac's 88th quatrain gives a good
measure of Gorgibus's dishonesty, which is very similar to
Orgon's in breaking faith with his daughter and the man to
whom she has been promised:

> Songe longtemps avant que de promettre:
> Mais si tu as quelquechose promis,
> Quoique ce soit, et fût-ce aux ennemis,
> De l'accomplir en devoir te faut mettre.

As Molière composed quatrains in this tradition for the
Confrérie de l'Esclavage de Notre-Dame la Charité in 1665,
it seems reasonable to suppose that Orgon's attitude to his
previous consent to Mariane's marriage to Valère can be
found wanting by the same standard. There are, of course,
many important ways in which Molière differs from the
devotional currents invoked here (e.g. in filial obedience as
an absolute requirement). But the main difference is doubtless the way in which he is able to exploit the tergiversation
of Gorgibus and Orgon for comedy, through the contra-
dictions in their attitude and the scope which their tergiversation offers for comic mime. For the satire of such
Pharisaical bigots, it is not necessary to look beyond the
mainstream Christian traditions identified by Molière himself.

The other speech on which it may be helpful to comment
is Tartuffe's declaration of love to Elmire in Act III, scene
3, beginning:

L'amour qui nous attache aux beautés éternelles
N'étouffe pas en nous l'amour des temporelles . . . (l. 933 ff.).

As Tartuffe wishes to become Elmire's lover without ceasing to appear devout, his declaration reflects both devotional attitudes and conventional gallantry in a masterly literary pastiche involving fusion and parody of contemporary devotional poetry and *vers galants*.

Clearly Tartuffe contradicts the sort of devotional stance implicit in (say) Gabrielle de Coignard's apostrophe to her desires:

> Sans plus vous arrêter aux choses temporelles . . .
> Il faut chercher au Ciel les grâces éternelles.[8]

But there may be more hesitancy than need be over the basic idea invoked by Tartuffe. Jacques Scherer, for instance, observes: "Cette conception de la beauté et de ses reflets me semble vaguement platonicienne."[9] But other scholars have also noted that the speech echoes the Psalmist's theme "the Heavens declare the glory of God," as one may read in the new Pléiade edition (I, 1356). Doubtless also a valid point, but the Neoplatonism of the passage is more specific and probably more satirical than generally realized.

A *Tesoro di concetti poetici* published in Venice in 1610 contains a section of poems by Petrarch, Annibal Caro, Bembo, d'Azia, and the two Tassos under the rubric "Per la bellezza della donna si può ascendere alla contemplazione del summo bene."[10] This represents a still rare expression of Ficinian Neoplatonism, which held physical passion (including intercourse), as well as the morally perfective "Platonic" love, to be "honestus" and in keeping with the "imago divina" (cf. Levi, p. 237). The full Ficinian implications were not always present in recurrences of this theme in France, but there is no shortage of recurrences. Couton mentions Cardinal Bellarmini's *De ascentione mentis in Deum per scalas rerum creatarum* (1615), of which he notes also three French translations. But look how the theme recurs, physical passion sublimated, in Lannel's *Roman satirique*, where Philanton writes to Aminthe, who has left him for a convent, a decision he has come to approve and imitate:

> Mais par le moyen de tant de merveilles [vos beautés], qui vous avaient acquis un empire sur toutes mes affections, je

> découvre l'éclat de la dignité de celui de qui vous les tenez, et m'en sers comme de degrés pour élever mon esprit en la considération de son excellence, admirant l'ouvrier par le mérite de ses œuvres (p. 170).

Du Bosc also alludes to this Neoplatonist theme in the chapter "De la beauté" of *L'Honnête Femme*, where the power of natural beauty to perfect through love is contrasted with artificial beauty aids:

> La gorge et le sein de Théodote athénienne étaient si agréables, que Socrate même en devint amoureux. Ce sont des traits ou des charmes qu'il ne faut pas chercher par artifice ni posséder par vanité: la Nature en gratifie quelques personnes à dessein de contenter les yeux, et d'élever les esprits jusques à l'amour de celuy qui est la source de toutes les perfections humaines (I. 153).

Hardly a plea for the "nudité de gorge" to which Tartuffe alludes upon his first entry, and which is defended in the *Cabinet satirique;*[11] but the passage does suggest the extent to which a Franciscan moralist of the mid-century could interpret physical passion as morally perfective.

This stanza from Lingendes's "Stances sur une jeune courtisane" also seems worth quoting in connection with Tartuffe's assertion: "Le scandale du monde est ce qui fait l'offense, / Et ce n'est pas pécher que pécher en silence" (ll. 1505–6), though the idea is familiar through Régnier's Macette:

> Celle qui fait du mal se peut dire innocente
>   En le tenant caché,
> Mais quand on fait du mal et qu'après on s'en vante,
>   On fait double péché (l. 103).

It is not difficult to see that Tartuffe, by denying sin altogether, adds intellectual *libertinage* to such a libertine notion, illustrating his hypocrisy. It seems equally obvious that Molière, who creates comedy by allowing the declaration to be overheard, is not voicing any libertine view of his own through Tartuffe.

But the most appropriate background to Tartuffe's declaration I have met occurs in a book well known to have been used by Molière, Cotin's *Œuvres galantes* (Paris, 1663), the acknowledged source of Trissotin's poems in *Les Femmes savantes*. An anonymous sonnet published by Cotin with his own commentary to a lady correspondent combines the themes "the Heavens declare the glory of God" and "a woman's beauty lifts the soul up to her creator." Although Scherer, I think mistakenly, states in his remarks on Tartuffe's declaration that "le platonisme est plutôt lié, au XVIIe siècle, à une pensée libertine" (p. 159), the sonnet is a rather playful attack on intellectual *libertinage* through appeal to the physical passion dear to the sensual libertine:

Vous, à qui notre foi paraît une imposture,
Qui doutez des secrets que son voile a couverts,
Qui ne connaissez point de maître à l'Univers,
Et qui croyez qu'ici tout roule à l'aventure,

Pouvez-vous voir des Cieux la brillante structure,
Le constant mouvement de tant d'astres divers,
Le retour des étés, et celui des hivers,
Sans confesser qu'un Dieu règne dans la nature?

Certes si pour sortir de votre aveuglement
Tant de fortes raisons sont un faible argument,
Je m'en vais vous guérir de cette erreur mortelle:

Incrédules esprits, accourez en ce lieu;
Quand vous verrez Philis si charmante et si belle,
Vous verrez bien qu'elle est le chef-d'œuvre d'un Dieu.
    (p. 308)

Though Cotin does admit that the poet "est d'une piété assez extraordinaire," it is one he endorses for the lady:

Il est de bon sens, d'adorer ainsi la Divinité dans ses plus parfaits ouvrages. En effet, Madame, si l'homme est le chef-d'œuvre des mains divines pour la grandeur et la hardiesse du dessein, qu'est-ce que sera la plus ravissante femme du monde pour sa beauté? (p. 309)

A woman's beauty shows design; and design, a designer, as paintings imply a painter (Titian, Correggio, and Champaigne are mentioned). Indeed Cotin is delighted that this "belle méditation", as he continues,

me met bien à couvert du reproche qu'on m'a voulu faire, que je m'arrêtais trop à regarder les belles personnes (p. 310).

Cotin was not one to exclaim "Couvrez ce sein que je ne saurais voir" (l. 860), to judge by his "Vers libres," "Pour une belle gorge" ending:

> Amour, en ma faveur viens mettre sur ses yeux
> Le voile qu'elle a mis sur sa gorge d'albâtre (p. 426).

But there can be no doubt about the Neoplatonist framework in which the abbé's contemplation of beauty finds its justification. The "Réponse au sonnet" continues:

> Il s'y faut arrêter, Madame, pour s'élever à la première beauté dont les autres sont descendues. En l'état où nous sommes, on ne peut voir le Créateur qu'en ses créatures; et c'est dans les plus parfaites qu'on le voit plus parfaitement . . . (p. 320).

L'abbé Cotin is of course aware "qu'il y a des insensés qui abusent de la beauté" (pp. 320–1); and this is precisely what, within the Neoplatonist calculus, Tartuffe attempts to do. His amorous declaration to Elmire parodies love poems and devotional poems related to the calculus.

There is one more point of interest, though it does not materially affect the interpretation of *Tartuffe*. In reviewing *Les Femmes savantes* for *Le Mercure galant* of 12 March 1672, Donneau de Visé mentions the "applications de cette comédie":

> une querelle de l'auteur, il y a environ huit ans, avec un homme de lettres, qu'on prétend être représenté par M. Trissotin, a donné lieu à ce qui s'en est publié. . . .

It is known that the abbé Cotin, despite Molière's denial of this "application," had said disobliging things about Molière in his satires; and it is thought that he may have preached against *Tartuffe* in his unpublished sermons. This is a matter to which I give a little more attention in my edition of *Les Femmes savantes*, where attention is again called to well-known analogies between the roles of Tartuffe and Trissotin as parasites and impostors who deceive victims willing to be deceived because they are already victims of self-deception.[12] The eight years mentioned by Donneau de Visé in 1672 takes us back to the creation of *Tartuffe*; and though the texts to which I invite attention are by no means a proven source for Tartuffe's declaration, they do suggest why, whether or not Molière meant to satirize Cotin personally in the earlier play, that clergyman may have been particularly sensitive to certain aspects of the comedy. It does then seem reasonable to conclude that, if *La Guide des pécheurs* helps link Orgon with other Pharisees like Gorgibus, Cotin's *Œuvres galantes* furnishes another link between Molière's principal conscious hypocrites, Tartuffe and Trissotin.

Over against Tartuffe and Orgon Molière sets Cléante, sometimes taken as a *raisonneur*, in any case an eloquent spokesman in his great set speech in Act I, scene 5, added in the 1667 revision. Too little attention has perhaps been given to the opportunity for Orgon, during this speech, to mime impatience, frustration, aggression, tergiversation, indifference, and resolution. Until recently too little attention was also given to the philosophical implications of some of Cléante's lines, which J. L. Kasparek has admirably illuminated in his *Molière's "Tartuffe" and the Traditions of Roman Satire.*[13] Contrary to the view that the vogue of neo-Stoicism tends to be dissipated and rejected after about 1650 in France, Kasparek interprets Cléante as a Stoic *vir bonus*, substantiating his interpretation with an explanation of the allusions made in lines 385–86:

> Regardez Ariston, regardez Périandre,
> Oronte, Alcidamas, Polydore, Clitandre.

Clearly one might imagine a production in which Cléante merely displays the rhetorical mastery of the Doctors of *commedia dell'arte*, bashing words and dropping names, while Orgon mimes impatience. But the allusions if followed up suggest more, as Kasparek puts it so well:

> Cléante is well-chosen to be Molière's satiric voice. His name and his character are derived from the Stoic sage Cleanthes, a pupil of Zeno, the founder of Stoicism. [His] exemplars of virtue [include] Aristo and Alcidamas, Greek philosophers of the Stoic and Sophist schools, and Periander, one of the seven sages. . . . Equal proof is provided by his language; his vocabulary is that of philosophy; appearance (336); bounds

(341); reason (341); excess (*trop*, 341); knowledge (352); virtue (388) (p. 60).

Even without Kasparek's arguments for supposing that Molière knew about these philosophers it is clear that the allusions are too coherent to have been names dropped at random, while Orgon's sarcastic reference to Cato in line 349 is a pointer to this aspect of what follows in the speech.

But the language of Cléante's speech is also to some extent reminiscent of the Gospel texts in which Christ condemns Pharisees and hypocrites. It is not a question of verbal reminiscence, which would scarcely have been tolerated, though the hypocrite's "dehors plâtré d'un zèle spécieux" of Cléante's line 360 seems near enough—when the whiteness of Paris plaster is recalled—to the hypocrites denounced by Christ as "des sépulcres blanchis" (Matthew 23:27, quoted from the Jerusalem Bible). Hypocrites are called, elsewhere in Matthew 23, blind guides who will neither enter the Kingdom nor allow others to do so. They are condemned for making formal observances while lacking "la justice, la miséricorde et la bonne foi." Such strictures by Christ seem to fit, if not exactly Cléante's speech, at least the implications of the play in context. Consider Orgon's enthusiastic account of his first encounter with *Tartuffe*:

> Il attirait les yeux de l'assemblée entière
> Par l'ardeur dont au Ciel il poussait sa prière;
> Il faisait des soupirs, de grands élancements. . . .
> Et quand je refusais de le vouloir reprendre [un don],
> Aux pauvres, à mes yeux, il allait le répandre (ll. 285–98).

Tartuffe's behavior on this occasion as narrated by Orgon is precisely that of hypocrites described by Christ in Matthew 6:1–5 while warning his followers to behave otherwise:

> Gardez-vous d'afficher votre justice devant les hommes, pour vous faire remarquer d'eux. . . . Quand donc tu fais l'aumône, ne va pas le claironner devant toi; ainsi font les hypocrites, dans les synagogues et les rues, afin d'être honorés des hommes. . . . Et quand vous priez, n'imitez pas les hypocrites: ils aiment, pour faire leurs prières, à se camper dans les synagogues et les carrefours, afin qu'on les voie.

Of this part of the preparation Molière might have written of his hypocrite what he writes in the *Préface* about Tartuffe's *entrée en scène:* "on le connaît d'abord aux marques que je lui donne."

Perhaps I am not the first to have observed that, in the midst of Christ's strictures against Pharisees and hypocrites in Matthew 23, occurs the famous prediction: "Quiconque s'élèvera sera abaissé, et quiconque s'abaissera sera élevé." Tartuffe's ambition, from his claims to nobility discussed in Act II, scene 2, to attempt in the last act to get possession of Orgon's house, is so much a part of his character that it is perhaps unnecessary to stress that the hypocrites denounced by Christ share that failing. It might be possible to construct an argument by which in the course of the play Orgon is shown to have been humbled before being exalted again at the denouement, while Tartuffe is progressively more and more exalted before he is humbled in the end. *Tartuffe* to that extent would be an imaginative enactment of Christ's prophesy, a temporal approximation of reversals fully realizable only in eternity. There can be no doubt that Tartuffe at least does exalt himself and that at the denouement he is humbled.

The denouement of *Tartuffe* has attracted much commentary, a great deal of it unfavorable. To the extent that what goes before is deemed realist, a sudden change for the better has seemed implausible. To the extent that the Bourbon monarchy and/or Louis XIV has been out of favor politically, the Exempt's speech has seemed grossly flattering. There is a certain amount of evidence to suggest that such a personal intervention as Molière stages through the Exempt in Act V is at least poetically consistent with royal practice, because the king is known to have intervened in a number of private cases in the 1660s, some involving complaints about his rule. But rather than realism or flattery, the denouement of *Tartuffe* seems to me to represent a celebration of kingship, not so much as it was even in those early days of Louis XIV's personal reign, as kingship as it ought to be.

There is a long tradition in France of the king as the source and upholder of justice, as in the famous emblem of

Saint Louis dispensing justice personally beneath a royal oak. In one of the first performances in the theatre in which *Tartuffe* was first performed in five acts, the *Ballet de la Prospérité des armes de la France* (1641), an entry brought on Minerva, "déesse de la Prudence," and the goddess Justice, both decorated in the arms of the dauphin, the future Louis XIV. But above all the Astraea theme associating European monarchs with the return of Justice, as Vergil had done for Augustus Caesar in the fourth Messianic *Eclogue*, recurred from reign to reign and from country to country. "Queen Elizabeth I as Astraea" by the late Frances Yates is perhaps the best known study of the question.[14] In France in the early seventeenth century Honoré d'Urfé reflects the same tradition with respect to Henri IV, while Ariosto had used the Astraea theme in *Orlando furioso*—the poem which gave the theme of the *Plaisirs de l'île enchantée* festival in which the first *Tartuffe* was performed—to celebrate the emperor Charles V, the great Hapsburg ancestor of the young king celebrated in *Tartuffe*. On the level of poetic aspirations mythically projected, the Astraea theme is associated with the return of a Golden Age, a myth of particular appeal whenever a new reign appears to be bringing a new order from political chaos and civil war. Thus Malherbe's *Prière pour le Roy allant en Limousin*, drawing syncretistically upon both the classical theme of the Golden Age and the Old Testament Messianic tradition, celebrates the reign of Henri IV with a stanza opening: "Nous sommes sous un Roi si vaillant, et si sage." The Exempt's intervention at the denouement of *Tartuffe* beginning "Nous vivons sous un Prince ennemi de la fraude . . ." is best taken as within that same tradition. It does not merely flatter, because the ideal which it expresses is an admonishment also to kings. It is dramatically powerful because it projects, in a coherent poetic form, aspirations for justice of mythic dimensions onto a recognizable historic present.

10

"La Scène du Pauvre" of *Dom Juan* in Context

Few scenes in Molière's theatre are more provocative than "la scène du Pauvre" in *Dom Juan*. The following commentary, in which an attempt is made to extend literary analysis to stagecraft, proposes an interpretation in which individual lines are related to the context of the scene as a whole, the scene to the context of the play, and the play itself to the larger context of life in France in the early years of the reign of Louis XIV. First the scene:

DOM JUAN, SGANARELLE, UN PAUVRE

Sganarelle
Enseigne-nous un peu le chemin qui mène à la ville.

Le Pauvre
984   Vous n'avez qu'à suivre cette route, Messieurs, et
tournez à main droite quand vous serez au bout de la
forêt; mais je vous donne avis que vous devez vous tenir
sur vos gardes, et que depuis quelque temps il y a des
988   voleurs ici autour.

Dom Juan
Je te suis obligé, mon ami, et je te rends grâces de
tout mon coeur.

Le Pauvre
Si vous voulez me secourir, Monsieur, de quelque
992   aumône?

Dom Juan
Ah! ah! ton avis est intéressé, à ce que je vois.

Le Pauvre
Je suis un pauvre homme, Monsieur, retiré tout seul
dans ce bois depuis plus de dix ans, et je ne manquerai
996   pas de prier le Ciel qu'il vous donne toute sorte de biens.

Dom Juan
Eh! prie le Ciel qu'il te donne un habit, sans te mettre
en peine des affaires des autres.

Sganarelle

Vous ne connaissez pas Monsieur, bon homme; il ne
1000   croit qu'en deux et deux sont quatre, et en quatre et
quatre sont huit.

Dom Juan

Quelle est ton occupation parmi ces arbres?

Le Pauvre

De prier le Ciel tout le jour pour la prospérité des gens
1004   de bien qui me donnent quelque chose.

Dom Juan

Il ne se peut donc pas que tu ne sois bien à ton aise?

Le Pauvre

Hélas! Monsieur, je suis dans la plus grande nécessité
du monde.

Dom Juan

1008   Tu te moques: un homme qui prie le Ciel tout le jour
ne peut pas manquer d'être bien dans ses affaires.

Le Pauvre

Je vous assure, Monsieur, que le plus souvent je
n'ai pas un morceau de pain à mettre sous les dents.

Dom Juan

1012   Voilà qui est étrange, et tu es bien mal reconnu de
tes soins. Ah! ah! je m'en vais te donner un louis d'or
tout à l'heure, pourvu que tu veuilles jurer.

Le Pauvre

Ah! Monsieur, voudriez-vous que je commisse un
1016   tel péché?

Dom Juan

Tu n'as qu'à voir si tu veux gagner un louis d'or ou
non: en voici un que je te donne, si tu jures. Tiens. Il
faut jurer.

Le Pauvre

1020   Monsieur . . .

Dom Juan

A moins de cela, tu ne l'auras pas.

Sganarelle

Va, va, jure un peu; il n'y a pas de mal.

Dom Juan

Prends, le voilà, prends, te dis-je; mais jure donc.

Le Pauvre

1024   Non, Monsieur, j'aime mieux mourir de faim.

Dom Juan

Va, va, je te le donne pour l'amour de l'humanité.
Mais que vois-je là? Un homme attaqué par trois autres!
La partie est trop inégale, et je ne dois pas souffrir cette
1028   lâcheté.

(*Dom Juan, ou le Festin de Pierre*,
W. D. Howarth, ed., Oxford, Blackwell, 1958, pp. 35–36)

"La scène du Pauvre" is one of the most comic, but also
perhaps one of the most misunderstood, scenes in Molière.
Suppressed in provincial performances following the withdrawal of *Dom Juan* from the stage of the Palais-Royal in
Paris after an initial highly successful run of fifteen performances (February 15th to March 20th, 1665), the scene
was mutilated in early French editions and replaced by an
anodyne seduction scene in Thomas Corneille's verse version of *Le Festin de Pierre* (1677) which took the place of
Molière's prose comedy in the repertory of the Comédie-
Française until 1847. No one doubts that the "scène du
Pauvre" was bold and controversial in its own time; but its
original outlines and its art are best understood in the light
of the relevant theatrical, social and political circumstances
in which Molière chose to create a scene related to the
tragicomic material of the Don Juan legend but with no real
source there and evidently scandalous to some of his contemporaries.[1]

Context

Warned at the end of Act II that he was being pursued by
twelve horsemen (including Dom Carlos, to whose aid he
rushed at the end of this scene), Dom Juan abandoned his
dalliance with the peasant girls and fled with Sganarelle to
the nearby woods, where they lost their way: whence
Sganarelle's request for direction in the first line of our
passage, which is the second scene of Act III. While
Molière's use of stage time and space is imaginative (and the
scene-shifting machinery at his disposal dispenses with any
need to observe the strictest "unity of place"), it seems

likely (as M. R. Pintard has recently argued) that the action of Act III should be assumed to take place on the afternoon of the day begun in Act I, with Act IV following later the same evening and Act V on the evening of the following day.[2] The allusion in Act II to the horsemen and the discovery later in Act III of the tomb of the Commandeur indicate that (in contrast with earlier versions of the Don Juan legend, in which different parts of the action take place at widely separated times and places) Dom Juan and Sganarelle have not wandered further than classical verisimilitude would allow in the few hours assumed to separate the different acts.

Like Dom Juan's exit at the end of the scene to fight the brigands offstage—an exit which dispenses with "extras" while observing the *bienséances* limiting violence on stage—, the relation of this scene to the rest of the action in a relative unity of time and place reflects Molière's adaptation to fashionable contemporary French dramatic theory and practice of a legend which reached him from Spain by way of Italian comedy and French tragicomedy. Unlike the Spanish original, Tirso de Molina's *El Burlador de Sevilla* (if that play, which Molière seems not to have known, was the original), *Dom Juan* is not concerned with the theological question of whether repentance *in extremis* or attrition without contrition is futile. For Molière's Dom Juan never repents. Such a perspective, partly restored by Thomas Corneille in *Le Festin de Pierre*, had been largely lost in Molière's immediate sources: Cicognini's burlesque *Il Convitato di pietra*, an anonymous *commedia dell'arte* scenario of around 1658, and two five-act French tragicomedies in verse, both entitled *Le Festin de Pierre*, one by Dorimond (1659) and the other by Villiers (1660). By contrast, even in the "scène du Pauvre" where faith is an issue, Molière's *Dom Juan* is conceived more in a social than a religious frame of reference.

The meeting of Dom Juan and Sganarelle with Un Pauvre fits into a series of encounters which comprise the essential action of the comedy. It is a further "coup de pinceau" in the portrait of a rake so comically sketched by Sganarelle in the first scene of the play (ll. 77–79): not a stage in a "rake's progress," not a development of character, but an illustration the hyperbolism of which can surprise while fulfilling the comic expectations aroused in the exposition.

The relation of the "scène du Pauvre" to the rest of the action is best understood by analogy with the *comédie-ballet*, a genre invented by Molière through the fusion of comedy (including elements of satire, *commedia dell'arte* and farce) with the *ballet de cour*, a courtly and partly amateur form of *divertissement* quite distinct from modern professional ballet. In Molière's time the *ballet de cour* was characterized by a succession of *tableaux* in which verse commentary, costume, music and dance were normally related to a central subject or theme, but not necessarily structured in terms of plot, e.g. *Le Ballet des Incompatibles* danced by Molière's troupe at Montpellier for the Prince de Conti. In *Les Fâcheux* (1661), Molière's first *comédie-ballet*, Eraste ("amoureux d'Orphise") is repeatedly interrupted en route to a rendez-vous by a succession of importunate bores, the "fâcheux" of the title. Now *fâcheux* does not necessarily mean *raseur*. A "fâcheux" may well be a bore less by nature than by circumstance (e.g., another's haste); he may also of course importune a greater bore than himself. It is a question of point of view. The structure of *Dom Juan* as recast by Molière to include episodes like the "scène du Pauvre" reflects not only the temporal structure of the *comédie-ballet* generally by its use of loosely connected scenes and possible reuse of actors in different minor roles, but also the spatial structure of *Les Fâcheux* in particular insofar as it assembles on stage a succession of incompatible or contrasting characters.

It is no accident that this encounter follows hard upon the discussion of faith in the preceding scene, to which Sganarelle alludes in lines 999 ff., and but shortly precedes the first of the miracles, the Statue's nod later in the act. It is also worth remarking that Dom Juan is never present, in this scene or elsewhere in the play, without Sganarelle. But the specific interpretation urged upon the analogy of *Les Fâcheux* is that, by asking alms of Dom Juan, who rejects any sort of obligation to other people, Le Pauvre becomes for him—like Done Elvire in Act I, Pierrot in Act II, scene 3, and the successive entries in Act IV (M. Dimanche, Dom Louis, Done Elvire again)—very much a "fâcheux." Nor is it difficult, in the social conditions Molière knew, to conceive of a beggar in such a role, as the section on "Background" should make clear.

Décor

Producers have of course staged this scene in various ways. But the "Marché de décors pour *Dom Juan*" dated 3 December 1664, provides a notion of the perspective set originally used in this part of Act III:

> Plus une forest consistant en trois chassis de chaque costé dont le premier sera de dix-huit pieds et les autres en diminuant (an illusionist device to suggest perspective), et un chassis fermant sur lequel sera peint une maniere de temple entouré de verdure.[3]

Like some of Sganarelle's examples in the burlesque debate on medical and religious beliefs in the preceding scene (e.g., "ces arbres-là, ces rochers," l. 951), the references to the "forêt" and to "ce bois" by Le Pauvre and to "ces arbres" by Dom Juan (ll. 986, 995, 1002) are intelligible in terms of this set and invite appropriate gestures. The scene-shifting machinery used in the original performances did not discover the "chassis fermant" or backcloth depicting the Commandeur's tomb before scene five of this act, when Dom Juan exclaims: "Mais quel est le superbe édifice que je vois entre ces arbres?" (ll. 1219–20).

There was no particular novelty in either perspective set or use of machinery; both had been used in January 1641 for the inaugural performance (of Desmarets's *Mirame*) on that very stage, then the Grande Salle de Spectacle du Palais-Cardinal, and repeatedly thereafter, especially for *ballets de cour* and operas in which the "merveilleux" or supernatural played an important part (as in this play). Nor is the forest setting of the scene unusual, since it was frequent in seventeenth-century tragicomedy, pastoral, and comedy, including *Le Médecin malgré lui* in which another

Sganarelle appears as a woodcutter later disguised again as a doctor. Although in the latter part of the seventeenth century there was a tendency for French writers to prefer parks and formal gardens to wild nature, forests still covered most of France. Even in the Paris region (which the peasants' dialect in Act II and certain details of this scene suggest more readily than the nominal setting in Sicily), what Saint-Simon calls "l'immense plain pied d'une forêt toute joignante"[4] at Saint-Germain and other forests like those at Saint-Léger, Montmorency, Compiègne, and Fontaine-bleau—far larger than at present—were almost contiguous. Among the millions who found shelter in the real forests of Molière's France were both brigands like those who (after a warning from Le Pauvre in ll. 986–88) appear offstage at the close of this scene and men like Le Pauvre himself.

The presence of an illusionist *décor* made a poetic evocation of the forest unnecessary.

Costumes

To a spectator, one of the most obvious facts about this scene is the disguise of two of the three actors, Dom Juan and Sganarelle. They have not simply exchanged outfits as proposed at the end of Act II (a detail of the legend): Molière effects instead a *coup de théâtre* at the beginning of Act III by allowing Dom Juan to appear "en habit de campagne" and Sganarelle "en médecin." The latter traditionally wears a long black gown and a high conical peaked black hat, the "attirail ridicule" mocked in the preceding scene by Dom Juan, who cannot imagine where it might have been dug up (ll. 864–65), and which owes more to comic fantasy than to observation.[5] Disguise is of course a common feature, on either side of the Channel, in seventeenth-century theatre; and its use here may be, as Jean Rousset argues, a baroque feature of the play (quoted by Howarth, ed. cit., p. 87). But, in contrast with the disguises and mistaken identities in *El Burlador de Sevilla* and the versions of the legend which Molière adapted, in our play it is primarily a comic one. Granted that the hero's disguise as a pilgrim in the plays of Dorimond and of Villiers may have suggested the "scène du Pauvre" and the following encounter with Dom Carlos, those authors use the episode to depict him as odious, since it is by means of the disguise that he hypocritically disarms (and in Villiers's play treacherously murders) his pursuer. Like Dom Juan's teasing and his disconcerting rescue of his pursuer, Sganarelle's "attirail ridicule" surely helps to situate this scene in a different register.

As far as the Don Juan legend is concerned, Sganarelle's disguise originates with Molière. In Molière's theatre, it looks back to an early farce, *Le Médecin volant* and heralds a line of doctor comedies: *L'Amour médecin, Le Médecin malgré lui, Monsieur de Pourceaugnac, Le Malade imaginaire*. To this scene, it brings an atmosphere of farce, a theatrical fantasy which even after the medical satire of the preceding scene has ended continues to distance comically the whole of the action and all three characters. Dom Juan's disguise enhances the irony of Sganarelle's rejoinder: "Vous ne connaissez pas Monsieur, bon homme . . ." (l. 999); and disguise heightens the incongruity of Sganarelle's panic at the end of the scene.

Dom Juan's taunt in line 997 is most meaningful if his suggestion to pray for a suit implies that Le Pauvre is in rags, a costume whose possible significance is discussed in the following section.

Background

The France of Molière's time counted more paupers than Parisians. John Lough quotes an observation by a doctor at the not very large town of Blois who in 1662 could write: "Depuis trente-deux ans . . . je n'ai rien vu qui approche de la désolation . . . non seulement à Blois où il y a quatre mille pauvres . . . mais dans toute la campagne."[6] In such circumstances compassion is a possible and very proper reaction. But, incessantly set upon by beggars, travellers could also find their requests for money more importunate than piteous, as indeed a tourist may do today in third-world countries where mendicity is common. Such appears to have

been the reaction of Malherbe, of whom Racan and Tallemant des Réaux tell the following story:

> Quand les pauvres lui disaient qu'ils priaient Dieu pour lui, il
> leur répondait "qu'il ne croyait pas qu'ils eussent grand crédit
> auprès de Dieu, vu le pitoyable état où il les laissait, et qu'il
> eût mieux aimé que M. de Luynes (the prime minister) ou M.
> le Surintendant (des Finances) lui eût fait cette promesse."
> (quoted by Howarth, ed. cit., p. 90).

Perhaps dramatizing this anecdote, Molière allows his Dom
Juan to exploit the same paradox, which depends upon the
assumption of a just and omnipotent God.

But Le Pauvre in *Dom Juan* is not simply a pauper. In the
so-called "non-cartonné" copies of the first edition (Paris,
1682) he had a name: *Francisque;* and in the first performances his costume may well have suggested the habit of the
Franciscans, to whom the name seems to allude. The text in
any case makes it clear that Le Pauvre is not indigent
against his will, say through poor health or unemployment.
Two *répliques* (ll. 994–95 and 1003–04) make it absolutely
clear that his retreat from society more than ten years earlier had been deliberate and that his poverty has a definite
religious significance. Le Pauvre is unmistakably a hermit
and a mendicant.

This is a fact of special significance. In 1664, Colbert had
initiated measures to reduce the privileges of the monastic
and mendicant orders in reaction to what he considered the
"trop grand nombre de prêtres, moines et religieuses."[7]
Such a reform encountered vigorous opposition, not only
from the Compagnie du Saint-Sacrement but from other
devout people who felt that it threatened the ancient Christian ideals of monasticism and solitary retreat. In 1665 the
nuns of Port-Royal were, for other reasons, under pressure
from the Crown; and the so-called solitaires of Port-Royal
(who had translated among other things the *Vies des Saints
Pères des déserts*) were in hiding. In such a context, Dom
Juan's patronizing taunt to Le Pauvre, " . . . tu es bien mal
reconnu de tes soins" (ll. 1012–13), must—however galling
to some—have seemed topical comedy to others. And the
scene may reflect commitment to Colbert's policy.[8]

Like the whole question of Molière's religious views, the nature of Dom Juan's *libertinage* is much debated; and doubtless part of the appeal of Dom Juan lies in a certain enigmatic quality that probably arises from a deliberate intention on the part of the author to create an ambiguous character. But while admitting that some of Dom Juan's lines (e.g., ll. 196 ff., and 1847 ff.) can be cited as evidence to the contrary, the arithmetical faith to which Sganarelle alludes in lines 999–1001 may best be taken as dramatic shorthand confirming the atheism implied by Sganarelle in the exposition. The equation used by Dom Juan in the preceding scene (repeated here by Sganarelle) is associated with the name of Maurice de Nassau (d. 1625), the Prince of Orange who, according to Guez de Balzac and Tallemant des Réaux, advised his deathbed confessor "que 2 et 2 font 4, et 4 et 4 font 8" (quoted by Howarth, ed. cit., p. 89), a by no means isolated attitude in the seventeenth century. Although the concept and term *atheism* can represent a variety of disbeliefs, to express Dom Juan's attitude one may prefer the vaguer term *libertinage*, which can mean free thought or nothing more than loose morals. But the associations surrounding Dom Juan's equation, the tone of this and other scenes, and the final absence of any repentance suggest not a character conscious of deliberate sin (a *libertin* in the moral sense), but one characterized without religious belief (a *libertin* in the intellectual sense, an atheist like Maurice de Nassau). Specifically, Dom Juan is characterized with reference to what as early as 1630 the author of the most widely disseminated treatise on manners in seventeenth-century France, Nicolas Faret, had referred to in *L'Honnête Homme* as the "nouvelle et orgueilleuse secte d'esprits forts," whose lack of faith deprives them, *ipso facto*, of *honnêteté*, since in his view it was only through blindness and pride that they

> osent bien porter leur impiété jusques à nier une chose que les oiseaux publient, que les choses les plus insensibles prouvent, que toute la Nature confesse, et devant qui les Anges tremblent, et les Démons ployent les genoux.[9]

The difference is that in the preceding scene of *Dom Juan*, it is not so much the *esprit fort* as the superstitions Sganarelle whose understanding had seemed "petit et aveugle" and whose reasoning had appeared "grossier et ridicule" (ibid., p. 56). *Inde irae.*[10]

In the "scène du Pauvre" Dom Juan also departs in other recognizable ways from the *honnêteté* generally characteristic of Molière's more romantic roles, especially his faithful lovers. If Dom Juan possesses the noble birth which Faret considers so advantageous to the *honnête homme* (p. 9), his behavior turns it to his own disadvantage, as Dom Louis suggests in Act IV. Although in his rescue of Dom Carlos he displays the courage expected of the *honnête homme*—whose chief professional activity was war—, that act and the resulting *quiproquo* must be considered in the context of the dramatic action as a whole; and one recalls Faret's reflection that prowess of itself is no adequate guarantee of *honnêteté*, since "ceux qui joignent la malice à la valeur, sont ordinairement redoutés et haïs comme des bêtes farouches . . ." (p. 14). Above all Dom Juan departs from *honnêteté* in the "scène du Pauvre" through excessive *raillerie*. Like the inconstant lover, the *Railleur* is a seventeenth-century commonplace—in life and in the theatre—as exemplified notably by Mareschal's comedies *L'Inconstance d'Hylas* (1635) and *Le Railleur* (1638). By his gibes, Dom Juan no doubt exposes himself as well as the hermit to ridicule, inasmuch as the *honnête homme* does not tease the unfortunate, who mocked might attract more sympathy than a *railleur*.[11]

In the context of the action—if one can anticipate the section on interpretation—both *railleur* and *raillé* in this scene are held at a comic distance; both are treated in a manner certainly less farcical than Sganarelle, who distances the action from life, but none the less comic because it allows a certain amount of sympathy for all three of the contrasting attitudes dramatized in carefully differentiated styles: the transcendent, rather naïve faith of Le Pauvre (the ambiguity of whose prayers for the *prosperity* of others is brought out by Dom Juan); Dom Juan's callow mockery and implied denial of transcendency (introduced by Sganarelle's partial repetition out of context of the equation from their earlier conversation, a frequent comic device in Molière, as in ll. 313 ff. of this play); and Sganarelle's own ridiculous mixture of faith and superstition inconsistently held and specifically belied in line 1022, a peripety which in the context of the scene can satisfactorily be taken only as comically grotesque.

As the temptation of Le Pauvre is a focal point of the scene, it is important that the bribe offered by Dom Juan to induce him to blaspheme, a *louis d'or*, was a great deal of money: the first ones issued by Bullion in 1640 were worth 10 francs (later 24 francs, then 20 francs). Imagine $100 bills. By way of contrast, Pierrot's wager in Act II, scene 1, consists of thirty-four coins, any one of which a pauper might have expected as an offering; and the total amount, clearly an important sum for Pierrot, is only ten *sous*, a twentieth of a *louis d'or*. M. Dimanche's visit in Act IV suggests that Dom Juan's gesture with the coin is an act of prodigality; but to any pauper (and to the theatre public) the offer of a *louis d'or* must have been startling.

On the other hand, the purely secular risks of blasphemy were considerable, not through the survival of medieval attitudes, but because new statutes were introduced in Molière's adolescence. Except for brief periods in the reigns of Saint-Louis and François Ier, blasphemy had not been punishable in France by physical mutilation until 1636, when an edict by Louis XIII condemned

> les blasphémateurs de Dieu, de la Vierge et des Saints jusqu'à la quatrième fois inclusivement à des amendes redoublées; pour la cinquième, à être mis au pilori; pour la sixième, à avoir la lèvre de dessus coupée; pour la septième, à perdre la lèvre de dessous; et, pour la huitième, à avoir la langue arrachée.
>
> (quoted by Allier, p. 215)

Renewed and verified by Parlement in 1639, this edict was one of the first confirmed by Louis XIV upon assuming his majority in 1651; and the penalties were reconfirmed by Parlement in 1655.

Ten years later, in 1665, the provisions of the edict were not an idle threat. Actual sentences had been harsher than the penalties provided. For nearly forty years the powerful clandestine Compagnie du Saint-Sacrement—doubtless the "parti dévot" or "cabale des dévots" to which Dom Juan refers in his ironic praise of hypocrisy in Act V, scene 2— had made it its business to seek out and destroy heresy and impiety of all kinds. A pamphlet published in 1655 discloses that the Compagnie was especially concerned about blasphemers (thought to attract plague, flood, famine, etc.) and sought to make examples of them "dans toutes les occasions" and "avec beaucoup de ferveur" (Allier, p. 215). Such zeal went not unrewarded: a pamphlet of 1661 reveals that as early as March 1655, one Claude Poulain was, for blasphemy,

> condamné à être tiré de la prison de Senlis à jour de marché et conduit nu en chemise, la torche au poing, la corde au col, attachée sur une claie au cul d'un tombereau, au devant de la principale église de Senlis, et là faire amende honorable, puis être conduit au marché pour y être pendu et étranglé, son corps et son procès brûlés et réduits en cendres, et les cendres jetées au vent . . . (Allier, p. 217).

Similar sentences were passed on a number of others in the later 1650s; and in June, 1661, a certain Jean le Vert, was convicted of blasphemy and

> condamné à faire amende honorable, à avoir la lèvre de dessus et celle de dessous fendues, à être rompu vif, son corps brûlé et ses cendres jetées au vent (ibid., p. 217).

No wonder that, as one reads in Rochemont's *Observations sur une comédie intitulée "Le Festin de Pierre"* (1665) reprinted with various editions of the play, "cet art de jurer de bonne grâce, qui passait pour un agrément du discours dans la bouche d'une jeunesse étourdie, n'est plus en usage. . . ."[12] Clearly it was unwise as well as unholy to swear in the wrong company.

The Compagnie du Saint-Sacrement, which Mazarin had very nearly succeeded in dissolving before his death in 1661, had a final burst of activity between the spring of 1664 (when it was active in forcing the withdrawal of *Tar-*

tuffe) and some time after the first run of *Dom Juan*. On 17 January 1665, just a month before the latter opened, the Compagnie met at the home of the marquis de Laval to discuss ways of obtaining further reconfirmation of the penalties against blasphemy, penalties duly confirmed by an edict eventually promulgated in September 1666. The new edict also provided heavy fines upon witnesses to blasphemy convicted of failing to denounce it and attractive rewards for those witnesses who did (Allier, p. 418).

If an edict of September 1666 is too late to have influenced Molière in writing the "scène du Pauvre"—and we do not know whether he had got wind of the specific plans of the "cabale"—, its provisions reflect an atmosphere of espionnage and denunciation to which Dom Juan alludes in Act V, scene 2:

> Je ferai le vengeur des intérêts du Ciel, et, sous ce prétexte commode, je pousserai mes ennemis, je les accuserai d'impiété, et saurai déchaîner contre eux des zélés indiscrets . . . (ll. 1746–49).

Is it really too farfetched to propose that in the "scène du Pauvre" Dom Juan, in disguise, may to some have seemed like an *agent provocateur*, one of such "zélés indiscrets"? It is true that Dom Juan's "provocative proposition" offers, as Professor Howarth points out, a parallel with the known behavior of the Chevalier de Roquelaure, a libertine imprisoned for impiety in the late 1640s at the instigation of Saint Vincent de Paul: "hearing a poor man blaspheme in public, he rewarded him and offered to pay him more if he would blaspheme more outrageously" (ed. cit., p. 90). But in the altered context of the 1660s might not Dom Juan's offer have evoked, for some of the first public at least, not only rakes like Roquelaure, but the informers who piously denounced him?

Interpretation

As the preceding sections imply, the interpretation of this scene cannot be separated either from questions of staging or from the background of the play. There can be little doubt, however, that whatever comedy the scene contains plays upon some of the major anxieties of Molière's time. But if a range of possible implications can be suggested in terms of contemporary preoccupations, and certain interpretations definitely excluded as anachronistic, detailed analysis of the scene and of the *characters* who appear in it depends very much upon interpretation of their *roles*. And on a number of crucial points a student is as free to decide for himself as any critic or producer of the play.

One neglected fact has a considerable importance. If Le Pauvre exits at line 1025, followed by Dom Juan after his last speech, the only character present throughout the scene is Sganarelle, the role originally played by Molière himself. This analysis has assumed that Sganarelle is no less a participant in the action than either of the other two characters; and clearly he dominates the end of the scene—which continues until Dom Juan returns with Dom Carlos—when he has the opportunity to mime panic as he hides perhaps in full view of the audience (a spectacular use of the conventional *liaison des scènes*). But there are suggestions, particularly in Rochemont's *Observations*, that Sganarelle's participation earlier in the scene should not be limited to his outlandish disguise and three *répliques*. Rochemont complains of Molière's "grimaces" and "gestes" as an actor in the role of Sganarelle, whose exhortation to Le Pauvre to blaspheme a little can be read in the light of Rochemont's complaint that Molière

> rend la majesté de Dieu le jouet d'un maître et d'un valet de théâtre, d'un athée qui s'en rit, et d'un valet, plus impie que son maître, *qui en fait rire les autres* (italics mine).

No less than the farcical disguise discussed above, the broadly comic mime associated with Molière's acting must have ensured that the whole scene was initially played in a comic register.

The extent to which Dom Juan was also conceived as a comic character, obviously in a different style, depends upon an actor's reading of the role.[13] I have argued that—like so many of Molière's title roles—Dom Juan is clearly not an *honnête homme*, that his callow attitude in this scene is inspired in part by the traditional comic role of the *railleur*, and that it offers certain analogies with the *marquis ridicules* presented by Scarron and Molière in a number of comedies.[14] Much depends, of course, upon the manner in which Dom Juan thrusts the *louis d'or* upon Le Pauvre at line 1018 ("Tiens"), teases with it at line 1021, and thrusts it forward again two lines later ("Prends, le voilà, prends, te dis-je"). Nor can Dom Juan's style be separated from the response of Le Pauvre. Should the latter turn his back upon Dom Juan at line 1024? And does Dom Juan hand the coin to him at line 1025, or throw it after him? The scene is more comic if, after protesting "j'aime mieux mourir de faim," Le Pauvre has to pick up the money from the stage floor. But Dom Juan could be made more ridiculous if, breaking with tradition, Le Pauvre does not accept the gift at all.

Silence in the theatre is also important, like rests in music. How long a pause should there be between lines 1025 and 1026? And to what extent should the surprise mimed by Dom Juan in exclaiming "Mais que vois-je là?" reflect genuine astonishment? Should the line be taken instead merely as a pretext for breaking off an unsatisfactory conversation? It cannot be the latter if Le Pauvre has already exited. On the other hand, it seems likely that Dom Juan's celebrated phrase "je te le donne pour l'amour de l'humanité" (l. 1025) spoken to—or perhaps after—Le Pauvre has for the speaker no humanitarian connotations. Phrased in antithesis to the conventional "pour l'amour de Dieu," it implies that the money is offered, not in recognition of any religious (or humanitarian) obligation, but to flout the hermit's faith.

There is a further caution. The scene is delicately balanced, so that (as in any dramatic encounter) the interpretation of one character influences all the rest. Too little dignity in Le Pauvre, too much coarseness in Dom Juan, too much farcical byplay from Sganarelle, diminishes the symbolic value of the confrontation; too much dignity in Le Pauvre, a hard or brittle Dom Juan, an inert Sganarelle, can dissipate the comic.

Conclusion

The argument for a comic interpretation of this scene rests in the main upon a concept of the play's structure, its social background, current political activity, Molière's characteristic use of distorted repetition, and what we know from contemporary documents about his own style of acting in the role of Sganarelle, strongly influenced by the grotesque mime of farce and *commedia dell'arte*. But it also involves his adaptation of legendary material—the French tragicomedies in particular—in which the prototypes of Dom Juan in similar circumstances were cast as cowardly, treacherous, and unredeemedly odious. Molière chose instead, by a process not without analogy with travesty or low burlesque, to depict a character whose mockery and too narrow sympathies—for he not only taunts Le Pauvre, but betrays members of the opposite sex (Done Elvire, the peasant girls), of other classes and conditions (Pierrot, M. Dimanche), of another generation (Dom Louis), assisting only a man of his own age and condition whom he had already offended (Dom Carlos)—proclaim his lack of *honnêteté*.

As the "scène du Pauvre" fits into a series of Dom Juan's encounters with "fâcheux," it is more structurally related to the play as a whole than sometimes allowed; and by bringing together in this scene three "incompatibles," Molière succeeds in illustrating not only their mutual incomprehension and failure to communicate across different orders of thought, but also the comic incongruity latent in the inner "contrariété" or self-contradiction of each of the characters individually. The scene may also fit into another structure of the play: episodes alluding to matters which the recently revived Compagnie du Saint-Sacrement found particularly objectionable, such as Sganarelle's praise of tobacco (doubtless snuff) and Done Elvire's broken vows in Act I, Pierrot's wager in Act II, and the duel arranged (by "direction of intention") in Act V. This structure would be especially relevant if there is an allusion in this scene to the "zélés indiscrets" openly satirized in Act V, and also if it reflects

Colbert's efforts to "diminuer doucement et insensiblement les moines de l'un et l'autre sexe" (quoted by Allier, pp. 415–16). We now know, in any case, that the structure of *Dom Juan* is not slapdash. The play was not put together in great haste, as once assumed. The "Marché de décors" shows that in early December 1664, fully ten weeks before the opening, Molière was in substantial possession of his subject. There is evidence in this scene for the conclusion now that the dialogue is coherently related not only to the conceptual themes of the comedy as a whole, but also to the spectacular stage decoration for which it was written and to which so little attention has been paid in the twenty years since details of its main features were published.

Beyond such considerations, the "scène du Pauvre" is a crucial episode in a play where the heavenly perspective is always present—as in baroque tragicomedies and religious paintings—from Sganarelle's first allusion to "le courroux du Ciel" in the exposition to the miraculous denouement. And this is true—though the implications are obviously different—even if (as seems likely) the miracles are parodied, a point on which, as upon Dom Juan's atheism, contemporary opinion is divided.[15] Yet the tone of the "scène du Pauvre" is so different from that of providential tragicomedy that Dom Juan's taunts focus comically, rather than compassionately, the ambiguity of an ascetic ethic by which an indigent hermit can offer prayers for the prosperity of those who give him money. In particular, the taunt ". . . tu es bien mal reconnu de tes soins" rephrases thematic material already introduced in Act II, scene 3, when Sganarelle receives a clout intended for Pierrot, whom he has tried to protect, along with the jibe: "Te voilà payé de ta charité" (l. 716)—a jibe that might have been made a little earlier to Pierrot, who had rescued Dom Juan, as later on to Dom Louis or Done Elvire, all of whom are hurt in their efforts to help Dom Juan. Louis XIV is said to have countered objections to the role of Dom Juan on the grounds "qu'il n'est pas récompensé."[16] Perhaps the most significant thing about the "scène du Pauvre" is that, unless Dom Juan's *louis d'or* is looked upon as providential, Le Pauvre is not rewarded either. The comic peripety of Sganarelle's incitement to blasphemy after extolling faith (l. 1022) suggests, moreover, that there is no necessary connection between religious conviction and conduct—an interpretation shocking in the context of much seventeenth-century thought, but by no means incompatible with the "zélés indiscrets" of Act V or the line of Molière's characters who unconsciously exploit religious faith in order to crush others and gratify themselves: Gorgibus in *Sganarelle*, Arnolphe in *L'Ecole des Femmes*, Orgon in *Tartuffe*. Independently of possible satire of mendicants, *esprits forts*, cowards, and/or zealots (for plays mean different things to different points of view), the *lazzi* of this scene do not diminish its significance by being comic. On the contrary, as so often in Molière, they focus its furthest implications. His *burlesque* of tragicomic material amounts to more than a travesty of a theatrical tradition, and the total meaning of the scene is greater than the sum of its parts. On such important issues as the working of providence and the relation of faith to morals Molière discards the common assumptions of the tragicomic genre to offer new insights which together imply—by a denial of the opposites commonly debunked—a world in which providence, asceticism, and superstition are less important than *honnêteté*—the recognition of man's social responsibilities.

I I

The Literary Context
of *Le Misanthrope*

I

1. To judge from a note in *L'Information littéraire*, there appears to be a persistent misconception concerning the relation of *Le Misanthrope* to other literature of Molière's time. "Les critiques de notre temps sont d'accord," writes M. Pierre Bourdat, "pour affirmer que la pièce est une création personnelle, qu'elle n'est puisée à aucune source," a judgment supported by reference to M. Donnay ("on n'y signale aucune imitation") and to D. Mornet ("*Le Misanthrope* ne doit à peu prés rien à personne").[1] That critics—some critics—have been prepared to make such an assumption about a writer so widely accused of plagiarism by his contemporaries, a writer reported moreover as having remarked on the *Galère* scene of *Les Fourberies de Scapin*, "je reprends mon bien partout où je le trouve," strikes me as rather odd. Certainly it is no secret that in *Le Misanthrope* Philinte alludes to "Ces deux frères que peint *L'Ecole des Maris*" (l. 100) and reuses a number of lines from *Dom Garcie de Navarre*, or that Eliante's most famous *réplique* paraphrases Lucretius. G. Rudler's edition of the play (Oxford: Blackwell, 1952) contains a useful table of the borrowings from *Dom Garcie* (pp. 146–47), together with two earlier French imitations of Lucretius's lines taken from works known to Molière, Faret's *L'Honnête Homme* and Scarron's *Jodelet duelliste* (p. 145), passages to which I shall return in section 9. A structural analogy with *Les Fâcheux* is often remarked. In their well-informed edition of *Le Misanthrope* (Paris: Editions sociales, 1963), E. Lop and A. Sauvage quote from a host of contemporary authors to situate the text of the play. *Les Valentins* of Guilleragues, texts by Méré, Faret, Balzac, Saint-Evremond, La Mothe Le Vayer's *Prose chagrine* (1661)—already discussed by R. Jasinski in *Molière et "le Mi-*

santhrope" (Paris: Nizet, 1951)—are discussed as relevant context in their introduction and notes.[2]

The most cursory survey of critical writings on *Le Misanthrope* suggests other *rapprochements*. But M. Bourdat is right to suggest that Mornet's *à peu près* invites further research, which could well begin precisely with Corneille's comedies, notably *Mélite*. We meet there for the first time, I think, in a French comedy the sort of pseudo-Greek names reminiscent of pastoral, and used both to "distance" the action of the comedy and to relate it obliquely to a definite social context, which in *Le Misanthrope* Molière exploits as an established convention. For what Corneille calls a "peinture de la conversation des honnestes gens" in *Mélite* provides comedy based on young characters belonging largely to the same social world and "d'une condition au dessus de ceux qu'on voit dans les Comedies de Plaute et de Terrence," a conception which, unlike Molière, Corneille could not take for granted. The *rapprochement* is clearer when one recalls that in *Mélite* there is no obstacle to the lovers' plans in the form of parental opposition (cf. *La Veuve*, II, 4, ll. 636 ff., and contrast most of Molière's comedies besides *Le Misanthrope*). Moreover, like Alceste (and Dom Garcie) Corneille's Eraste is a *jaloux*. Like Oronte, Tirsis courts with a sonnet. Letters atrributed to Mélite cast her wrongly as a *coquette*, while La Nourrice describes the sort of *coquette* Célimène will be (ll. 1203 ff.). Though Doumic saw a source for Molière's Arsinoé in the Arsinoé of *Nicomède* (Lop and Sauvage, ed. cit., p. 110), the opening lines of the scene in which Cloris meets Mélite for the first time (IV, 2):

> Je cheris tellement celles de votre sorte,
> Et prends tant d'interest en ce qui leur importe,
> Qu'aux fourbes qu'on leur faict je ne puis consentir,
> Ny mesme en rien sçavoir sans les en advertir,

anticipate in some ways Arsinoé's famous visit to Célimène in Act III, scene 4, of *Le Misanthrope*. Finally, Tirsis, believing himself deceived by Mélite, declares that his feet, which used to bear him to see her without help from his eyes,

> Me porteront sans eux en quelque lieu desert
> En quelque lieu sauvage à peine descouvert (ll. 1001–02)

where he means in the more violent sense—to which, significantly, there is no allusion by Alceste at the end of *Le Misanthrope*—to finish his days. The context of Alceste's declarations differs of course from Tirsis's; and the "endroit écarté" mentioned in Alceste's last speech is not, I think, really reminiscent of the sort of distant places—inspired by the recent voyages of discovery—evoked by Tirsis. That "endroit écarté" fits rather into a less heroic framework discussed below in section 7.

It is hard to believe that such *rapprochements* have gone unnoticed, but as far as I know they have gone unpublished. Admirers of *Le Menteur* in particular must also have reflected that, before Molière, Corneille glimpsed the comic potential of a scene in which a jealous lover calls to quarrel. For Alcippe's visit to Clarice in Act II, scene 3, of *Le Menteur* to some extent anticipates Alceste's "méthode . . . toute nouvelle" of courtship in his first scene with Célimène (Act II, scene I). If we add the scene of *La Veuve* adduced as a source by M. Bourdat, *Le Misanthrope* can already be suspected to stand less in isolation from contemporary comedy than sometimes assumed, even if we pass over *La Place royale* with its suggestive subtitle, *L'Amoureux extravagant*, and other Cornelian comedies.

When we reflect how much Alceste's relations with Célimène depend upon an amplification of the *dépit amoureux*, an obvious connection with Molière's other comedies and with the *commedia dell'arte* is established—established, not incidentally, as Du Bois provides a link with farce, but in the very fabric of the play. It is known, moreover, that the name Célimène had furnished the title of one of Rotrou's plays, that Célimène's portrait of Cléon is clearly adapted from Villiers's *Les Coteaux ou les Marquis friands* of 1665 (as indicated by Lop and Sauvage, ed. cit., p. 149), that Scarron had staged a *Marquis ridicule* before the *petits marquis* of *Le Misanthrope*. We may add that in Scarron's *L'Héritier ridicule* (upon which Molière is well known to have drawn for *Les Précieuses ridicules*) Hélène is abandoned in Act V, scene 4, by three suitors rather as Célimène is exposed and abandoned at the end of *Le Misanthrope*, and that one of the marriages arranged in Desmarets's *Les Visionnaires* (upon which Molière drew for *L'Ecole des Femmes* and *Les Femmes savantes*) breaks down, like the one proposed for Alceste and Célimène, because Artabaze is too exclusively "amoureux ce luy mesme" (S.T.F.M. ed., ll. 2002, 2022). We can then be certain that, whatever its originality, the characterization, themes, and dramatic techniques of *Le Misanthrope* are firmly grounded in the dramatic literature of the seventeenth century. Mornet was wrong. The play owes a great deal to other people; it is an intensely personal work, not because it is drawn from no source, but because its sources are exploited, amplified, adapted, given new and greater life.

2. I do not know whether the anonymous *Carite* mentioned by H. C. Lancaster may be considered a further source of *Le Misanthrope*. But this *tragicomédie pastorale*, in which courtiers are disguised as shepherds, provides another link with dramatic literature, and specifically with the conventions of pastoral and what may be called "le théâtre romanesque." In *Carite*, writes Lancaster

> the two girls resemble, respectively, the two friends of the *Misanthrope*, Célimène and Eliante . . . the hero, Florestan . . . has nothing about him of the diffident pastoral lover, but represents to a certain extent the type later made famous by Alceste.[3]

This *rapprochement* contains the seed of a most fruitful line of inquiry. For much of the comedy in Alceste's attitude toward Célimène springs from an inversion of the attitudes of the pastoral lover and from Alceste's identification—always selective and partial—with the *romanesque* lover.

To make a case there is no need to go beyond a comedy well known to have been exploited by Molière, Rotrou's *La Sœur* (from which he is known to have adapted some of the pseudo-Turkish jargon of *Le Bourgeois Gentilhomme*). More *romanesque* than *Le Misanthrope*, *La Sœur* presents an outlook against which Alceste's attitude toward Célimène can be measured, particularly if we compare his demand in Act V, scene 3, that Célimène consent

Au dessein que j'ai fait de fuir tous les humains,

> Et que, dans mon désert, où j'ai fait vœu de vivre,
> Vous soyez, sans tarder, résolue à me suivre,

with an offer freely made in *La Sœur*, Act II, scene 1, by
Aurélie to Lélie, to whom she is secretly married:

> Proposez-moi l'horreur des plus affreux déserts,
> Des plus sombres forêts, des plus pénibles mers:
> Je vous suivrai sans peine au bord des précipices;
> Tous travaux avec vous me seront des délices.

Though he doesn't seem to be proposing either dark forest or
distressing seas, Alceste clearly expects Célimène to react in a
similarly *romanesque* way, to behave like a heroine of comedy,
like an Aurélie.[4]

Alceste's quixotic demand is a measure of his extravagance.
A few lines before he had warned—ambivalently—that he
would show "que c'est à tort que sages on nous nomme" (l.
1755). And this demand makes clear how much he lacks what
Nicolas Faret, among others, had referred to in *L'Honnête
Homme* (first published, 1630) as the "tranquillité des Sages,"
the Stoic *apatheia* which Faret had sought to show one can
preserve within a worthwhile social role. Alceste is comic
partly because he has not followed his misanthropy to its
logical conclusion in retreat, but doubtless more so because,
while clinging to a *coquette's salon*, he is not really concerned to
solve the problem of preserving peace of mind and personal
integrity within a social context. Faret had proposed a solution by outlining a way in which—if he adopts sensible manners and plans—"le Sage peut au milieu des vices et de la
corruption conserver sa vertu toute pure et sans tache" (Paris,
1639, p: 62). Alceste seeks instead to escape into one of the
characteristic attitudes of *romanesque* fiction and to take
Célimène with him—without regard to the cost to her—by
demanding a similarly *romanesque* gesture on her part. It is no
part of my argument that *Le Misanthrope* is without moralist
concerns. But it seems fair to comment that at the denouement Alceste is portrayed as turning his back on the solution
to one of his problems proposed in *L'Honnête Homme* because
his head is turned by too much fiction. In this respect he fits
into a tradition illustrated by Cervantes's sad-faced knight,

Sorel's—and Thomas Corneille's—"Berger extravagant," the more literary of Desmarets's "visionnaires" and Molière's own "précieuses ridicules."

3. I venture this *rapprochement* with *La Sœur* the more confidently because in the scene cited Aurélie had just reminded Lélie of herself as one

> Qui, sans aucun bien, sans nom, sans connaissance,
> Pour support, pour amis, pour parents, pour époux,
> Pour tout refuge enfin, ne reconnaît que vous.

Rescued by Lélie in good *romanesque* tradition, Aurélie is in fact in precisely the sort of position in which Alceste would like to see Célimène (ll. 1425–28):

> Oui, je voudrais qu'aucun ne vous trouvât aimable,
> Que vous fussiez réduite en un sort misérable,
> Que le Ciel, en naissant, ne vous eût donné rien,
> Que vous n'eussiez ni rang, ni naissance, ni bien.

There is an obvious analogy with Arnolphe's attitude to Agnès in *L'Ecole des Femmes*, an attitude demanding a Griselda role for the wife and a role for the husband like that of Perseus snatching Andromeda naked from the rocks and from the monster. That we can now see sexism and perhaps latent sadism in such an attitude should not obscure its immediate source for Alceste in the *romanesque* comedy of Molière's youth, one of whose attitudes Alceste seeks to relive at the expense of Célimène.

Alceste's wish to find Célimène wholly bereft, his demand for her to leave the world for him, inverts the attitude of lovers in the pastoral, tragicomic and gallant novel traditions, lovers prepared to give all for love and to consider the world well lost. Just how pervasive was the theme of "all for love" on the French stage in the mid-seventeenth century can be indicated by reference to part of a declaration by Timocrate to Eriphile in Thomas Corneille's *Timocrate*, which a decade before *Le Misanthrope* enjoyed the best box-office success of the century:

> Renoncer pour l'amour au soin de sa fortune,

> N'est que le faible effet d'une vertu commune;
> On a vu mille amants dans ses moindres douceurs
> Trouver la pente aisée au mépris des grandeurs,
> Et pour l'objet aimé, sans que rien les étonne,
> Quitter parents, amis, sceptre, trône, couronne . . .

(Act II, scene 4). In P. Corneille's *Rodogune*, for example, Seleucus's offer and request to Antiochus in Act I, scene 1: "Pour le Throsne cédé cédez moy Rodogune" (l. 123) forestall a message dictated in similar style by Antiochus in the previous scene, "Que pour cette beauté ie luy cède l'Empire" (l. 92) (ed. J. Scherer [Paris: Droz, T.L.F., l. 946]). Significantly, however, the brothers realize how much sacrifice on the part of Rodogune such self-sacrifice for love would involve, and in Act III, scene 4, they generously ask her instead to choose in the same man her husband and her king. Among other texts exemplifying this attitude, we may cite one of Jupiter's speeches to Alcmène in Rotrou's *Les Sosies* (known to be a principal source of Molière's *Amphitryon*). In Act III, scene 2, Jupiter tries—ambivalently—to woo Alcmène as a lover while disguised as her husband:

> Pour moi si, souverain des dieux et des mortels,
> Je voyais cet objet au pied de mes autels,
> M'en laissant adorer, je croirais faire un crime;
> Je voudrais de son dieu devenir sa victime,
> Et je croirais du prix de la terre et des cieux
> N'acheter pas assez un regard de ses yeux.

The gallant lover typified in Jupiter's pose would give the world for his love. In *Le Misanthrope*, even Alceste is touched in Act I, scene 2, by an old song offering to forfeit Paris in a similar spirit. But in reality he expects Célimène to give up the world and Paris for him. No wonder she exclaims in l. 1421, "Non, vous ne m'aimez point comme il faut que l'on aime." There is at any rate an obvious contrast between Alceste's vain wish, and the gallant offer to share his modest fortune with Henriette, which in *Les Femmes savantes* Clitandre makes in response to the *fausses nouvelles* which precipitate the denouement.

Whether or not Alceste's role involves travesty of specific scenes, it represents such a striking inversion of the sort of *romanesque* and gallant attitudes adduced from *La Sœur, Les Sosies,* etc. that it is hard not to read parts of it as parodistically related to such attitudes. At the very least, Alceste *as a lover* provides an overdose of "les jalousies conçues sur de fausses apparences, les plaintes, les désespoirs" indicated by Madelon as part of the gallant lover's role, and none of the "Billets-Doux, Petits-Soins, Billets-Galants et Jolis-Vers" whose lack in a lover seems so lamentable to Cathos in scene 3 of *Les Précieuses ridicules,* and which Célimène seems to relish from her other suitors. If then, as I suspect, Alceste's wish to find Célimène bereft and dependent upon himself for rescue in ll. 1425 ff. involves a form of parody, it would be wrong to accept M. Maurice Descotes's assertion that, "Alors, certes, Alceste n'est pas comique, ni par la situation où il se trouve, ni par les sentiments qu'il éprouve."[5] Alceste may well have been cast as comically inverting, in this situation, "romantic" feelings familiar to theatre-goers.

4. To conclude this rapid survey of ways in which *Le Misanthrope* is related to the theatre of its time, we may return to its well-known borrowings from *Dom Garcie de Navarre,* and in particular to the letter scene reworked from *Dom Garcie,* Act II, scene 5, in *Le Misanthrope,* Act IV, scene 3. Rudler is never more perceptive than when he remarks that Alceste "commence par quatre vers d'imprécations bouffonnes qui sentent d'une lieue la parodie (1281–84) [Ils viennent de *Dom Garcie*] comme si Molière avait voulu donner le *la*" (ed. cit., p. xxxiv). These are the lines beginning: "Que toutes les horreurs dont une âme est capable" in either play.

For Rudler, however, the impression of parody is rapidly effaced, so that "le pathétique de la situation vous prend." Yet parody, rather than pathos, seems to me a better guide throughout this scene, and not least when Alceste produces Célimène's letter: "Jetez ici les yeux, et connaissez vos traits" (ll. 1324 ff.). It is less important here, I think, that Molière reworks material from *Dom Garcie*—the identical lines are scrupulously distinguished in Rudler's appendix from those that are merely similar—than that the letter scenes in both comedies are comic developments of a situation in a well-known tragedy in which a furious *jaloux* is answered in a similar way, the opening scene of Mairet's *Sophonisbe*. Confronting Sophonisbe with a letter, Syphax demands:

> Desaduoüras-tu point ces honteux caracteres,
> Complices & tesmoins de tes feux adulteres?

Calmly she replies: "Non, Sire, ils sont de moy, je ne le puis nier. . . ."[6]

In such a scene as Mairet's—with a background of invasion, death, altered fortune, heroism, sublimated love and suspected adultery—the spectator may or may not be gripped by "le pathétique de la situation." In a judgment that inverts Rudler's reading of Alceste's letter scene as "pathétique," a critic of the *Annales dramatiques* criticized Voltaire for retaining a letter scene in his adaptation of Mairet's *Sophonisbe*, since, he says, "rien n'est moins tragique que la colère d'un mari contre sa femme qui écrit à un amant."[7] Clearly interpretation is crucial, demanding no less tact in the tragic than in the comic actor. I would argue, however, that Alceste—and indeed Dom Garcie—are intended through parody to exploit the comic potential in the sort of letter scene devised by Mairet for its tragic scope (mime of jealous rage). The material is recast in situations where there is no peril to life and—since in the comedies the *jaloux* are not even husbands—no tragic theme of adultery. On this argument, Alceste's role in the letter scene is not "pathétique," but very precisely heroï-comic. How else are we to interpret Célimène's remark: "Vous êtes, sans mentir, un grand extravagant" (l. 1335)?

Readers of the first edition were reminded of something later readers tend to forget. The *Lettre écrite sur la comédie du "Misanthrope"* attributed to Donneau de Visé and published as a preface to the first edition of the play (1667), and as an appendix to their edition by Lop and Sauvage, mentions no pathos in connection with Alceste. Instead it draws attention to the admirable theatricality of his role, for "les chagrins, les dépits, les bizarreries et les emportements d'un misanthrope étant des choses qui font un grand jeu, ce caractère"—referred to a few lines later as "ce ridicule"— "est un des plus brillants qu'on puisse produire sur la scène" (ed. cit., p. 211). Among French moralists it is not difficult to find supporting evidence, as the section of Du Bosc's *L'Honnête Femme*, "Melancolie mere le plus souvent d'extravagance que de sagesse" (from the *Table* of Part I, first published, Paris, 1632, quoted here and later from the Rouen edition, 1643).

5. Equally fruitful results await research into the non-dramatic literature of Molière's time, and this may be particularly valuable in situating Alceste's attitudes. We know, for example, that Alceste is criticized by Philinte for affecting "Cette grande roideur de vertus des vieux âges" which, he says, "Heurte trop notre siècle et les communs usages" (ll. 153–54). This would seem to indicate sources in Antiquity for Alceste's behaviour; and unsuspected sources do indeed exist, as Alceste's famous lines in the first scene

> et je hais tous les hommes,
> Les uns parce qu'ils sont méchants et malfaisants,
> Et les autres pour être aux méchants complaisants
> (ll. 118–20)

no doubt represent a brilliant—and unsuspected— rephrasing of one of *Les Apophtegmes des Anciens* translated by Nicolas Perrot d'Ablancourt—the author of the "belles infidèles"—and published in Paris by Thomas Jolly in 1664:

> TIMON, surnommé le Misanthrope, à cause qu'il haïssoit les hommes, disoit pour raison, Que c'est que la moitié n'en valoit rien, et que l'autre ne valoit guère, *A cause qu'elle ne haïssoit pas assez les méchans* (p. 344).

In this volume, Demosthenes is reported as saying, "Qu'il n'y avoit rien de plus rude aux honnestes gens, que de ne pouvoir dire leur sentiment en toute liberté" (pp. 103–04). Elsewhere Lysander replies to a Persian that the best gov-

ernment is "Celle où chacun est traité selon son mérite . . .
ou bien, où les dignitez sont la récompense de la vertu. . . ," and so
on.

Perhaps we should refer to this conception of Alceste's
"roideur" part of his quarrel with Célimène in the letter
scene of act IV, where she asks:

> D'où vient donc, je vous prie, un tel emportement?
> Avez-vous, dites-moi, perdu le jugement?

and Alceste answers:

> Oui, oui, je l'ai perdu, lorsque dans votre vue
> J'ai pris, pour mon malheur, le poison qui me tue . . . .
> (ll. 1315–18)

For Socrates had warned Xenophon that the "poison" of a
fair person is more dangerous than scorpions, which only
wound upon contact, while beauty strikes from afar: "de
quelque endroit que l'on puisse l'appercevoir, elle lance sur
nous son venin, & nous renverse le iugement." Xenophon
accordingly is warned to flee any such person without looking back—advice Alceste hardly takes to heart.[8] Obviously
it is not necessary to assume that Alceste's lines, identical
with a passage in *Dom Garcie*, are directly inspired by
Xenophon, or that the volume of *Morales* cited is the only
channel through which the *Memorabilia* could have reached
Molière. This possible source nonetheless offers another
striking example of the way in which Alceste is characterized with respect to traditions only partially assimilated
and inconsistently applied. *Inde vis comica.*

Alceste's apparent indifference to criticism may offer yet
another—and our last—link between his antic deportment
and the conception of his role in terms of "cette grande
roideur des vertus des vieux âges." For Epictetus, writing
"Contre l'opinion que le vulgaire a de nous," had pre-
scribed:

> "Si tu veux profiter en sagesse, ne te mets pas en
> peine, si pour les choses estrangeres, tu es estimé
> fou ou sot (ibid., p. 14).

Alceste's attitude is more energetic:

> Tous les hommes me sont à tel point odieux,
> Que je serais fâché d'être sage à leurs yeux (ll. 111–12)

And once again *rapprochement* is profitable. For it reveals that Alceste's attitude, full of hatred and hostility, is far too concerned with opinion—his own misanthropist view of others, and theirs of him—to be more than a caricature of the Stoic *sage's* indifference. No wonder that Philinte, who according to the *Lettre* preface of 1667 is "un homme sage et prudent" whose "sagesse" is brought out through confrontation with Alceste (ed. cit., pp. 211–12), exclaims: "Mon Dieu, des mœurs du temps mettons-nous moins en peine . . ." (l. 145). Among modern moralists, Faret had remarked in *L'Honnête Homme* that *Sages* "ont premierement la paix avec eux-mesmes et la sçavent entretenir avec le monde" (ed. cit., p. 61). La Rochefoucauld—thinking perhaps of this problem—would add: "C'est une grande folie de vouloir être sage tout seul."[9]

6. Among the active moralist traditions with respect to which it is possible to situate the attitudes represented in *Le Misanthrope* should certainly be mentioned one which guaranteed frequent editions—often together—of Mathieu's *Tablettes* and Pibrac's *Quatrains*. Both works enjoyed a wide diffusion in the French literary culture of the seventeenth century, and both are mentioned by Molière in the first scene of *Sganarelle*. For certain of Mathieu's *Tablettes*, with Boileau's early satires and other texts, must be part of (or may represent) the satirical tradition critical of the Court and Paris assimilated by Molière and fused with personal observation in *Le Misanthrope*, to cite only *Tablette* xlv from the second part:

> N'aimer rien, craindre tout, dissimuler le vice,
> Savoir accomoder son cœur en cent façons,
> Refuser l'amitié, et offrir le service,
> Sont des galands en Cour les premières leçons.

And it may be that in Alceste's plan to "rompre en visière à tout le genre humain" (l. 96) we have a specific reminiscence of *tablette* II, xlvii:

> Qui veut plaire à la Cour ses affaires se trompe,
> Si avec l'hardiesse et l'ardeur il n'est prompt:
> Car enfin qu'importun à tous la tete il rompe,
> Il faut premièrement qu'il se rompe le front.

Once again, if this is right, Alceste is made to recall the grand gesture, but not the conditions and not the price. The satire of Court circles in *Le Misanthrope* is not new, but a brilliant amplification of themes long current in French moralist verse and adapted to new circumstances.

With Pibrac we are on more solid ground, at least for Alceste's belated recollection in lines 1089–90:

> Et qui n'a pas le don de cacher ce qu'il pense
> Doit faire en ce pays [la Cour, l. 1091] fort peu
> de résidence

which seem to recall Pibrac's *quatrain* cv (or another statement in the same tradition):

> Ne voise au bal, qui n'aymera la danse,
> Ny au banquet qui ne voudra manger,
> Ny sur la mer qui craindra le danger,
> Ny à la Cour qui dira ce qu'il pense,

advice which, if we take Célimène's company of courtiers as representative of Court circles, Alceste has so far ignored. Among other *rapprochements*, Alceste's claim "J'ai pour moi la justice . . ." (l. 1492) flies in the face of *quatrain* lxxxiv: "juge ne donne en ta cause sentence . . . ." Pibrac's *quatrain* xxvi, "Vertu qui gist entre les deux extrèmes", on the other hand, seems very much the sort of ethic behind Philinte's lines: "La parfaite raison fuit toute extrémité . . ." (ll. 151 ff.), and not least because both Pibrac and Philinte stress self-reliance in a social context: *aurea mediocritas*.

Alceste's "roideur" finally, is none the less comic for lacking self-control. Just because it is a widely disseminated commonplace we can set over against the misanthropist's vociferous censure of others Pibrac's maxim (after *Proverbs*, xvi, 32; Horace, *Odes*, II, ii, 9–12, etc.): "Vaincre soymesme est la grande victoire" (xlvii). In the absence of such self-mastery—to refer again to the *Lettre*-preface—"les chagrins, les dépits, les bizarreries et les emportements d'un misanthrope . . . font un grand jeu." Alceste is made to mime his failure to grasp a traditional ethic which continued to nourish responses in the classical decades. It need not follow from the fact that Molière wrote as an actor that his writings—and his acting—had no ethical content.[10]

7. Behind the "désert" theme as it appears in *Le Misanthrope* lie not only the theatrical threat of a Tirsis and the no less theatrical offer of an Aurélie, but an abundant poetic literature which Alceste characteristically distorts in declaring—in a *coquette's* reception room—his intention "De fuir dans un désert l'approche des humains" (l. 144) or to retire to what he terms "mon désert, où j'ai fait vœu de vivre" (l. 1763). *Mutatis mutandis*, these threats can be situated better by reference to the disappointed Damon in Boileau's *Satire I* than to any sort of specifically religious retreat, like those of the solitaries of Port-Royal-des-Champs in their "désert" in the Vallée de Chevreuse. I certainly see no suggestion of any asceticism like that evoked in *Dom Juan* by Le Pauvre, who is cast as a religious hermit and a mendicant. Alceste's projected "désert" is more literary, with distant roots perhaps in that ironic second epode of Horace (*Beatus ille qui procul negotiis*) and immediate associations with a French tradition opposing the tranquility of the country to the corruption of Paris and the Court: *tædium curiæ*.

Among many texts that could situate his theme, none perhaps do so better than a sonnet adressed to Faret by Maynard in the *Recueil de 1646*, beginning

> Je donne à mon desert les restes de ma vie,
> Pour ne dépendre plus que du Ciel et de moy.

Disenchanted, the poet asks the author of *L'Honnête Homme* to approve his "retraite" and allow him to die "Dans le mesme Vilage où mes peres sont morts." On Faret's advice, he had frequented the fair court of Henri IV and leaves it with regret,

> Mais les ans m'ont changé. Le Monde m'importune,
> Et j'aurois de la peine à vivre dans un lieu,
> Où toujours la Vertu se plaint de la Fortune.[11]

In other sonnets Maynard develops such themes. One in particular celebrates "mon Desert où rien ne m'importune" and the poet's love of virtue, while deploring "La cour. . ./ . . . où le grand merite est souvent mal-heureux" (p. 35; cf. others, pp. 37, 43–44). An epigrammatic sonnet views Paris as "le pais de tout le monde", opposed to the "petit Desert qui *le* cache," later mentioned as "une terre sauvage" and "un Village / Que la Carte ne connoist pas" (p. 55). This last *désert* indeed seems remote enough to include places like Alceste's "endroit écarté" (l. 1805).

Most of Maynard's sonnets on the "désert" theme have a neo-Stoic flavor and further situate Alceste's behavior with respect to a *sagesse* he affects without attaining. But Maynard also strikes a pastoral note, as in a variant to the sonnet "Je donne à mon desert le reste de ma vie," which reads "Je veux vivre berger le reste de ma vie" (ed. cit., p. 305). Witness too the epigram

> Si la Bergere que je sers
> Revient jamais dans ces Desers . . . (p. 85).

Since Alceste's retreat is prompted not only by corruption at Court, but also by Célimène's independence, it would be a mistake to dismiss this overtone of the "désert" theme. Indeed it brings us back to the comic duality of Alceste, who misconceives himself, not only as virtuous *Sage*, but as pastoral lover rejecting Paris for love.

8. The epigram provides a further fertile field for research into the sources of *Le Misanthrope*, most obviously for its numerous verbal *portraits* in Act II, scene 5, and elsewhere. We may begin with Célimène's *portrait* of Timante (ll. 586 ff.):

> C'est, de la tête aux pieds, un homme tout mystère,
> Qui vous jette, en passant, un coup d'oeil égaré,
> Et, sans aucune affaire, est toujours affairé.
> Tout ce qu'il vous débite en grimaces abonde;

> À force de façons, il assomme le monde;
> Sans cesse il a, tout bas, pour rompre l'entretien,
> Un secret à vous dire, et ce secret n'est rien;
> De la moindre vétille il fait une merveille,
> Et, jusques au bonjour, il dit tout à l'oreille.

So far as I know, it has never been noticed that this *portrait* is substantially a paraphrase of Martial's epigram *In Cinnam* (Book I, no 89). In Marolles's bilingual edition of Martial's epigrams (Paris, 1655), it had been translated as *Contre Cinna*, as follows:

> Cinna, tu dis toûjours quelque chose à l'oreille des gens: tu n'y oublies pas mesme ce qui est connu du peuple. Tu ris à l'oreille, tu y fais des plaintes, tu y mesles des reprimades, tu y pleures. Tu chantes aussi à l'oreille, tu y portes tes jugemens: tu t'en approches mesme quelquefois pour n'y rien dire du tout, et tu y cries *tout d'un coup*. Ce vice est-il si fort enraciné dans ton ame, Cinna, que tu celebres mesme souvent les loüanges de Cesar à l'oreille? (I, p. 107)

This epigram was also paraphrased by Bussy-Rabutin:

> En Damon tout est mystère,
> De tout il fait des secrets.
> Il dit tout bas, que le Soleil éclaire,
> Que le temps est chaud, qu'il est frais.
> Cette manie est sans pareille,
> Il en fait son unique emploi;
> Il trouve tant de goût à parler à l'oreille,
> Qu'il feroit à l'oreille un éloge du Roi.[12]

In comparison with Marolles and Bussy, Célimène's portrait of Timante is strikingly abstract. "Bonjour" is the only content of his speech. Hyperbolism in Célimène's *caractère* Timante is also less marked than in Bussy's version. But above all, in Célimène's, political allusion is absent, and that despite the fact that, in his edition of Martial, Marolles adds a note to this epigram explaining that the epigrammatist "reprend le vice de Cinna, qui estoit un flateur et un calomniateur"—a remark linking the epigram, and *portrait*, clearly enough to the theme of sincerity in *Le Misanthrope*. For Alceste complains of both flattery and calumny—"un livre abominable," ll. 1500 ff.—as opposites to the *franchise* he affects. Yet Célimène suggests no motivation for the extraordinary conduct she satirically evokes.

Possible motivation is suggested, however, by d'Aubignac's discussion "Du mot à l'oreille," section XII of *Les Conseils d'Ariste à Célimène, achevé d'imprimer* 1 March 1666, three months before the première of *Le Misanthrope* and favorably reviewed in the *Journal des Savants* for 5 April 1666—a text which shows associations of the name Célimène with a moralist current:

> Nous trouvons assez souvent dans les compagnies, des gens qui se plaisent à dire toûjours quelque mot à l'oreille d'vne Dame auprés de laquelle ils seront assis, & je doute que tout le monde approuve celle qui le souffre. . . .

For, d'Aubignac continues, what is "honeste" can be said aloud; what is not, a lady should not hear. "Vn Poëte Romain," he adds

> se mocque d'vn Courtisan de son siècle qui faisoit mystère de tout, & qui ne manquoit iamais de conter à l'oreille de tous ceux qu'il rencontroit quelque action genereuse ou quelque belle parole de l'Empereur, comme si les loüanges d'vn Souverain, veritables ou fausses, ne devoient pas estre publiées tout haut: à plus forte raison doit-on condamner celuy qui feroit un secret à quelque Dame d'vn entretien loüable & digne d'une bonne compagnie; & l'on doit encore moins souffrir celuy qui l'entretiendroit ainsi secretement de quelque impudence, ou pour mieux dire, elle ne le doit iamais endurer (pp. 93–94).

Doubtless this passage suggests the particular sense in which Molière's Célimène is made to adapt a Classical epigram which enjoyed a considerable fortune at the time. As *Les Conseils d'Ariste à Célimène* suggests in so many other ways, the *médisance* of Molière's *coquette* at this moment in the action is also a counterattack against a clearly diagnosed and specific transgression against *honnêteté*.

A similar process can be observed if we compare Célimène's *portrait* of Cléon with the source indicated in Villiers's *Les Coteaux* by Lop and Sauvage (ed. cit., p. 149). For however comically he may be mistaken, Villiers's Thessandre has a clear idea of what he is trying to do with his "cuisine en fort bonne odeur": ". . . près beaucoup de gens tenant lieu de mérite," he says, "Elle est cause souvent qu'ils vous rendent visite"—personal politics of ostentation, by which he seeks to please the ambitious and to win respect through generosity. In her portrait of Cléon, Célimène is once again more brilliant and more shallow, which is no doubt what Molière wished her to be.

Célimène's portrait of her friend Damis, considered an "honnête homme" and "assez sage" by Philinte (ll. 632–3), is also rooted in epigram, especially the four central couplets:

> Depuis que dans la tête il s'est mis d'être habile,
> Rien ne touche son goût, tant il est difficile;
> Il veut voir des défauts à tout ce qu'on écrit,
> Et pense que louer n'est pas d'un bel esprit,
> Que c'est être savant que trouver à redire,
> Qu'il n'appartient qu'aux sots d'admirer et de rire,
> Et qu'en n'approuvant rien des ouvrages du temps,
> Il se met au-dessus de tous les autres gens.

For Damis is what contemporary epigrammatists—and Boileau in his *Discours au Roi*—called a *Censeur*. In this, of course, Damis resembles Alceste, whose role doubtless calls for a comic reaction on his part based on awareness of the resemblance, since he erupts a few lines later and draws from Célimène his own *portrait*.

In the absence of specific sources, certain of *Les Epigrammes* of Gombauld (1657) may represent a current relevant to the *portrait* of Damis and to the conception of the misanthropist himself. First, two epigrams on *Censeurs*. No. lv reads:

> Toy qui vas souvent où se trouvent
> Ces Censeurs qui n'espargnent rien:
> Demande-leur ce qu'ils approuvent,
> Et tu les empêcheras bien.

Determined to "n'épargner rien" (l. 88), Alceste is clearly conceived in this tradition, an impression strengthened by no. lx:

> Charles censure toute chose,

> Il ne gouste ny Vers ny Prose,
> Et c'est un Juge à redouter.
> Du moins il se le persuade;
> Mais puisqu'il ne peut rien gouster,
> Il est sans doute bien malade.

Similarly, nothing pleases Damis, while Philinte explicitly refers to Alceste's dissatisfaction with the whole of the environment as "une maladie" which everywhere "donne la comédie" (ll. 105–06).

Like Damis, and Gombauld's Charles, Alceste is a *censeur* "des ouvrages du temps," and notoriously of Oronte's sonnet in Act I, scene 2. In the play, Alceste's attitude is implicitly linked to self-love ("Je veux qu'on me distingue. . . ," l. 63), a link explicit in Gombauld's epigram no. lxx, entitled *Amour de soy-mesme*:

> T'offenses-tu s'il a repris
> Les plus beaux lieux de tes Escrits,
> Avec une insolence extrême?
> Et n'aperçois-tu pas en luy
> Qu'il est si ravy de luy-mesme,
> Qu'il ne sçauroit louer autruy?

Indeed in the background of this epigram a scene is implied very like Oronte's stormy reception of Alceste's outspoken reaction to his sonnet.

If it be objected that Philinte also is present, there is a source for his role, too, in Gombauld's *Epigrammes*, beginning with his role as a friend to Alceste. "Moi, votre ami?," exclaims Alceste (l. 8), a reaction suggested perhaps by Gombauld's epigram no. I, *Amis*, which concludes:

> Et je ne hais rien tant au monde
> Que la plus-part de mes amis.

It is, of course, as a flatterer that Philinte has offended, behavior particularly abhorred by Alceste, as the latter goes on to explain:

> *Et je ne hais rien tant* que les contorsions
> De tous ces grands faiseurs de protestations,
> Ces affables donneurs d'embrassades frivoles,
> Ces obligeants diseurs d'inutiles paroles . . . (ll. 43–46).

Molière may not have found his rhyme in Gombauld, but he clearly found in *Les Epigrammes* some of his themes and some of his rhythms (italics mine)—and that notwithstanding the fact the whole of Alceste's encounter with Oronte *as a flatterer* could be a comic dramatization of Faret's attack in *L'Honnête Homme* upon "ces opiniastres faiseurs de complimens": "Surtout à vne ame franche, et qui croit que chasque parole qu'elle dit par bien seance oblige sa foy, c'est vne gehesne bien tyrannique que la rencontre de cette sorte d'esprits embarassans" (ed. cit., p. 128). One need not have danced the *Ballet des Incompatibles*, or staged *Les Fâcheux*, to see the scope here for comic mime—or that the actor is here to mime a *morale*.

Molière may also have found in *Les Epigrammes* of Gombauld one of his comic situations, the scene precisely in which Philinte is caught between the *censeur* Alceste and Oronte *as a poet*, epigram no. ci, *Honeste homme et mauvais poete* (though to be sure Gombauld's Eraste is given as more virtuous than Oronte):

> Eraste ayme la Vertu,
> Il est de bonne famille;
> Sa Sœur est fort belle fille,
> Et lui propre et bien vestu,
> S'il m'accoste en ta présence,
> Damon, je souffre l'offense
> De ton regard de travers.
> Soudain ta colère esclatte:
> Quoy! veux-tu que je le batte
> Pource qu'il fait mal des vers?

Once again, a scene is suggested; an encounter invites dramatic treatment, comic treatment, grimace and mime. Not the least interesting line is the allusion to a stick not used, the sort of question Célimène will ask Alceste: "Dois-je prendre un bâton pour les mettre dehors?" (l. 464). In epigram and comedy there is the same irony, the same hyperbole, an analogous allusion to—and distance from—the traditional stick evoked doubtless more in terms of theatrical farce than of social repression.

For Oronte as a flatterer, compare Dorante's remarks to

Lisidor in Pierre Ortigue de Vaumorière's *Art de plaire dans la conversation* published in Paris in 1688 with a *privilège dated 1677:*

> [. . .] toutes ces Cérémonies, et ces protestations d'amitié ne seroient pas seulement regardées comme une dissimulation; on pourroit même les considérer comme des crimes et des trahisons, si ces termes dont on use à tout moment n'avoient perdu leur première force, et que leur trempe, [. . .] ne se fût amolie par un long usage. Mais on s'est accoutumé à ne prendre plus ces paroles à la rigueur. L'on voit tous les jours des gens qui s'embrassent, se baisent, et se font mille offres, comme s'ils étoient les meilleurs Amis du monde; et qui, un moment après, avoüent sans honte qu'ils ne se connoissent presque point. Cependant il faut suivre cet usage, au lieu d'entreprendre de le changer. C'est moins nôtre vice, que celui de notre siècle, et tout ce que peuvent faire les gens sages, est de s'en servir avec discrétion et retenue. Quand tout le mode tombe dans une faute, personne n'en doit être blâmé, et quelque extravagante que puisse être une mode, un homme seroit encore plus extravagant s'il refusoit de s'y assujetir" (Suivant la Copie imprimée à Paris, 1692, pp. 25–26).

There were several editions of this work, which appeared also in English. For Oronte's role as importunate poet, see Bussy-Rabutin's version of another of Martial's *Epigrams* (ed. cit., I, p. 262):

> Dieux! que vous êtes importun
> Par vos vers que vous voulez lire!
> Vous en accablez un chacun;
> Oronte, on n'y peut plus suffire.

And Alceste's repeated "Je ne dis pas cela" may be a reminiscence of Mme Bouvillon's comic repetition of that phrase in Scarron's *Le Roman comique* (Part II, chapter 10).

Such epigrams and other reminiscences do not account for the quality of Molière's comedy. But, with the other texts indicated, they begin to make clear to what an extent even in *Le Misanthrope* Molière's observation of social reality is mediated by and dependent upon a variety of literary traditions whose assimilation and restatement is apparent in many passages long regarded either as self-expression or personal observation. Gombauld's epigrams, by a poet who frequented the most fashionable of aristocratic circles, also bring us up against a hard fact concerning the point of view implied by the satire of *salon* society in the *portrait* scene and elsewhere in *Le Misanthrope*. Molière's satire is demonstrably developed in large part from techniques and themes current in such aristocratic *salons* themselves, a fact which invites caution in assuming that Molière's point of view is "bourgeois and libertine," as recently argued by John Cairncross in *Molière, bourgeois et libertin* (Paris, Nizet, 1963).

I cannot leave this section on the epigram without reference to one by Sarasin addressed to the Prince de Conti, written possibly at a time when both he and Molière were protected by that notable in the early 1650s, almost certainly between 1648 and 1652, and entitled *A un Grand qui s'était moqué d'un ruban gris et vert:*

> Monseigneur, puisque vous raillez
> Du vert et du gris que je porte,
> Souffrez au zèle qui m'emporte
> De vous dire que vous faillez.
> Le vert, cette couleur jolie,
> Est un blason de la folie,
> Comme le gris l'est des douleurs.[13]

Probably Conti took the poet's colors heraldically and made fun of them as a pretentious claim to aristocratic breeding. Alceste's costume contained both colors: "haut de chausses et juste-au-corps de brocart rayé or et soie gris, doublé de tabis, garni de rubans verts" (Rudler, ed. cit., p. 69). René Bray devotes a brilliant page to Molière's apparent preference for the color green, which he and Armande used in so many costumes and in so much interior decorating (op. cit., pp. 199–200), a discussion extended by Descotes (op. cit., pp. 92–93). Sarasin's epigram does not of course prove that Alceste's "rubans verts" are intended as symbolic in this sense, but it is unmistakable evidence of awareness of such a tradition very much nearer to Molière than the hitherto cited *L'Archisot* of 1605 in which green is the "couleur des bouffons et des fous" (Bray, p. 199). However suspect the rhyme word "jolie," it also attests the fashion for green in a milieu frequented by Molière before his return to Paris.

9. Before concluding this survey of sources of *Le Misanthrope*, I would cite, not a new one, but perhaps the most famous of all, the paraphrase of *De rerum natura*, IV, ll. 1153 ff., in Eliante's "favorables noms" passage of *Le Misanthrope*, Act II, scene 7:

> La pâle est aux jasmins en blancheur comparable,
> La noire à faire peur, une brune adorable . . . (ll. 717–18).

Daniela Dalla Valle is not the first scholar to cite this passage in support of the hypothesis that Molière accepts the new Gassendist Epicurism: "por boca de Eliante, Molière hasta cita a Lucrecio . . . ."[14]

But to historicize an attitude it is not sufficient to identify a paraphase: whereas Lucretius's passage is rightly referred to as developing the blindness of lovers, Eliante's point is rather their *complaisance*. Such an attitude, which Alceste has just rejected, is a theme given considerable development by seventeenth-century theoricians of *honnêteté*. In *L'Honnête Homme*, Faret allows that the courtier's *complaisance* in describing the object of another's affection may "en ce poinct seulement pancher vu peu du costé de la flatterie, avec quelque sorte de legitime excuse . . ." (ed. cit., pp. 141–42). "Elle n'aura point de deffaut," Faret continues, "qu'il ne desguise par quelque terme d'adoucissement: Si elle a le teint noir, il dira qu'elle est brune . . ." (p. 142). And the most delicate *complaisance* should be scrupulously observed in all dealings with women, who "ont l'esprit tendre à se picquer des plus petites contestations qui s'opposent à leurs sentiments" (p. 199). Admittedly Du Bosc had warned against excessive *complaisance* in the second part of *L'Honnête Femme* (first published in 1634): "Tantost elle donne de beaux noms aux choses les plus laides, appellant la temerité vu grand courage, l'auarice vne œconomie . . ." (ed. cit., II, p. 9). But Du Bosc makes it clear that this is, like excessive frankness, a culpable extreme, while some *complaisance*, he says, is necessary to civility and to society

(II, pp. 28–35). Dramatists and satirists, moreover, had long been aware of the comic potential of a *réplique* like Eliante's. In the first act of Lope de Vega's *Fuenteovejuna* Frondoso develops a somewhat similar rhetoric of euphemism:

> Andar al uso queremos:
> al bachiller, licenciado;
> al ciego, tuerto; al bisojo,
> bizco; resintido, al cojo,
> y buen hombre, al descuidado . . . . (ll. 292 ff.),

rhetoric which Laurencia promptly stands on its head: "al hombre grave, enfadoso," etc. In a French comedy well known to Molière, Desmarets de Saint-Sorlin writes such a *réplique* into the role of Alcidon in *Les Visionnaires* (I, 7) to characterize—and satirize—that character's excessive *complaisance*, while in the first scene of *Jodelet duelliste* Scarron—in a very different spirit—satirizes seducers by letting Dom Félix describe his approach to women in a similar manner: "Aux petites, je dis que leur corps est adroit . . . ." The satirist or *censeur* instead cannot, as Boileau remarks in the *Discours au Roi*, "D'un nain faire un Atlas, ou d'un lâche un Hercule"—an attitude which Alceste exaggerates.

If now we return to the context of Lucretius's passage, where the analysis of dreams turns toward a discussion of love, we find that he insists upon the blindness of lovers to support his view that a man should (*scilicet* in the interest of Epicurean clarity and tranquillity) avoid love's obsessions by casting what Lucretius calls its liquor indiscriminately into any male or female bodies ("et iacere umorem conlectum in corpora quaeque," IV, l. 1065), an attitude which Molière's faithful lovers implicitly reject (the romantically comic Cléonte is the more sympathetic for exemplifying Lucretius's point about lovers' blindness—rather than following his advice—in *Le Bourgeois Gentilhomme*, III, 9). Certainly it is not one that Eliante favors. The presence in *Le Misanthrope* of a passage adapted from Lucretius does not then show that Molière has Epicurean leanings (though this might be argued on other grounds). It merely shows that, like other contemporary writers, he knew how to adapt a well-known *locus* in a Latin classic to new ends: to comic effect and to a quite different, but culturally significant, contemporary concept, that of *honnêteté*—a concept of social harmony to which a measure (but not an excess) of *complaisance* is vital. In the thematic structure of the play such *complaisance* points on two levels to an acceptable middle way between the language of empty flattery exemplified by Oronte, Acaste and Clitandre and the censorious *franchise* of Alceste. Verbally, Eliante suggests praise instead of criticism, praise that Du Bosc had distinguished from flattery and commended as socially beneficial, as permitting the amplification of good qualities without dishonesty (II, p. 37). Spiritually, her solution *commends* an ideal of love entirely absent from Lucretius's *critique* of its distorting influence, a love which "Aime jusqu'aux défauts des personnes qu'il aime." This positive concept of love is certainly not Lucretian and—*mutatis mutandis*—nearer Montaigne's love of Paris, warts and all, though we can no more expect *verrues* or *taches* in Eliante's lines than for such a character in Molière to have rendered Lucretian adjectives like *fœtida* and *mammosa*.

In his *Preceptes galans* (Paris, Barbin, 1678), L. Ferrier takes up this theme in still a different spirit, inspired no doubt partly by Eliante and—for the remark on eyes— Cléonte in *Le Bourgeois Gentilhomme* (III, 9): familiarity will bring tolerance, or at least recourse to flattery, here conceived as lucid and well-meaning (even if there is some irony):

> Quand l'Amour dans un cœur vient seulement de naître,
> Il n'est point de defaut qu'il ne scache connaître,
> Mais dès qu'à soûpirer on s'est accoûtumé,
> On ne voit que vertus dans un objet aimé:
> Ou du moins un Amant s'imposant à luy même,
> Paroît ingenieux à flater ce qu'il aime,
> Et chatoüillant son cœur par des éloges faux,
> Sous des noms adôucis colore ses defauts.
>   A l'agréable Brune il compare La Noire,
> De la blonde à la pâle il prodigue la gloire,
> Trouve les yeux petits, brillans & pleins de feux,
> Et les grands sans vigueur tendrement langoureux,

Honore d'une taille & libre & dégagée,
Celle que jusqu'aux os la maigreur a rongée,
Et donne l'agrément d'un parfait embonpoint,
A celle que la graisse enfle & n'embelit point.
(pp. 81–82)

Lucretius's notion of distorted vision has here completely disappeared in favour of *complaisance*, and under Molière's visible influence.

To conclude this section, in Eliante's *réplique* Molière has adapted Lucretius's rhetoric, significantly altering it to fit the contemporary French canon of *bienséance*. Its altered conclusion shows that on this point he entirely rejects the original Epicurean ideology, while analysis of the context reveals its use in search of a solution to a current social problem, not a personal and physiological one. If I have expanded this point, it is because the sort of question it raises is vital to the study of comparative literature or cultural historiography. Such aspects of continuity can only be properly assessed through a concomitant analysis of context and change.

10. To sum up, numerous sources and other contextual or intertextual evidence suggest that Molière's comic vision in *Le Misanthrope* is neither isolated nor remote from the literary preoccupations of his contemporaries: dramatists, satirists, poets and moralists. Molière's observation of contemporary society is demonstrably expressed through a variety of assimilated literary traditions, traces of which are everywhere apparent in the text of his comedy, which reflects the literature of its time quite as much and perhaps more directly than it reflects the life of that time. This is not to argue that *Le Misanthrope* is, in any deep sense, the less personal or the less original for its innumerable sources, which are rewritten, transposed, inverted, contradicted. Nor does this really teach us where Molière found his rhyme. It suggests instead that once again, and even in this great comedy, we must think of originality not so much in terms of games with different balls, but of a writer who placed some of the same balls differently, often better. It

should make us cautious in assuming that satire of a privileged class must necessarily arise from a point of view outside that class. It should also make us sceptical of arguments assuming that the mere identification of a source in a complex work of itself discloses an attitude. Above all, it suggests that we need not approach Molière's art in this comedy as being exclusively the work of either an actor, or a poet, or a moralist. The actor who transposed and invented material for *Le Misanthrope* was also a poet steeped in French and Latin poetic traditions, one whose talent and invention can be analysed and assessed with reference to a host of specific sources. The playwright who selected material to mime from Faret, Maynard, Gombauld, Martial, Pibrac and other poets and moralists was also himself a moralist, none the less insightful (on the contrary) for being also a great poet and a great comedian.

In his "Oraison funebre de Molière" in *Le Mercure galant* (IV, 1673), Cléante rightly saw a great author because of "la beauté de ses Ouvrages . . ." and the "bons effets qu'ils ont produits"; and a great actor, because he acted well himself and directed the acting of others well (pp. 291 ff.). Bouhours begins his *Tombeau de Molière:*

> Ornement du Théâtre, illustre acteur,
> Charmant Poète, illustre Auteur . . .,

and suggests that, with others, "L'homme ennemi du genre humain . . . N'[a] pas lu tes écrits en vain."[15] I hope to have demonstrated in this essay that if indeed Molière was the "grand Peintre moral" celebrated by *Le Mercure galant* (IV, p. 311), it is partly because he adapts, exploits, and re-creates a host of literary traditions and notably because *Le Misanthrope* is, among other things, a splendid amplification and dramatization of medieval *topoi* such as *aurea mediocritas* and *tædium curiæ* which reached him through neglected channels like Pibrac, Mathieu, Racan, Maynard and others. Doubtless this is why Cléante could say in his "Oraison funèbre" (p. 294): "le Defunt n'estoit pas seulement un habile Poëte, mais encore un grand Philosophe. Philosophe,

me direz-vous, Philosophe!" which opens a perspective on
the future.

II

Why did Molière make "la maîtresse du Misanthrope . . .
une jeune veuve, coquette, et tout à fait médisante"? The
"Lettre sur la comédie du *Misanthrope*" (probably by Donneau de Visé) published with the first edition doubtless
makes the main points concerning her coquetry and her
school for scandal:

> . . . la maîtresse du Misanthrope est une jeune veuve, co-
> quette, et tout à fait médisante. Il faut s'écrier ici, et admirer
> l'adresse de l'auteur: ce n'est pas que le caractère ne soit assez
> ordinaire, et que plusieurs n'eussent pu s'en servir; mais l'on
> doit admirer que, dans une pièce où Molière veut parler con-
> tre les mœurs du siècle et n'épargner personne, il nous fait
> voir une médisante avec un ennemi des hommes. Je vous
> laisse à penser si ces deux personnes ne peuvent pas naturelle-
> ment parler contre toute la terre, puisque l'un hait les hom-
> mes, et que l'autre se plaît à en dire tout le mal qu'elle en
> sait.[16]

Full of admiration for Molière's skill and judgment, the
Lettre develops this appreciation:

> Le Misanthrope, seul, n'aurait pu parler contre tous les hom-
> mes; mais en trouvant le moyen de le faire aider d'une
> médisante, c'est avoir trouvé en même temps celui de mettre,
> dans une seule pièce, la dernière main au portrait du siècle. Il
> y est tout entier, puisque nous voyons encore une femme qui
> veut paraître prude opposée à une coquette, et des marquis
> qui représentent la cour: tellement qu'on peut assurer que,
> dans cette comédie, l'on voit tout ce qu'on peut dire contre les
> mœurs du siècle (p. 212).

Neglecting the ambiguity of Donneau de Visé's last lines
concerning a play which Molière never performed at Court,
we can thank him for sketching what still seems the basic
structure of *Le Misanthrope*. At once like and unlike Alceste,
through the dissimilarity of her humor (old sense) Célimène

plausibly assures Alceste's incongruous encounters with incompatible characters, while by a comparable outspokenness, she continues and varies the satire of contemporary society. Yet Molière achieves comedy too by the incongruities of their own relationship, in which the very similarities—Alceste's tirades against Célimène, Célimène's polemical portrait of Alceste—emphasize their incompatibility as lovers who make war, not love. At the same time, by coupling *misanthrope* and *médisante* Molière suggests a latent affinity in *amour-propre* between Alceste's *franchise* and Célimène's *médisance*. It is this latent affinity in *amour-propre* which, as the characters interact, comically manifests an incompatibility not only in their relations with each other, but also within each character himself. Nowhere is this more apparent than in Célimène's *médisance:* a powerful weapon in the service of coquetry as she charms all but the sternest of her admirers in the "scène des portraits," it is later turned against her in the portrait-letters, so that partly through Alceste—whose spirit of contradiction she cleverly exposes at the end of the "scène des portraits"—she is undone by precisely the sort of *médisance* on which the most brilliant moment of her coquetry is founded.

The attraction that Célimène holds for Alceste, as he and other characters recognize, indicates a basic *contrariété*, or self-contradiction, in his character, which reflects a problem of concern to contemporary moralists. Though Molière is careful to situate his comedy, not at Court, but in a *salon* where the marquis "représentent la cour," some of Saint-Evremond's "Observations sur la maxime qui dit qu'il faut mépriser la fortune et ne se point soucier de la cour" (1668) seem pertinent:

> Je ne trouve donc pas estrange en ce cas là qu'un honneste homme méprise la Cour, mais je trouve ridicule qu'il se veüille faire honeur de la mépriser.
> [Il] a beau faire le Philosophe, sa Philosophie m'est suspecte de vanité. Je ne suis point la dupe de ces hypocrites de Cour qui preschent les autres sur la retraite, et qui ne peuvent se persuader qu'elle soit un bien. . . .[17]

Alceste ridiculous, not for despising courtly life, but for

glorying in his distaste for it, is not an implausible reading. The hypocrisy which Saint-Evremond sees in such an attitude has interesting implications for the conception of the misanthrope and his relation to other characters and themes in Molière: self-deception is no less "metaphysically" hypocritical in connection with frankness or "sincerity" than with piety, or snobbery, or hypochondria.

Such self-deception irritates Saint-Evremond:

> Il y en a d'autres qui ne me déplaisent pas moins: ce sont ceux qui ne peuvent quiter la Cour, et qui se chagrinent de tout ce qui s'y passe. . . .
> Ils regardent comme une injustice tout le bien et tout le mal qu'on fait aux autres; ce n'est point assez de meriter d'estre heureux pour éviter leur envie; mais assez d'estre mal-heureux pour attirer leur pitié (ll, 147–8).

Célimène's circle provides Molière with ample scope for developing in Alceste precisely the sort of *ridicule* diagnosed by Saint-Evremond.

That there is a basis in contemporary medical theory for Alceste's characterization was abundantly demonstrated by R. Jasinski in *Molière et le Misanthrope* (1951). But I know of nothing that illustrates better the relation of Alceste's humor to Célimène's, and that of both humors to theories of *honnêteté*, than the chapter "De l'humeur gaye, et de la melancolique" in Du Bosc's widely circulated treatise *L'Honnête Femme:*

> les plus excellentes des humeurs gayes, [sont] celles qui approchent le plus de la Melancolie, & entre les Melancoliques celles qui sont plus voisines de la Gayeté. Parce qu'estant ainsi temperées, les premieres seront plus discrettes, & les autres moins austeres & moins importunes.[18]

If the *honnête femme*, or the *honnête homme*, has an *humeur gaye*, or *enjouée*, it is tempered with melancholy, and vice versa. For his comedy, Molière's characterization does just the reverse, isolating Alceste's melancholy and making it extreme, while conferring upon Célimène the most striking and absolute attributes of the *humeur gaye*, so that their confrontation negatively outlines an *honnête* temperament by excesses on either side, while preserving some of the charm of either humor in something of its pure state.

For Du Bosc, *Gayeté* is better than melancholy, as far as conversation is concerned, because it possesses "quelque chose de plaisant." But women of this temperament, he warns, are "sujettes à de grandes fautes: parce que si la raillerie dont elles se meslent ordinairement, est agreable à quelques-uns, elle en offense plus qu'elle ne contente." The particular relevance of this analysis to the characterization of Célimène (whether one assumes that Molière knew the text or simply that it represents a system of ideas relating individual characteristics to social behavior to which he had access) becomes evident in the observation that such humors have "plus d'esprit que de jugement." At first, Du Bosc continues, they seem to have "quelque lumière, mais qui est fausse ou ne dure pas long-temps sans estre esteint. Elles se laissent surprendre, manque de ne prevoir pas d'assez loin aux affaires d'importance." For if Célimène's coquetry is very precisely an effort to measure con-sequences—in terms of her lawsuit and general reputa-tion—ostentatiously neglected by Alceste, her *médisance* is not; and Du Bosc's analysis exactly fits the short-lived bril-liance of the portrait scene followed by Célimène's disgrace when her indiscreet letters are brought home to her in the last act.

If *L'Honnête Femme* seems far-fetched, consider the advice in *Les Conseils d'Ariste à Célimène, sur les moyens de conserver sa réputation, achevé d'imprimer* 1 March 1666 three months be-fore the premiere of *Le Misanthrope*, a text from which I argued earlier the significance of Célimène's portrait of Timante, and to which I shall return to explore many other ways in which it can help interpret her situation. Here suffice it to say that Célimène's failure in the comedy to follow advice that Ariste offers the other Célimène makes it almost seem as if Ariste had told *her* so, in section 11 "Com-ment il faut parler des hommes":

> n'en dites jamais rien qui vous en puisse faire des ennemis; car quand on les a raillez aigrement, & que l'on n'a point feint [= hésité] d'en médire, de publier leur défauts & d'insulter à leur

disgrace, ils ne demeurent pas dans le silence, quand ils le
sçavent; il n'y en a point qui fassent profession d'vne patience
assez Philosophique ny assez Chrestienne, pour ne se pas ven-
ger . . . (pp. 86–87).

However, in *L'Honnête Femme* Du Bosc also attacks what
he considers excessive *franchise:*

> . . . n'est-il pas vray que cette grande franchise à parler [que]
> plusieurs louent, ne vient pas le plus souvent d'vne integrité
> de meurs, mais d'opiniastreté, de vanité, & d'imprudence?
> Nous prenons plaisir à contredire, parce que la crainte d'estre
> vaincus nous fait trouuer de la complaisance à contredire la
> verité mesme (II, 27).

La Rochefoucauld puts something of the same idea rather
more neatly in his *Maximes:* "La vertu n'irait pas si loin si la
vanité ne lui tenait pas compagnie." The Franciscan and the
former *frondeur* suggest the moralist significance of
Célimène's ironic portrait of Alceste: "Et ne faut-il pas bien
que monsieur contredise?" (669 ff.).

Yet Alceste cannot be reduced to mere "esprit con-
trariant" by a vexed Célimène, nor his aspiration to virtue
reduced to mere vanity along the lines of La Rochefoucauld's maxim. In this respect, the continuation of Du
Bosc's analysis presents a particular interest:

> Toute fois ie veux que cette humeur aigre ne vienne pas d'vn
> mauuais Principe, c'est au moins vn mauuais effect d'vne
> bonne cause. Ceux qui sont si rudes & si peu complaisans,
> sont dignes de compassion, quoy qu'ils soyent sçavans & ver-
> tueux. . . .

Such is the response that Alceste has elicited from spectators and readers intermittently for three centuries. For
like Du Bosc, Molière appears to have approached the problem with no less insight than La Rochefoucauld, firmly
linking the strenuous proclamation of virtue to self-love,
but with greater respect for the total character, greater tolerance, more humanity, a more charitable vision. At the
same time, in contrast with Du Bosc, Molière's comic
characterization arises from awareness of a more complex
motivation. Alceste involves no simple alternative: either
"integrité de meurs," on the one hand, or stubbornness, con-

ceit, imprudence, on the other. In Alceste rather Molière
dramatizes ways in which such abstractly incompatible aspects of character relate and interact simultaneously within
the same personality, not as successive passions, but with a
complex emotional wholeness: *honnête homme* in some respects, ridiculous in others, according to the basic insight
expressed by Dorante in *La Critique de l'Ecole des femmes*
(scene 6).

It is this complexity that Eliante's analysis of Alceste
brings out:

> Dans ses façons d'agir il est fort singulier,
> Mais j'en fais, je l'avoue, un cas particulier,
> Et la sincérité dont son âme se pique
> A quelque chose en soi de noble et d'héroïque.
> C'est une vertu rare au siècle d'aujourd'hui,
> Et je la voudrais voir partout comme chez lui (1163–68).

How carefully Eliante separates the ideal of sincerity "en
soi" from Alceste's manner, "fort singulier." And
significantly her words "dont son âme se pique" lend themselves to judgment against La Rochefoucauld's maxim: "Le
vrai honnête homme ne se pique de rien." No spurious
idealization of Alceste's sincerity minimizes the self-love
and the self-deception with which it is accompanied in the
play—in Alceste himself, and in other characters: for
Oronte in admiration of his own sonnet, the marquis in
admiring the figures they cut at Court, are no less sincere
than Alceste. Molière does not lose the ideal of sincerity by
depicting it in association with aggression, or fatuousness,
but defines it in laughter.

Turning now to the scene (Act III, scene 4) in which
Molière introduces Arsinoé, "une femme qui veut paraître
prude opposée à une coquette," we find Du Bosc's chapter
"De la vraye et de la fausse probité" no less helpful. Since,
as Du Bosc argues, "les mauuais desseins ont besoin d'vn
beau masque," he outlines a diagnosis of false probity the
main lines of what are similar to Célimène's analysis of
Arsinoé's motives:

> . . . comme la fausse Probité tesmoigne de l'excez pour em-
> brasser la vertu, elle en tesmoigne aussi pour fuir le vice: elle

contrefaict l'amour & la haine. Elle veut paroistre
scrupuleuse: mais si elle a le scrupule sur le frõt, elle a le
libertinage dans l'ame. . . . que faudra-t'il dire de celle qui est
entierement libertine au dedans, & seulement scrupuleuse à
l'exterieur, ou pour mieux dire, qui ne montre de scrupule
que pour avoir plus de licence? (II, 164–65).

There is greater art in Célimène's counter-attack upon
Arsinoé, the most scathing of all her portraits, beginning
"A quoi bon, disaient-ils, cette mine modeste . . ." (ll. 937
ff.). But surely it is relevant to the interpretation of
Molière's position, and Célimène's, that both mask image
for religious hypocrisy and the central valuation of false
piety had been current for more than a generation in a
popular Franciscan manual of *honnêteté*, which also states
that—like Arsinoé—:

> La fausse Probité n'est non plus capable de faire vne correc-
> tion, que de la recevoir: elle n'est pour cela ny humble ny
> charitable. C'est icy la pierre de touche, pour la vraye & pour
> la fausse vertu des Dames: Celles qui sont bõnes en effet, ai-
> ment la correction; celles qui ne le sont qu'en apparence, le
> hayssent & la mesprisent: elles sont ennemis de tout ce qui
> peut leur leuer le masque (II, 167).

Arsinoé is characterized with all three of the main traits of
false probity suggested in *L'Honnête Femme:* exaggerated
show of virtue, excessive scruples concerning Célimène,
and resistance to criticism. Thus independently of religious
considerations, Célimène's counterattack on Arsinoé—like
her portrait of Timante—also satirizes a lapse of *honnêteté*,
one outlined by a Franciscan moralist, who however had
advised against "la guerre aux Hypocrites" (I, 94)—advice
by which we may measure the distance between Du Bosc
and Molière while outlining the multiple and striking
similarities.

The immediate background of the "scène à faire" between *coquette* and *prude* is suggested, however, in the
eighth section of d'Aubignac's *Les Conseils d'Ariste à
Célimène*. The author observes in particular:

> I'ay veu des conversations toutes occupées sur la difficulté de
> sçavoir . . . si l'on doit plus estimer vne Coquette declarée qui
> dans la verité ne fait point de mal, qu'vne fausse Prude qui

sçait cõserver vn Amant, sans que l'on y connoisse rien . . .
(pp. 68–69).

If in this great scene Molière develops, with sure comic and
dramatic touch, the sort of acid encounter already exploited
by Corneille in *Mélite* Act IV, scene 2, there can be little
doubt that he does so in response to an active moralist
discussion.

On Alceste's jealousy, and its contrast with his
"heroism," I note Ariste's *sentence* in Beys's tragicomedy *Le
Jaloux sans sujet* (1636): "Vn cœur genereux n'en est guere
capable" (III, 1, p. 41). But in terms of Alceste's jealousy of
Célimène, Béatrix's complaint in Chevalier's comedy of
1662, *Les Barbons amoureux et rivaux de leurs fils*, is even more
suggestive of possible audience expectations concerning
such a theme:

> Certes, le beau garçon, vous estes admirable!
> Vous vous fâchez Amant; mary, vous seriez diable.
> Vous deviez mieux cacher vostre méchante humeur,
> Vn Amant ne plaist pas quand il fait le Censeur;
> Lorsqu'il se voit entrer la ialousie en l'ame,
> Il ne se doit iamais charger d'aucune femme . . . (II, 5, p. 26).

Quite apart from the use Molière made of the main idea of
this play in *L'Avare*, his Célimène would appear to share
some of Béatrix's reactions.

It is a central thesis of Nicolas Faret's *L'Honnête Homme*,
that by adopting sensible manners "le Sage peut au milieu
des vices & de la corruption conserver sa vertu toute pure &
sans tache" (ed. cit., p. 62). And in his essay on *Self-
Reliance*, R. W. Emerson makes the point that "It is easy in
the world to live after the world's opinion; it is easy in
solitude to live after our own; but the great man is he who
in the midst of the crowd keeps with perfect sweetness the
independence of solitude." Alceste's uncommitted, unself-
critical, and self-deceptive idealism illustrates a conspicu-
ous failure even to try, which can be measured effectively
either against Faret's concept of "sagesse" or Emerson's idea
of greatness.

That for Célimène the challenge was immeasurably
greater will be appreciated by readers at all familiar with

the history of feminism in France in the seventeenth century, and in particular with the fact that, unlike *L'Honnête Homme*, *L'Honnête Femme* makes no suggestion whatever for an independent career, that is, a career outside marriage and the family.

No social or moral problem—neither hypocrisy, nor medicine, nor even perhaps cuckoldry—more persistently held Molière's attention than feminism, from *Les Précieuses ridicules* to the Angélique of *Le Malade imaginaire*. Without prejudice to the fuller discussion of this problem written for the introduction of my own edition of *Les Femmes savantes* for the Clarendon French Series (Oxford University Press), we can now propose precise answers to further questions about Célimène: why did Molière make her a widow of twenty? and why did he call her Célimène?

The general way in which Célimène's widowhood is related to the status of women in seventeenth-century French society is well understood, since widowhood assured an independence which neither wives nor unmarried daughters (especially under twenty-five) could normally enjoy, together with a respectability denied independent women who did not marry or enter the Church—unless of course she were one who had the rank and wealth of the Grande Mademoiselle, which no other woman had. The advantage of making a young widow the heroine of a comedy without the traditional obstacle in the path of the lovers' marriage had of course been illustrated by Corneille in *La Veuve*. And it is one of the insights of *Le Misanthrope* that the obstacle to any marriage between Alceste and Célimène is wholly inward, in self-love.

However, the particular feminist implications of the widow of twenty for Molière's public have not to my knowledge been explained. A precise significance is suggested by the following demand for the liberation of unmarried women made by Lucrèce in Chappuzeau's *Académie des femmes* (1661), also published as *Le Cercle des femmes* (1663), in Act III, scene 3:

> Que l'on les emancipe; & si l'on veut i'appreuue
> Que chacune à vingt ans ayt le brevet de veuue.

> Qu'elle soit sa maistresse, & suiue son humeur
> Et ne dépende plus d'vn pere ou d'vn tuteur.

Since *Le Cercle des femmes* is an acknowledged source of *Les Femmes savantes*, on which Molière is thought to have begun work as early as 1668, it seems likely that he was struck by this passage even earlier and chose to exploit an extremist revendication in the characterization of Célimène. But it may be that the claim was sufficiently current among *précieuses* for Molière to have met it independently of the text cited, in which case Célimène's age and status would embody and dramatize a *précieuse* aspiration.

Even if Chappuzeau's Lucrèce does not faithfully reflect *précieuse* aspirations, which she may to some degree caricature, the implications are none the less significant. *Le Cercle des femmes* is a dramatic verse version of the same author's prose work of the same title, sub-titled *Entretien comique tiré des Dialogues d'Erasme* (Lyon, 1656), a work containing, as the "Argument" indicates:

> l'entreuuë d'vn Docteur & d'vne femme sçauante, les intructiõs du premier à vn rustaut de village pour devenir Gentilhomme, & les merueilleuses regles que le beau sexe se veut desormais prescrire . . . des pièces tres-fortes, tres-adroitement cõduites, & en vn mot tout à fait du temps.

In its two states, then, *Le Cercle des femmes* appears to be an important channel through which the medieval and Renaissance "querelle des femmes" reached Molière, along with some of the wit and moralist preoccupations of Erasmus. But, since the "brevet de veuve à vingt ans" is neither in the *Entretien comique* of 1656, nor in *Le Senat des femmes*—as Erasmus's dialogue appears in Chappuzeau's translation of *Les Entretiens familiers d'Erasme* published in Paris by Billaine in 1662—, the different adaptations by Chappuzeau suggest that the intellectual climate in which the notion of a "brevet de veuve à vingt ans" could be put forward and/or caricatured is significantly different from what it had been even seven years earlier, let alone in Erasmus's own time. *Le Cercle des femmes* is also a striking illustration of the way in which the comic theatre in Molière's time drew upon moralist literature and in particular upon that still largely uncharted genre of the classical period, the dialogue. However, the heroine of Scarron's story "A trompeur, trompeur et demi" in *Le Roman comique* is also a widow of twenty—suggesting concomitant "romantic" associations.

At the same time the confrontation confirms the surer theatrical touch of Molière and the greater complexity of his comic vision in linking *atrabilaire amoureux* with *coquette médisante*, in contrast with even a talented writer like Chappuzeau, who was content to follow Erasmus's dialogue in simply coupling like to like: the *Docteur* (or pedant) Hortense and the *Femme savante* Emilie. No striking contrast brings out the latent similarities in characters that on the surface appear to be totally different, which as indicated earlier is one of the brilliant insights of *Le Misanthrope*.

That moralist concerns as well as romantic associations may be implied by the name Célimène, previously considered in relation only to Rotrou's comedy *Célimène* of 1636, is suggested by d'Aubignac's *Les Conseils d'Ariste à Célimène*, to which I shall now devote the rest of this chapter. For despite the obvious difference that d'Aubignac's Célimène is a young wife, her separate establishment in her own apartments and general independence offer many analogies with the situation of Molière's heroine. *Les Conseils d'Ariste à Célimène sur les moyens de conserver sa réputation* was favorably reviewed in the *Journal des Savants* for April 5, as follows:

> Ce livre a cela de singulier, que sans perdre le temps à traiter les maximes qui sont de la connoissance de tout le monde, & qui se trouvent tant de fois rebattuës dans les Autheurs qui ont escrit de la Morale, il s'attache aux particularitez qui concernent la conduite d'une jeune Dame, & regle ses conseils sur toutes les circonstances de la vie commune & sur les actions ordinaires du beau monde. Les regles sont fondées sur l'honnesteté, & sont escrites d'un style agreable. Si les esprits libres se plaignent qu'elles ne tendent qu'à ruyner la galanterie, les sages reconnoistront qu'elles retranchent seulement de la societé les choses que la modestie n'y peut souffrir. . . . cet ouvrage sort de la main d'un homme qui s'est acquis l'intelligence des bons livres, & qui connoist parfaitement la vie de la Cour (p. 100).

The anonymous author, now thought to be the abbé d'Aubignac, relates that he proposed for Célimène "l'exemple de la sage Arthenice, à qui," he continues, "vous devez, avec la naissance, vne partie de l'estime que vous avez acquise" (p. 4). Arthenice is of course a common anagram for Catherine in the seventeenth century, after Malherbe, Racan, and the heroine of *Les Bergeries*. But it is not impossible that this is an allusion to the most famous Arthenice, Mme de Rambouillet, in which case our Célimène would likely be her best known daughter, Julie d'Angennes, who married the duc de Montausier in 1645. If we accept the author's assertion in the first section, "je n'écris que pour vous, comme je n'ay parlé qu'à vous" (p. 8), that is, that he did not initially write for publication, and if we further note that the *privilège* is dated 15 January 1656 ten years before publication, this identification is not implausible, though it is made tentatively and as the point of departure for new research. It would, however, help account for the early identification of Alceste with Montausier, made despite the manifest implausibility of such a "key."

For present purposes, the important thing is that the author envisages the new bride established in the grand style, in her own apartments, like the princesse de Clèves in the novel, and like Célimène of *Le Misanthrope* except that the latter no longer has a husband. D'Aubignac's point that, married and more experienced, his Célimène will be more exposed to amorous advances applies *a fortiori* to the Célimène of the comedy. For men, he indicates in section 4, "Du choix des visites," will all have a go at her:

> c'est une conqueste que tous entreprennent, croyant qu'il est glorieux d'en avoir eu la pensée, quand on ne l'auroit pas obtenuë. . . . tous ceux qui vous respectent ne travailleront qu'au moyen de vous perdre, & plus ils vous témoigneront de zele, de deference & de soins, plus en devez-vous juger les approches funestes à votre reputation (pp. 30–31).

That in Molière's comedy the marquis's courtship and Arsinoé's report reflect the same background, need hardly be specified. But as far as Célimène's relations with Alceste in the play are concerned, and her point (Act II, scene 1) that she would be unwise simply to turn away her other suitors, I note d'Aubignac's recognition that a woman of a Célimène's rank is not free to choose her company exclusively among people with "une réputation entière & bien approuvée."

If, however, d'Aubignac continues, it is impossible to know an *honnête homme* by sight or report, since "les plus vicieux se couvrent d'vne fausse vertu, & le jugement du public est vn mauvais garand de la verité," Célimène can at least avoid those "qui font vanité de leurs débauches, qui prennent la generosité pour vne fierté du vieux temps & la sincerité pour vne foiblesse, les impudens, les perfides, les imposteurs, les violens" (p. 32). Thus, since the *petits marquis* of *Le Misanthrope* clearly "font vanité de leurs débauches" and take Alceste's "generosité pour vne fierté du vieux temps & la sincerité pour vne foiblesse," there can be no doubt that the substance of Alceste's complaints to Célimène in Act II, scene 1—though not the manner, which actors interpret in different styles—, indicates both the way and the extent to which Célimène herself departs from a recognized norm of *honnêteté*.

Yet the failure of Molière's Célimène to adopt the sort of life style advised for d'Aubignac's Célimène is responsible for some of the former's difficulties, which give rise to several of Molière's most comic scenes, notably in connection with what the author of *Les Conseils* calls "visites frequentes ou assiduitez," the subject of an explicit warning in section 5: ". . . Celimene, il ne faut pas souffrir qu'aucun d'eux se rende auprés de vous plus assidu que les autres" (p. 34). In the play, of course, this is precisely what all of Célimène's suitors, and especially Alceste and Oronte, attempt to do. Ariste warns the Célimène of *Les Conseils* that such frequent visits "vous familiariseront avec vn homme qui d'abord ne vous auroit pas esté supportable; elles vous découvriront des qualités loüables dont vous ne vous seriez jamais appercçeuë . . .," leading to a *complaisance*, which in turn "vous engagera d'accorder insensiblement des privileges dont la suite ne peut estre que tres-fâcheuse, quand elle demeureroit innocente . . ." (pp. 36–38). For such a man will always be underfoot, making other suitors jealous and ready to ruin her reputation. In *Le Misanthrope*, Alceste's relations with Célimène seem to have reached just such a stage, as witness his familiarity in her home, his insistence upon seeing her alone (533), his threat to outstay the other suitors (742), the general rudeness of his possessive attitude toward his hostess, and her final loss of reputation.

If a general analogy is accepted between *Les Conseils* and *Le Misanthrope*, Ariste's advice to Célimène for dealing with anyone who has established himself on such a basis of familiarity will be of particular interest. For it may cast a more favorable light on the behavior of Molière's Célimène:

> rompez ces assiduitez [Ariste advises] par tous les moyens que la societé publique vous pourra permettre; supposez vne affaire précipitée, vne visite d'obligation, vne obligation domestique. . . . il n'importe qu'il découvre apres qu'elles ne sont pas veritables; au contraire, il est bon que sans luy dire, il connoisse vostre dessein; & s'il s'en plaint, n'en rēdez que de legeres & de mauvaises raisons, mais avec des paroles obligeantes; pourveu qu'il n'en voye point d'autre mieux traité que luy, il pourra bien renoncer à la poursuite qu'il meditoit, mais il ne pourra jamais condamner vostre conduite (pp. 41–42).

Allowing for the marriageability of Célimène in the comedy (an important difference not to be minimized on grounds of the *bienséances*), and also for the outspokenness of a misanthrope, I would argue that this text sheds light favorable to Célimène on her public rebuke to Alceste in the portrait scene (569 ff.), as earlier on her insistence that Acaste come up (532), and on her later exit on the pretext of a letter to write (1037), etc. As in so many of her responses, there is an element of self-defense conducted in a manner about which the least that can be now said, is that it was independently advised in 1666 in a respectable work on manners and morals.

The defensive nature of Célimène's handling of Alceste becomes even clearer in the light of Ariste's advice in section 6, "De ceux qui viuent sans ceremonie," against according any man "le droit de vivre auprés de vous de cette

maniere que l'on appelle ordinairement, sans ceremonie
. . ." (p. 46) For this would harm Célimène's reputation, by
arousing suspicions of a "complaisance particulière" and
because any such man would seek to "découvrir jusqu'où
vous serez capable de l'endurer; & ceux qui ne seront pas
d'humeur de vivre de cette sorte, en feront des discours qui
ne pourront vous estre avantageux . . ." (pp. 47 ff.). Above
all Ariste warns Célimène that she will be unable either to
avoid altogether or to improve such men:

> Vous en rencontrerez qui ne seront pas capables de s'en corri-
> ger; ce sont des ames grossieres, ennemis de toute politesse,
> qui semblent n'avoir esté faites que pour estre logées en des
> corps rustiques . . . ils s'entretiennent mesme dans cette
> humeur & font gloire de cette mauvaise liberté; ils entrent
> dans vne compagnie, ils y demeurent, ils en sortét sans au-
> cune marque de leur naissance ny de leur dignité; ils parlent
> sans garder aucune mesure d'honnesteté; ils agissent de
> mesme; ils prennent pour vn genereux détachement de vaine
> ceremonie, ce que tout le monde appelle ordinairement
> brutalité; & ils n'ont rien de cette belle vie de Cour que leurs
> habillements & leur équipage (pp. 50–51).

Although there is much in Alceste that transcends this
polemical portrait of "ames grossieres," it suggests something of the background of Eliante's acknowledgment that
"Dans ses façons d'agir il est fort singulier." Alceste is not
of course such an extreme case. He tries in Act I, scene 2, to
avoid direct comment on Oronte's poem, etc. But Ariste's
warning is one further justification of the reactions of
Molière's Célimène to Alceste.

Indeed, if as I have argued elsewhere, Alceste's accusa-
tions in the first letter scene (Act IV, scene 3) have a parodic
quality, Célimène's response to them may well be considered in the light of Ariste's counsel to the other Célimène
on dealing with men "sans ceremonie":

> Ce que vous avez donc à faire avec eux est d'observer plus de
> ceremonies qu'avec les autres, & de faire connoistre par vostre
> conduite que tous leurs emportemens sont des actes de l'im-
> pertinence qui leur est naturelle, & non d'vne intelligence qui
> vous y fasse prendre quelque part (pp. 51–52).

Célimène's line 1335 in the play would seem to fit such a

suggestion: "Vous êtes, sans mentir, un grand extravagant."

Even Alceste's failure to obtain a prolonged private talk with Célimène—granted obvious analogies with *Les Fâcheux*—may reflect her response to the sort of consideration urged by Ariste on her namesake in *Les Conseils*, section 24:

> . . . faites au moins que jamais [quelque témoin] ne vous perde de veuë; car si celuy qui vous fait visite, vous a découvert des sentimens que vous ne deviez pas approuver, il ne manquera pas, quand vous serez seuls auec luy de les faire éclater en soûpirs, en plaintes, en extravagances . . . (p. 182).

Then section 25 of *Les Conseils* advises "Comment il se faut gouverner avec celuy qui paroist chagrin." Since *chagrin* is a word favored by Alceste, I note that Ariste advises his Célimène that she should never "demander à celuy qui sera seul avec vous quelle est la cause de son chagrin," repeating: "Celimene, ne vous enquerez jamais de l'estat de son cœur; laissez-le dans cette ingenieuse melancholie . . ." (pp. 185–86).

On the other hand, since Molière's Célimène is a *coquette*, she does not follow the sort of advice offered by Ariste in section 26 "De la complaisance envers ceux qui ont de bonnes qualitez," which is that Célimène must not assume "devant eux vne humeur trop enjoüée, ny qu'il semble que vous vouliez divertir leur mauvaise humeur . . .," because he has seen women show "petites complaisances" to frequent visitors: "elles les regardoient avec des yeux assez doux pour faire soupçonner le cœur d'estre vn peu tendre; elles les entretenoient agreablement . . ." (pp. 190–91). For such behavior might be misleading.

It might also lead to a declaration, the subject of section 27, "Comment se gouverner envers ceux qui se declarent," in which Ariste describes a melancholic's courtship:

> il aura les yeux tristes & le visage chagrin, il s'interrompra luy-mesme . . . & quelquefois il partira brusquement d'auprès de vous . . . il vous dira d'autres fois qu'il n'est pas bon de se familiariser avec vos yeux, que votre presence a beaucoup de

charmes, mais qu'elle est dangereuse, & qu'vn homme ne sera jamais plus mal-heureux qu'en vous aimant; il vous fera des discours entiers de la vertu . . . (pp. 202–03).

This description is so suggestive of Alceste's attitudes in Act IV, scene 3, that it should—given the other analogies indicated above—be considered a source of that scene in the traditional sense of the term, allowing us to see how Molière turns it into drama and into comedy.

I would conclude then that, without prejudice to the theatrical associations of the name Célimène, Molière probably chose it for the heroine of *Le Misanthrope* in part because of associations of a moralist nature connected with *Les Conseils d'Ariste à Célimène*, a text which sheds light often favorable to Molière's Célimène on the sort of situation in which the latter finds herself in the play.

That the name Célimène becomes associated with carelessness of reputation in later moralist literature is indicated by J.-B. Morvan de Bellegarde's *Reflexions sur le ridicule et sur les moyens de l'éviter où sont representez les differens caracteres & les mœurs de ce siécle*, first published in 1696:

Celimene se plaint toujours qu'on la déchire impitoïablement, & qu'on fait d'affreuses satires de sa conduite; elle n'a aucun soin de sa réputation; elle est trop indiscrette & trop étourdie pour s'assujettir aux précautions; elle est la premiére à s'applaudir de ses intrigues; elle parle librement de ses commerces & de ses avantures devant tout le monde; le Public suit son exemple, & se donne aussi la liberté d'en parler; A-t'elle droit de se plaindre?
(quoted from the 3e *édition augmentée Paris, 1698, p. 53*).

If, with other texts, *Les Conseils* leaves no doubt about the extent to which Molière's Célimène departs from *honnêteté*—in coquetry and in scandal—, it also suggests the many circumstances in which her responses are defensive in a socially acceptable way against a host of men who seek to take advantage of her situation, including Alceste. It would be foolish to claim too much for this sort of *rapprochement*, which has deliberately avoided any but the most summary sketch of the ways in which Molière transmogrifies his sources. I offer it, however, for what it is worth, to those sensitive to the abstract qualities of a great and somewhat ambiguous classic (the qualities that have made it a classic), but who also seek to understand such a classic in terms of an evolving cultural heritage and an observed social context.

I 2

From *Le Misanthrope* to Voltaire's *Prude* via Wycherley's *Plain Dealer*

The three comedies of my title stand in a close and acknowledged relationship to each other. Yet in many ways
they are unrecognizably different in technique, tone and
implicit values. There have been many studies of the migra-
tion of a comic subject, such as the blunderer or the liar.[1]
There have doubtless been more studies of repeatedly
dramatized myths and legends, such as Amphitryon and
Don Juan.[2] The late Tom Lawrenson and others (including
Voltaire himself) have studied the differences between *Le
Misanthrope* and *The Plain Dealer*.[3] But in the whole broad
field of inquiry into the translation and transformation of
dramatic subjects relatively little attention has been given to
the problem of reentry into a dramatic literature of a subject
adapted back into it from a successful foreign adaptation of
an earlier masterpiece in the same language. Yet reentry
presents different problems from those of adaptation or
readaptation within a single tradition; and the third adaptation in a series from French to English to French faces
obstacles not encountered by the third adaptation in a series
from Italian or Spanish into French and then into English.
Giraudoux readapts *Amphitryon 38* from earlier sources, including Molière's *Amphitryon* and some of its sources; but
neither the eighteenth-century French parodies nor the intermediate foreign adaptations (e.g. by Dryden and by
Kleist) seem sufficiently important for him that they ruffle
his handling of the French and classical traditions of the
subject. However, even if the intermediate versions of Amphitryon as a dramatic subject were more important to
Giraudoux than supposed, his conduct of the dialogue in
prose obviates some of the problems encountered by Voltaire in repatriating *The Plain Dealer* in verse.

Arguably those problems are also different from the ones met by Voltaire in adapting tragic subjects from English, such as *La Mort de César*, or indeed from earlier French tragedies. It is not clear that Voltaire's *Sophonisbe* suffers because a different version of the subject by P. Corneille comes between Voltaire's tragedy and the one by Mairet upon which it draws so conspicuously, though it may be that the general decline of Voltaire's reputation as a dramatist reflects a feeling that in handling the form of classical tragedy in five acts and in alexandrines Voltaire was less original than the seventeenth-century masters he follows. However, *La Prude* is not written in alexandrines, and decasyllables do not assure a wholly successful reentry of *The Plain Dealer* in *La Prude*.

This paper then deals with two adaptations. In the earlier, a masterpiece of English Restoration comedy, *The Plain Dealer*, first performed by the King's Company in London in December 1676, followed *Le Misanthrope*, created at the Palais-Royal theatre in Paris in June 1666, by just over a decade. In the later transformation, Voltaire is much more retrospective. Though apparently written early in 1740, *La Prude* was not performed until December 1747, in the private theatre of the Duchesse de Maine at Sceaux. There are various ways in which one might discuss the affiliation and transformations of *Le Misanthrope* in the later comedies: the shift from poetic comedy to one largely in prose and then back to Voltaire's decasyllables, for example. Or one might begin with Voltaire's opinion, expressed as early as the *Lettres philosophiques*, that Wycherley corrects the sole flaw in Molière's comedy: the want of plot and interest *(Dix-neuvième lettre)*. On that transformation my aim will be to show that the relation of *The Plain Dealer* to *Le Misanthrope* is more aptly described as the process of *contaminatio* (the original blending of multiple sources) than simply as one of *imitatio* or adaptation mainly from a single model. On the second transformation I shall suggest that the continuing vitality of *Le Misanthrope* prevented the successful readaptation into French of *The Plain Dealer*, partly because the French *bienséances* did not allow Voltaire (or he did not allow himself) to move further away from Molière in the use of jokes based on indecency (rather the reverse: *La Prude* is more decorous than *Le Misanthrope*) and partly because it was impossible to adapt Wycherley's wit into French verse without colliding with formulae previously used in similar contexts by Molière, from whom Wycherley derives some of his wit in the first place.

Addition of a subplot is a recurrent feature of English Restoration adaptations of French comedies. Wycherley introduces a romantic alternative to the corrupt Olivia, loved by Manly but unworthy of him, in the person of Fidelia. The latter follows Manly disguised as a sailor and at last is recognized and marries him, which fits the general pattern. There is of course an obvious precedent for the role of Fidelia in that of Viola in Shakespeare's *Twelfth Night*, ignored as a similar sort of page by Orsino, who sends her on his behalf to court Olivia, who falls for the disguised Viola. The Olivia of *The Plain Dealer* is corrupt as well as flirtatious, combining elements of the role of Arsinoé, the *prude* in *Le Misanthrope*, with characteristics of Célimène. Perhaps Molière had wished to contrast, in the scene in which Arsinoé confronts Célimène and each verbally portrays the other, types whose merits were argued in the *salons* of the day: the *coquette* careless of appearances but chaste in effect with the *prude* who denounces promiscuity but secretly practices it, as shown in the preceding chapter. Wycherley blackens Olivia well beyond either of those contrasted types, by depicting her as having betrayed a promise of marriage to Manly through marriage with his friend Vernish, with whom she has conspired to deprive Manly of his wealth entrusted to them. The scene in which Vernish attempts to rape Fidelia after he discovers that she is a young woman and the scene in which Manly cuckolds Vernish by substituting himself for Fidelia illustrate the complexities of plot and the relatively greater sexual license of the London stage compared with that of Paris in the classical period.

In the *Lettres philosophiques*, Voltaire comments more than once on the greater license of the London stage, which had

of course attracted sharp censure from English critics long
before Voltaire's visit to England in 1726 to 1729. Nor is it
surprising that he wished in adapting *The Plain Dealer* to
retain the main elements of Wycherley's more elaborate
plot: its ingenuity is what he appears most to have admired.
But he did not care or perhaps dare to imitate Wycherley's
licence even on a private stage. In *La Prude* Blanford is
closer to Manly than he is to Alceste except in the proprieties. Dorfise is a somewhat softer Olivia without
Célimène's wit. Adine, disguised as a young Turk, replaces
Fidelia disguised as a seaman. But Bartolin, who replaces
Vernish, makes no attempt to rape Adine when he discovers that she is a woman; nor does Manly's adulterous
revenge enjoyment of Olivia have any counterpart in *La
Prude*. Perhaps (residual difficulties notwithstanding) the
question of propriety guided Voltaire's somewhat unusual
preference for *The Plain Dealer* over Wycherley's *Country
Wife* as an illustration of English comedy. According to
Emmett Avery, there were only four performances of *The
Plain Dealer* in the seasons 1725–26 to 1729–30, when Voltaire was in London, thirty fewer than performances in
those seasons of *The Country Wife*, also adapted from
Molière (especially *L'Ecole des maris* and *L'Ecole des femmes*)
and produced competitively on both the London stages of
the day.[4] Voltaire certainly knew *The Country Wife*, because
he mentions it in the *Lettres philosophiques*. But perhaps he
was drawn to the character of Manly as a captain unvan-
quished in defeat, worthy in the face of ingratitude and
betrayal, deserving of the sort of ironic sympathy Voltaire
would later display in *Candide* for the unfortunate Admiral
Byng.

   Voltaire is, I think, correct in observing in the *Lettres
philosophiques* that Wycherley further complexifies his plot
by adding the litigious Widow Blackacre and correct to
suggest that she more closely resembles the Comtesse de
Pimbêche of Racine's *Les Plaideurs* than she resembles any of
Molière's characters, though lawsuits are a theme of *Le Misanthrope* and the Widow Blackacre is not without certain
qualities reminiscent of Mme Pernelle of *Tartuffe*, thor-

oughly naturalized and said by Manly to be "as vexatious . . . as a dozen Norfolk attorneys." The Widow Blackacre has no counterpart in *La Prude*, the wit of which does not involve the sort of farcical satire developed in such characters as the Comtesse de Pimbêche, Mme Pernelle and the Widow Blackacre. It is none the less interesting that Voltaire did undertake to write a witty comedy at the height of the vogue for *comédie larmoyante;* and if *La Prude* proved less successful in wit that Piron's *La Métromanie*, then maybe he could not readapt Wycherley's wit without introducing an unacceptable level of bawdy or colliding with Molière's comic phrasing. In shifting the scene of *Le Misanthrope* from Paris to London, Wycherley also substitutes for Alceste— who by his own admission is untried in the service of his country—a veteran captain, a man who has suffered in the service of his country, because he had lost a ship in the Dutch war. Voltaire also shifts the scene, but to Marseilles, so that in *La Prude* Blanford's naval associations are all with the Marine de Levant. Both shifts involve a move away from a *salon* offering an image of courtiers and courtly life such as *Le Misanthrope* provides down to the last polemical portrait. Wycherley's transformation opens out onto the new naval and commercial horizons often reflected in English Restoration comedy. Voltaire plunges his audience back into the old traditional Mediterranean comic associations, with effects such as Adine's Turkish disguise long associated with Molière and with Italian comedy. But he was not prepared to give this material the comic verve found in *L'Etourdi* and *Les Fourberies de Scapin*.

More significant perhaps even than this change of seas is the earlier sea change between the original Misanthrope and the Plain Dealer. Despite an evolving acting tradition and an occasionally aberrant critical heritage, Molière's title is to be taken literally: Alceste despises his fellow men, and is allusively linked (as shown in chapter 11) with the best known misanthropist of antiquity, Timon of Athens:

> et je hais tous les hommes,
Les uns parce qu'ils sont méchants et malfaisants,
Les autres pour être aux méchants complaisants (ll. 118–20).

It pays to be cautious in taking at face value anything said by Alceste or any other character in drama, but this interpretation is borne out by the *Lettre sur la comédie du Misanthrope* published as a preface to the first edition. Its author—probably Donneau de Visé—invites the reader to admire the fact that "dans une pièce où Molière veut parler contre les moeurs du siècle et n'épargner personne, il nous fait voir une médisante avec un ennemi des hommes." In other words, the Misanthrope no less than Célimène and her school for scandal is made both the vehicle and the object of satire. That Alceste was still perceived as an object as well as a vehicle for satire in the period after Molière's death is variously attested, but best perhaps by the *Tombeau de Molière* written by a Jesuit admirer of the social efficacity of Molière's satire, Dominique Bouhours, as noted in chapter 11: "L'homme ennemi du genre humain . . ./N'a pas lu tes écrits en vain. . . ."

Such was not the emphasis often placed in eighteenth-century French responses to Alceste, who came to be treated more sympathetically than Donneau de Visé indicates for Molière's own initial handling of the role, described as "plaisant, sans être trop ridicule." An important element in the transformation of Misanthrope into Plain Dealer characterizes the latter not so much as the enemy of the people as a victim of society, luckless in war, still more luckless in love and friendship. Perhaps such a transformation reflects the different contexts in which the two comedies were written. *Le Misanthrope* appeared toward the end of a period of peace that had, exceptionally, lasted in effect from the Peace of the Pyrenees some seven years earlier, a long time in the reign of Louis XIV for any peace to last. It is not then surprising that Alceste, though of the warrior class, had not yet proved himself in war or in administration, although the implications of this aspect of his characterization will vary with the age assumed for Alceste. Molière was forty-four when he created the role, and later interpreters have often (but not always) been actors of similar maturity. In *Molière et le Misanthrope* (Paris, 1951) René Jasinski assumes the age of Alceste to be twenty-six, and it can hardly be doubted that he is given as being at least of age, i.e. twenty-five or more. Alceste's age is not the subject of this essay, but clearly it matters to the atmosphere of his encounters with Célimène whether he is merely a few years her senior or more than twice her age. It matters also in any response to his brusque question to Arsinoé: "Quel service à l'Etat est-ce qu'on m'a vu rendre?" (l. 1054).

Manly's age may also be a problem, depending on whether one assumes his first command was in the Dutch War of 1672–74 (which seems likely) or in the earlier one fought in 1666–67. Otherwise the reader of *The Plain Dealer* is given help in "The Persons" of the play, where we are advised that Manly is of an "honest, surly, nice humour" and that he is "supposed first in the time of the Dutch war to have procured the command of a ship, out of honour, not interest, and chosing a sea life only to avoid the world." There is, I think, little or no irony in the name Manly, which suggests virility and (in the Machiavellian sense of *virtù*) virtue, which Manly displays in the two most obvious ways. *Manly* may interpret the name *Alceste*, which Molière may have found as that of a hero in a novel by his presumed namesake Molière d'Essertines, since it has similar associations suggesting "strong man." In *Le Misanthrope* Alceste may be named ironically, as a man manly in the wrong place and the wrong time and mainly with twits and women; and there may be additional irony in the unisex nature of the name, which was also that of a famous tragic character willing to renounce the world and die for her husband, Alcestis. However that may be, Manly is not a nobleman, in which respect he differs from Alceste, who must have been a *gentilhomme* to face trial in the Cour des Maréchaux. Manly has faced losses as a result of his service at sea and has no aristocratic privileges which depend upon no discernible function. Nor does he seek out a fashionable *salon* in which to advocate retreat from the world. Manly is no universal enemy of mankind turned lover in spite of himself, but a surly seasalt characterized by poor discernment in love and friendship, blind to treachery and deaf to sincerity. An integral part of the characterization of Manly,

and a significant difference between his character and that
of Alceste, involves the illusions which the Plain Dealer
entertains with respect to Olivia and to Vernish, whom he
wrongly exempts from his general disillusionment with the
world, a disillusionment shown to be wrongly rigorous and
too absolute. In *Le Misanthrope* Alceste is infatuated with
Célimène, but not obsessed with her and certainly not blind
to her faults. Much of the comedy of those incompatible
lovers depends upon the reproaches he makes as soon as he
approaches her. In *The Plain Dealer* the blind, obsessive
infatuation of Manly with Olivia and with Vernish more
closely resembles the infatuation depicted in another of
Molière's comedies: *Tartuffe*. That is, Orgon's infatuation
with the impostor, a model to which we must return.

First, as a caution against reduction in the *contaminatio*
proposed, let me observe that the detection of literary inspiration does not imply identity between the plays or parts of
plays compared. It does imply a continuity within a documented tradition, and it makes the task of identifying
change easier and its results more precise. I have suggested
that the literary inspiration of *Le Misanthrope* is far more
complex than used to be allowed, that Molière in that comedy has drawn upon a number of plays by Corneille,
Mairet, and Rotrou as well as upon earlier comedies of his
own. He exploits Gombauld's *Epigrammes*, Faret's *Honnête
Homme*, d'Aubignac's *Conseils d'Ariste à Célimène* published
shortly before the premiere, etc. *The Plain Dealer* would
appear to have a no less complex relation to earlier works in
English: to Shakespeare's *Timon of Athens*, to Jonson's
Epicoene, or the Silent Woman, to Shadwell's *Sullen Lovers*, a
comedy in which Stanford—the nearest counterpart to
Manly—is given as "a morose, melancholy man, tormented
beyond measure with the impertinence of people and re-
solved to leave the world to be quit of them." There can be
little doubt that *The Sullen Lovers* already echoes *Le Misanthrope* as well as the acknowledged debt to Molière's *Les
Fâcheux*, the hero of which, like Alceste, confronts a succession of impertinents. Of these English precedents, Jonson's
Epicoene—the first comedy revived on the Restoration

stage—is the most interesting, because Manly's character is partly inspired by the melancholy humor of his counterpart in that comedy, Morose, "a gentleman that loves no noise," as indeed is that of Stanford of *The Sullen Lovers*. But the connection does not end there. Both Kynaston, who created the role of Manly's friend Freeman—the wrongly mistrusted counterpart of Philinte in *The Plain Dealer*—and Mrs. Knep, who created Eliza, Olivia's cousin in *The Plain Dealer* who corresponds to Eliante in *Le Misanthrope*, had earlier appeared with great success in *Epicoene*.

In his diary for 7 January 1660/61 Samuel Pepys records that

> Kinaston, the boy, had the good turn to appear in three shapes: first, as a poor woman in ordinary clothes, to please Morose; then in fine clothes as a gallant, and in them was clearly the prettiest woman in the whole house, and lastly as a man; and then likewise did appear the handsomest man in the house.[5]

But when Pepys saw *Epicoene* again in 1668, Mrs. Knep was the silent woman; and the relation of dramatic illusion to sexual reality on stage was reversed. The practice imported from France of using attractive actresses as *jeunes premières* instead of the boy actors of the pre-Commonwealth stage had become thoroughly established in both of the London theatres. This matters theatrically in qualifying Wycherley's literary debt to *Twelfth Night* for the role of Fidelia. The cast that revived *Twelfth Night* in 1668 is not known, but like Epicoene at that date Viola must have been played by an actress. The original idea of Viola was a role for a boy, in transvestite disguise only in the first and last scenes of the play. The role of Fidelia from the beginning is written for a woman disguised as a youth until the denouement. But she does bring with her from *Twelfth Night* an element of romantic comedy: her marriage with Manly, with all that such denouements imply in the way of reconciliation and regeneration. That denouement is fundamentally different from that of either *Epicoene*, in which Morose escapes mock marriage to the sterile quiet of continued celibacy, or *Le*

Misanthrope, in which Alceste and Célimène are too self-absorbed to be marriageable, in contrast with Philinte and Eliante, who come to terms with love and with each other.

Clearly then Wycherley is more a transformer of Molière than a translator or even imitator. The relationship of *The Plain Dealer* to *Le Misanthrope* is complicated by important debts to an intermediate adaptation or partial adaptation, *The Sullen Lovers;* to at least three major English Renaissance comedies; and by common sources of the French and English comic traditions: the Attic figure of Timon of Athens, Lucian, Erasmus, Ariosto, the *commedia dell'arte*, etc. The interdependence of such traditions, and the independence of great writers within them, can be illustrated by reference to a single passage already quoted from Chevreau's *L'Ecole du sage*, the mid-seventeenth-century translation and adaptation of Joseph Hall's *Characters* (1608). The character of vice relevant to *Le Misanthrope* is the Malcontent, denounced for turning admiration for the virtues of a distant time—a Golden Age in the remote past or posterity yet to come—into scorn for the here and now. For the Malcontent despises only the present. Whatever is, is wrong. He rejects what he has because he wants something else. He thinks he has done a favor in not refusing a gift, which can scarcely equal his merit; or if it does, it is despised as flattery, and so on. Not the whole character of Alceste, nor nothing but his character, but suggestive enough in the series of "Characterismes of Vices" evidently exploited by Molière to make the point that there is no such element of the Malcontent in Manly, though Wycherley likely knew something of Marston's play *The Malcontent* and/or Joseph Hall's *Characters.* Surely, Jonson's Morose and Shadwell's Stanford notwithstanding, Manly is not such a misanthropic malcontent as Alceste, and he was conceived more as a vehicle than as an object of satire, whereas Alceste must originally have been intended as both.

If Manly is comic, it is not for morose or sullen love, but for his blind infatuation with Olivia, an infatuation impervious to Freeman's arguments and to Fidelia's affection. The most obvious precedent for this blindness is Orgon's obsession with Tartuffe, whether suggested directly by *Tartuffe* itself or by Medbourne's adaptation, *The French Puritan* of 1670, and/or the possibly less significant intermediate adaptation by Shadwell. Like Tartuffe, Olivia and Vernish (as his name suggests) are double dealers. They affect piety. They attempt to appropriate the money and cabinet entrusted by Manly to Olivia, just as Tartuffe abuses the *cassette* and the home entrusted to him by Orgon. Moreover, they are exposed at the end of Act V by a test or a device in which Olivia embraces Manly instead of Fidelia, farce for which there must be many precedents, but which in the context of these serious comedies and other apparent debts to *Tartuffe* may well be reminiscent of the termination of the great table scene in Act IV of that comedy: roughly analogous comic devices differently elaborated. It could be argued that Wycherley's scene in the dark is more comparable in some ways with the exposure of Béline toward the close of *Le Malade imaginaire*, also designed to expose an imposture and to cure an obsession. This rather reinforces my impression of a conceptual (and not just a technical) continuity from *Tartuffe* to *The Plain Dealer*. It is not, I think, controversial that in *The Plain Dealer* Wycherley draws upon other reminiscences of Molière. Act II, scene 2, reflects *La Critique de l'Ecole des femmes*. Manly's confidences to Vernish in Act V show that the author of *The Country Wife* (effectively a *contaminatio* of *L'Ecole des maris* and *L'Ecole des femmes*, markedly altered in atmosphere and values) had not forgotten Horace's confidences to his rival in *L'Ecole des femmes*.

I would however stress the conceptual debt to *Tartuffe*. Though more diffuse, it seems to me important; and so far as I know it has not been analysed in criticism of Wycherley. "C'est un homme, entre nous, à mener par le nez," Tartuffe assures Elmire with regard to Orgon in Act IV, scene 5; and with respect to Manly, Vernish assures Olivia: "I'll lead the easy, honest fool by the nose as I used to do" (Act IV, scene 2). Not the only apparent echo of *Tartuffe* in the lines of *The Plain Dealer*, but the best one to focus the fact that (unlike *Le Misanthrope*) both of these plays are largely involved with the interrelation of duplicity with an obsession which blinds the dupe to the motives of the duper, a self-absorption which leads to deception through self-deception. In *Twelfth Night* the self-absorbed self-deception of Olivia, and Alceste's combination of narcissism and infatuation in *Le Misanthrope*, are psychologically and dramatically quite different. Witness Alceste's angry exchange with the *petits marquis* over Célimène's school for scandal in Act II, scene 5. Clitandre professes "Madame sans défaut." Acaste adds, "Mais les défauts qu'elle a ne frappent point ma vue." But Alceste rejoins, "Ils frappent tous la mienne. . . ." Alceste is malcontent with everyone, even with the woman he loves. But in *The Plain Dealer* Manly is more like the Orgon of *Tartuffe* in that he fails to recognize the sincerity of characters who cherish him and the double-dealing of parasites who deceive him. Manly, Alceste, and Orgon all display a violent streak in their self-righteousness. Orgon seems to have been treated more satirically than Manly, though that depends to some extent on details of how the roles were played which we do not fully know. However, both Orgon and Manly are in the end rallied round, after the scales drop from their eyes, to an ethic more civil than the rigorism earlier associated with their infatuations. Both seem to have compensated, through ill-chosen individuals, for a general disgust with and rejection of society. In this way too they both differ from Alceste, though at the denouement hope is still held out for his reconcilement. In short, while absorbing the resentments of Shakespeare's Timon, and the dislike of company of Jonson's Morose, Manly shows nothing of the Malcontent detectable in Alceste, who seeks out frivolous company and vents his spleen upon it. The relation of Manly to Molière's comedies is better understood as involving a *contaminatio* in characterization involving also the Orgon of *Tartuffe*, because both share an obsessive self-righteousness which blinds them to the activity of hypocrites who play upon it.

It seems all the stranger that Voltaire did not notice this connection, but instead wrote in the *Lettres philosophiques* that London was full of Timons, but not Tartuffes, and that the subject of *Tartuffe* had been attempted on the London stage, but could not succeed there. Perhaps as an imaginative writer he nevertheless felt the analogy between Manly and Orgon, because Dorfise, his Prude, is somewhat reminiscent of Mme Pernelle, the irate mother of Orgon in *Tartuffe*. *La Prude*, little studied and perhaps underrated, as Voltaire's theatre tends to be, deserves close scrutiny. In *The Plain Dealer* Wycherley had expanded Molière's eight characters (and three extras) in *Le Misanthrope* to a full dozen characters and a host of atmospheric extras. By way of contrast, *La Prude* has only eight characters, with Le Chevalier Mondor alone representing the four impertinents of *The Plain Dealer*. Voltaire also restores the French unities, especially that of place, lacking the London freedom to shift scenes from forestage to scene area and back which was part of the disposition and related conventions of the Restoration theatres. In naming his hero Blanford, one wonders, is there an echo of Shadwell's Stanford of *The Sullen Lovers?* (If so, it is not one Voltaire would be likely to have acknowledged, given the poor literary reputation of that playwright, who deserves better.) Perhaps the name Mondor was suggested by the Mondor of Pierre Cerou's *L'Amant auteur et valet*, a striking success at the Théâtre Italien in February 1740 when Voltaire was writing *La Prude* and a comedy of outstanding popularity in the eighteenth century: indeed the first comedy of any sort known to have been performed in French in the area which is now the United States of America.[6]

If we limit comparison to the heroes, it is fair to say that Blanford lacks some of the savor of Alceste and the saltiness of Manly, which is not surprising, since they represent supreme achievements in comic characterization. It is a measure of the difficulty of Voltaire's task in attempting originality in his readaptation that, if we did not know that Alceste was one of the models for Manly, we would hardly recognize Blanford as a descendent. It is well known that "Manly" Wycherley assumed the name of his character, as if to reaffirm his crusty worthiness. But this is nothing like the sea change which transformed interpretation of Molière's Misanthrope. Originally played by Molière, as already observed, Alceste was "plaisant, sans être trop ridicule." But by 1740 subsequent actors had further attenuated the comic, indeed burlesque, elements written into the role for Molière's own performances, stressing the aspirations toward sincerity at the expense of his misanthropy and making him into an altogether more sympathetic hero, whose "message"—rather than the implications of a self-absorbed and self-deceptive character—was taken seriously. It is the merit of Maurice Descotes to have pieced together elements in the handling of the role, first by Baron at widely different times in his life, and by Baron's early eighteenth-century successors: Dancourt, Quinault l'aîné and Quinault-Dufrêne, which confirm this shift in valuation.[7] It is perhaps not so well known that there is a parallel shift offstage in the valuation of the concept and term *Misanthrope*, reflected in the title of the new periodical launched in 1711 by Van Effen in imitation of *The Spectator* of Addison and Steele: *Le Misanthrope*, intended as a periodical, which had several editions. The word has come to suggest, not the enemy of mankind, but an observer, a spectator, a man whose contribution was his moral vision. Whether or not one considers that actors and journalists lead public opinion, or merely reflect and follow it, or more likely do both, it is possible to perceive a transformation in the valuation of the idea of the *Misanthrope* in France by the early eighteenth century.

That is not of course the only important change in the transformations from *Misanthrope* to *Plain Dealer* to *La Prude*, as the titles suggest. Voltaire's successor to Alceste and to Manly is less important in *La Prude* than Dorfise, the prude herself, a female Tartuffe, doubtless indebted to Wycherley's Olivia and to Arsinoé, but not so much that she fails to be a striking character in her own right. The wheel has come full circle, and this brings us back, as it were—I am not suggesting this intention on the part of Voltaire—, to an apparent source for *Tartuffe*, "La Tartufe" of the mid-seventeenth-illustrated *Proverbes* published by

Lagniet: a female hypocrite crudely anticipating Arsinoé, in the cruel tradition of "l'horrible vieille" with perhaps a distant echo of Celestina.[8] If Alceste seems to block reconversion of Manly into Blanford, so Tartuffe seems to inhibit the reconversion of Olivia into Dorfise. *Contaminatio* from *Tartuffe* remains an important element in the two transformations which lead from *Le Misanthrope* via *The Plain Dealer* back to *La Prude*, positive in the hands of Wycherley, strangely embarrassing for Voltaire, as *Le Misanthrope* in other ways also seems to be. In the shift of the satirical thrust from the self-absorbed, aggressive, and outspoken malice of the original Alceste, object as well as vehicle of satire, to the satire of a woman's possessive hypocrisy in *La Prude*, the pivot on which the transformation turns is *The Plain Dealer*: not just Manly himself, but his relation to Vernish and especially to Olivia.

Notes

Notes to Chapter 1

1. A. Adam, *Histoire de la littérature francaise au XVIIe siècle*, 5 vols. (Paris: Domat, 1952), 3:383.
2. Molière, Œuvres, ed. E. Despois, 13 vols. (Paris: Hatchette, 1873), 1:381.
3. V. Pandolfi, *La Commedia dell'arte, storia e testo*, 6 vols. (Florence: Sansoni, 1651), vol. 5: *Gli Sdegni amorosi* of S. Frandaglia dal Val di Sturla, in the Fonds Coquebert de Montbret, p. 301; *Sdegni amorosi*, in the Scenari of the Correr Museum, Venice, p. 315; and *Sdegni amorosi* in the Scenari copied by Antonio Passanti for Count Casamarciano in 1700 and preserved in the Biblioteca Nazionale, Naples, p. 329.
4. *Dialogue de "Mépris et Paix,"* in G. Attinger, *L'Esprit de la Commedia dell'arte dans le théâtre français*, Publications de la Société d'histoire du théâtre (Neuchâtel: Librairie théâtrale, 1950), pp. 54–56.
5. C. Mic, quoted by Attinger, *L'Esprit de la Commedia*, p. 56.
6. La Rochefoucauld, *Maximes*, ed. J. Truchet (Paris: Garnier, 1967), p. 84 (1678 ed., no. 353). A number of other *maximes* offer pertinent analyses, which I will resist the temptation to quote: ed. cit., nos. 111, 163, 262, 263, 295, 326, 330. . . .
7. P. Nicole, *Traité de la comédie*, ed. G. Couton (Paris: Les Belles Lettres, 1961), pp. 42–43.
8. Cf. Nicole, *Traité*, ch. 2, p. 42: "la Comedie par sa nature même est une école & un exercice de vice, puis qu'elle oblige necessairement à exciter en soi-même des passions vicieuses."
9. Molière, *Le Bourgeois Gentilhomme*, ed. H. G. Hall (London: University of London Press, 1966), p. 42.

Notes to Chapter 2

1. Kant, *Critique of Judgment*, trans. J. H. Bernard (New York: Hafner, 1951), p. 176, quoted by M. C. Swabey, *Comic Laughter* (New Haven: Yale University Press, 1961), pp. 10–11.
2. J. Arnavon, *Notes sur l'interprétation de Molière* (Paris: Plon, 1930) and G. Michaut, *Les Luttes de Molière* (Paris: Hachette, 1925) in which the statement is made that in *Dom Juan* Molière introduces "de parti-pris, et pour ainsi dire de force, des lazzi, des couplets . . . ," p. 152; R. Bray, *Molière, homme de théâtre*, (Paris: Mercure de France, 1954). I have noted a polemical exaggeration of Bray's position, which, stated more moderately, is that "l'intention de Molière, la pensée qui donne à son œuvre la force et l'unité, ce n'est pas une pensée de moraliste, c'est une intention d'artiste," p. 36.
3. *L'Esprit créateur*, 6 (1966): 137–44.
4. For the probable attributions to Donneau de Visé of the *Lettre*, and its reliability in expressing views sympathetic to Molière and his milieu, see W. G. Moore, art. cit., and R. Robert, "Des Commentaires de première main sur les chefs-d'œuvre les plus discutés de Molière," *Revue des Sciences Humaines*, 21 (1956): 19–53.
5. Art. cit., p. 141.
6. Ibid., p. 142.
7. Moore, art. cit., p. 143.
8. For the background of this assertion see "The Literary Context of *Le Misanthrope*," chapter 11.
9. Quoted in R. Wellek and A. Warren, *Theory of Literature*, 3rd ed. (New York: Harcourt, Brace and World, 1956), p. 187. Cf. I. A. Richards: "What gives an image efficacy is less its vividness as an image than its character as a mental event peculiarly connected with sensation" (quoted ibid.).
10. *Traduction de l'Énéide de Virgile* (Paris: 1668; rpt. Amsterdam, 1700), p. 21.

11. Page references are to the text of the *Lettre* as published in Molière, *Œuvres*, vol. 4, ed. Despois and Mesnard (Paris: Hachette, 1878).

12. H. Munro, *The Argument of Laughter* (Melbourne: Melbourne University Press, 1951); C. Mauron, *Psychocritique du genre comique* (Paris: Corti, 1964).

13. Cf. his edition of *Tartuffe* and *Le Médecin malgré lui* (New York: Dell, 1962), p. 18.

14. Molière may not have known Cahaignes's *L'Avaricieux* (1580; modern edition by A. Gasté, Rouen, 1899). But a recent study of Larivey's *Les Esprits* suggests that this author prepares the way for Molière "a descrivere l'avarizia come un irremediabile attaccamento morboso, una passione profonda, non solo ridicola, ma anche penosa" (L. Petroni, "Traduzione e aspetti originali negli *Esprits* di Pierre de Larivey," *Atti dell'Accademia delle Scienze dell'Istituto di Bologna*, Classe di Scienze Morali, Memorie, 51–52 (1963–4): 31).

15. Ed. cit., p. 426.

16. (Berkeley and Los Angeles: University of California Press, 1962), p. 261.

17. *Le Malade imaginaire de Molière* (Paris: Plon, 1938), pp. 329ff.

18. "From Myth to Ideas—and Back," in *Ideas in the Drama*, ed. J. Gassner (New York: Columbia University Press, 1964), p. 63.

Notes to Chapter 3

1. Agne Beijer, "Une maquette de décor récemment retrouvée pour le 'Ballet de la Prospérité des armes de la France' dansé à Paris, le 7 février 1641. Etude sur la mise en scène au Grand Théâtre du Palais Cardinal avant l'arrivée de Torelli," *Le Lieu théâtral à la Renaissance* (Paris: Centre national de la recherche scientifique, 1963), p. 379.

2. C'est une attribution que nous développons dans une communication intitulée "*Europe*, allégorie théâtrale de propagande politique", qui éclaircit le rôle original joué dans le développement des divertissements de cour par Jean Desmarets, devenu plus tard Sieur de Saint-Sorlin (Colloque international du CNRS sur le Mécénat en France avant Colbert, 1598–1661, Paris, mars 1983, sous presse).

3. Rapprochement dû à John Varey dans une communication, "Plays for Great Occasions : the Relationship of Audience and Play at the Spanish Court" (Conference on Courts and Theatres of the Late Renaissance : England and Spain, University of Warwick, England, 12 March 1983).

4. Voir notre édition critique de cette pièce peu littéraire parue dans *Australian Journal of French Studies*, 9 (1972): 117–47, et l'étude plus récente de Harold C. Knutson, "Comedy as a 'School': The Beginnings of a Title Form," parue dans la même revue, 20 (1983): 3–14.

5. Voir à ce sujet notre article, "The Present State of Molière Studies," dans R. Johnson, Jr., Guy T. Trail, et Editha Neuman, eds., *Molière and the Commonwealth of Letters* (Jackson, Miss.: University Press of Mississippi, 1975), pp. 728–46.

6. C. E. J. Caldicott, "Observations supplémentaires sur l'histoire du Théâtre de l'Hôtel de Bourgogne," *Revue d'histoire du théâtre* 25 (1973), 1:241.

7. E. Gherardi, *Le Théâtre italien*, 6 vols., (Paris: 1741), 1:339. Notons qu'on localise cette anecdote à Rome. Il ne faut donc pas exagérer l'importance du fait que Scaramouche devait jouer à Paris devant un public qui ne parlait pas sa langue maternelle. Ce n'était pas le cas de Molière, et ce n'était pas non plus le cas de James Nokes, dont le jeu dans *Sir Martin Mar-All* (comédie de Dryden adaptée de *l'Etourdi* de Molière et de *l'Amant indiscret* de Quinault) à partir de 1667 ressemblait fort à celui de Scaramouche et de Molière, à en juger d'après le témoignage très connu de Colley Cibber (Nokes jouait l'étourdi) : ". . . he would shut up his mouth with a dumb studious pout, and roll his full eye into such a vacant amazement, such a palpable ignorance of what to think of it, that his silent perplexity (which would sometimes hold him several minutes) gave your imagination as full content

as the most absurd thing he could say upon it. . . . . I have seen him make with his looks (while the house has been in one continued roar for several minutes) before he could prevail with his courage to speak a word to [his servant]. . . ." (*An Apology for the Life of Mr. Colley Cibber*, cit. H. T. Swedenberg, Jr., et al, éd., *The Works of John Dryden* [Berkeley et Los Angeles, 1966] 9:353).

Le texte de *Sir Martin Mar-All* représente bien une influence de l'Italie sur la culture anglaise à travers la médiation de trois poètes français (car Voiture fournit quelques chansons). En serait-il de même du jeu de James Nokes? Ou est-ce un effet du hasard? En tout cas c'est bien le jeu de Nokes qui explique le déplacement du centre dramatique de la comédie du rôle du valet vers celui de l'amant étourdi.

8. *La Querelle de l'Ecole des femmes*, 1:57–58.

9. Citons Dorine, "Et cette large barbe au milieu du visage," *Tartuffe*, acte 2, sc. 2, v. 473; la phrase "un beau vieillard avec une barbe majestueuse" dans *l'Avare* (acte 2, sc. 5) est moins révélatrice. . . .

10. J. Duvignaud, *L'Acteur. Esquisse d'une sociologie du comédien* (Paris, 1965), pp. 61 seqq.

11. Il est curieux que dans sa relation d'une *représentation* de cette comédie-ballet La Fontaine écrive que Moliére "allait ramener en France / Le bon goût et l'air de Térence," réflexion suivie du vers : "Plaute n'est plus qu'un plat bouffon". Car les comédies de Plaute (bien plus que celles de Térence) étaient mêlées de musique et de danse. Ce vers est une raison de plus pour écarter le jugement hâtif que Molière eût appris de Scaramouche la bouffonnerie. Mais on peut se demander si, s'agissant d'une représentation, "l'air de Térence" ne comprend pas un élément supposé des représentations originales—un jeu sans masques qui met en valeur les visages, comme le nouveau jeu de Molière (auquel cas le mot "autrefois" des vers précédents renverrait non pas aux *Précieuses ridicules*, mais à *Sganarelle*). Nous n'en savons rien. Mais il est piquant de constater que les vers de *Phormio* qui soulèvent la question, 210 seqq., ont pu inspirer—à travers Horace, *Satires*, II, 3, vv. 316 seqq. le dialogue de la fable "La Grenouille qui se veut faire aussi grosse que le boeuf" (I, 3). W. Beare, *The Roman Stage*, 3e éd. (London, 1964), p. 307, conclut que les références "to facial expression . . . must have been directed to the imagination of spectators, aided by the tones and gestures of the actors. . . ." Mais le nouveau jeu de Molière a bien pu rappeler à l'imagination de La Fontaine un passage de *Phormio* dont le fabuliste s'est vraisemblablement souvenu un peu plus tard. . . .

Notes to Chapter 4

1. *Le Bourgeois Gentilhomme* (London: University of London Press, 1966); *Les Femmes savantes* (Oxford, Oxford University Press, 1974). L'orthographe de ces éditions a dû être modernisée.

2. "The Present State of Molière Studies," dans Roger Johnson, Jr., Guy T. Trail, et Editha Neumann, eds., *Molière and the Commonwealth of Letters* (Jackson, Miss.: University Press of Mississippi, 1975), pp. 734–37.

3. J. T. Stoker, éd., *Les Fourberies de Scapin* (London: University of London Press, 1971), pp. 18–19; M. Cuénin, éd., *Les Précieuses ridicules* (Genève : Droz/ Paris, Minard, 1973).

4. Tel mon regretté maître W. G. Moore, dans sa présentation de la collection "Studies in French literature," avant-propos de son *Racine : Britannicus*, (Londres: Arnold, 1960). Alvin Eustis parle des "rythmes laborieux" des *Femmes savantes*, qu'il cite d'après l'éd. Jouanny (Classiques Garnier) (*Molière as Ironic Contemplator* [La Haye, Mouton, 1973], p. 112); Jean Emelina établit même un tableau des interjections et des interrogatives dans *Amphitryon*, apparemment à partir de cette même édition. (*Les Valets et les servantes dans le théâtre comique en France de 1610 à 1700* [C.E.L.—P.U.G., 1975], p. 267).

5. Fredson Bowers, *Textual and Literary Criticism* (Cambridge, 1959), pp. 125–26.

6. M. Descotes, *Les Grands Rôles du théâtre de Molière* (Paris, 1960), pp. 152 seqq.

7. Il est vrai que Despois et Mesnard suppriment aussi les virgules de l'hémistiche de Tartuffe : "Cela certe est fâcheux." M. Couton fait imprimer *certes* avec *s* et sans virgules : "Cela certes est fâcheux." La modernisation même de l'orthographe ne va pas sans problèmes concernant le rythme des vers. *Certe* virgulé fait sans doute partie de la feinte onction du personnage.

8. On peut comparer la ponctuation du rôle du Maître de Philosophie avec celui encore de l'Apothicaire de *Monsieur de Pourceaugnac*, dont l'originale fut publiée par Ribou en 1670. L'Apothicaire, impatient, doit parler rapidement, sans réflexion, comme le suggèrent tant la ponctuation que le mot *vistement* de cette réplique de l'Acte I, scène 5 : "Cela est vray, à quoy bon tant baraguigner & tant tourner au tour du pot ? il faut sçauoir vistement le cours *(sic)* ou le long d'vne maladie" (p. 36). Pas de virgule avant &, ni à la page suivante : "il les traite & gouuerne à sa fantaisie. . . ."

9. A. J. Guibert, *Bibliographies des Oeuvres de Molière publiées au XVIIe siècle* (Paris, 1977), 1: 187.

10. Voir "The Literary Context of *Le Misanthrope*," (Chapitre 11).

Notes to Chapter 5

1. Molière's wordplay is, however, cleverly analysed by Alvin Eustis, who points to "puns and gag lines, paradoxes and epigrams, understatements and hyperboles, racy expression and word deformations" which fit the "Bergsonian category of the comic of words, since they are 'created by language.'" Not entirely by language, I would argue, but well put in a sparkling chapter on "Verbal Irony and Author's Irony" in his *Molière as Ironic Contemplator* (The Hague: Mouton, 1973), p. 21. J. H. Périvier, "Equivoques moliéresques: le sonnet de Trissotin" (*Revue des sciences humaines*, 38 [1973], pp. 543–54) brings out the erotic ambiguities of the sonnet and other lines of *Les Femmes savantes*.

2. Molière, *Oeuvres complètes*, ed. Georges Couton, 2 vols. (Paris: Gallimard, 1971) 2:1461–62.

3. See the edition by A. Gill: *Les Ramonneurs* (Paris: STFM, 1957).

4. Dorimond, *L'Escole des cocus, ou la precaution inutille*, ed. H. G. Hall, *Australian Journal of French Studies* 9 (1972):135–36.

5. See R. A. Weigert, "En marge des *Proverbes* de Lagniet," *Gazette des Beaux-Arts*, Sept. 1967, p. 177.

6. See Jacqueline Plantié, "Molière et François de Sales," *Revue d'histoire littéraire de la France* 72 (1972):902–27.

Notes to Chapter 6

1. Maurice Raynaud, *Les Médecins au temps de Molière* (Paris, 1862); François Millepierres, *La Vie quotidienne des médecins au temps de Molière* (Paris: Hachette, 1964); *Molière et la médecine de son temps*, (Centre méridional de rencontres sur le 17ᵉ siècle, 3ᵉ colloque de Marseille, *Marseille*, 1973, no. 95:105–95. See also John Cairncross, "Impie en médecine", *Cahiers de l'Association internationale des études françaises*, 1964, no. 16:269–84, discussed by Jacques Roger, pp. 301–03.

2. R. H. Shryock, *The Development of Modern Medicine* (New York: Knopf, 1947); Jules Guiart, *Histoire de la médecine française* (Paris: Nagel, 1947); J. Lévy-Valensi, *La Médecine et les médecins au XVIIᵉ siècle*, (Paris: Baillère, 1933); René Taton, ed., *Histoire générale des sciences*, vol. 2 : *La Science moderne (de 1450 à 1800)* (Paris: PUF, 1958): contains Emile Guyénot, "Biologie humaine et animale (au xviiᵉ siècle)", pp. 355–77, and "Médecine (au xviiᵉ siècle)," pp. 378–95.

3. Jean Riolan, *Manuel anatomique et pathologique*, new ed. (Lyons, 1682); Guy Patin, *Lettres*, ed. J.-H. Reveillé-Parise, 3 vols. (Paris, 1846). On Patin see also

Pierre Pic, *Guy Patin* (Paris, 1911), and Jacques Roger, "L'Univers médical de Guy Patin," in *Mélanges de littérature française offerts à Monsieur René Pintard* (Paris: Klincksieck, 1975), pp. 91–101. My primary sources also include Philibert Guybert, *Toutes les oeuvres charitables*, rev. ed. (Rouen, 1645).

4. Elizabeth W. Marvick, "The Character of Louis XIII: the Role of his Physician," *Journal of Interdisciplinary Studies* 4 (1974):347–74.

5. C. D. O'Malley, "The Medical History of Louis XIV: Intimations of Mortality," in John C. Rule, ed., *Louis XIV and the Craft of Kingship* (Columbus, Ohio: Ohio State University Press, 1969), pp. 148–50.

6. Molière, *Oeuvres complètes*, ed. Georges Couton, 2 vols. (Paris: Gallimard, 1971), 2:91–92.

7. A. J. Guibert, *Le Docteur amoureux. Comédie du XVIIᵉ siècle*, (Geneva: Droz [TLF, 91], 1960). See also P. Lerat, ed., *Le Docteur amoureux* (Paris: Nizet, 1973), with reviews of the former by A. Gill in *French Studies* 15 (1961): 54–57, and of the latter by G. Couton in *Studi Francesi* 19 (1975): 304–07.

8. Allardyce Nicoll, *The World of Harlequin* (Cambridge, England: Cambridge University Press, 1963), pp. 55–60.

9. See Robert W. Lowe, "Marc-Antoine Charpentier, compositeur chez Molière," *Etudes classiques*, 33 (1965): 34–41.

10. The dismissive mention of doctors in *L'Avare*, act I, scene 5, in which Valère doubts they can tell a feigned illness from a real one ("Y connaissent-ils quelque chose?"), is hardly an exception, that part of *L'Avare* is such a mixture of novelistic fantasy and farce. Once again Molière introduces a touch of medical satire into a dramatic subject which came to him without it.

11. M. Jurgens and E. Maxfield-Miller, continuation of their *Cent ans de recherches sur Molière* (Paris: Imprimerie Nationale, 1963) in *Revue d'histoire du théâtre*, 24, no. 4 (1972): 363–65.

12. Molière, *Le Malade imaginaire*, ed. Peter Nurse (London: Oxford University Press, 1965), pp. 12ff.

Notes to Chapter 7

1. Cioranescu also lists a dozen translations of different works of Joseph Hall published in French in Geneva by Théodore Jaquemot between 1626 and 1662, including a treatise with the appealing title: *Comparaison du pharisaïsme et christianisme* (1628).

2. Daniel Mornet noticed *L'École du sage* in connection with Molière: "Un prototype de *Tartuffe*," in *Mélanges E. Huguet* (Paris, 1940), pp. 308–12 (Cioranescu no. 19241).

3. Thus Erich Auerbach: "He [Tartuffe] plays his part execrably by exaggerating it beyond all reason. . . ." (*Mimesis*, trans. W. Trask, New York: Doubleday Anchor Books, 1957), p. 317, and Georges Mongrédien: "Il est incontestable que son faux dévot [La Bruyère's *Onuphre*] est mieux réussi, du point de vue purement psychologique, que le *Tartuffe* de l'auteur dramatique" (Idem, ed., La Bruyère, *Les Caractères* [Paris: Classiques Garnier, 1954], p. xiii).

4. That Molière was familiar with the word *caractère* in the sense of 'polemical portrait' is suggested by Dorante's line in *La Critique* (scene 5): "Je dirai que cela est digne du caractère qu'elle a pris; et qu'il y a des personnes qui se rendent ridicules, pour vouloir avoir trop d'honneur." Molière is quoted throughout from the new Pléiade edition, *Œuvres complètes*, ed. Georges Couton, 2 vols. (Paris: Gallimard, 1971).

5. Thus Jacques Guicharnaud: "Unlike Tartuffe, Orgon is not a hypocrite. He is sincerely devout." (Idem, ed., Molière, *Le Tartuffe* and *Le Médecin malgré lui* [New York: Dell, 1962], p. 20), and Raymond Giraud: "It [*Tartuffe*] portrays the helplessness of a good man victimised by a clever scoundrel' (*Encyclopedia Americana*, 1971 edition, s.v. "*Tartuffe*").

6. *La Guide des pécheurs*, composée en espagnol par le R. P. Louis de Grenade, de l'ordre de S. Dominique, traduite de nouveau en françois par Mr Girard, Conseiller du Roy en ses Conseils, Nouv. ed., reveuë & corrigée (Paris: 1668), pp. 726–27.

7. Saint-Évremond, *Œuvres en prose*, ed. R. Ternois, 4 vols. (Paris: STFM, 1962–69), 2:147.

8. Mircea Eliade, *Le Sacré et le profane* (Paris: Gallimard, 1965), p. 175. I would not like what is archetypal and indeed mythical in Molière (the aspect of his creativity which makes his plays infinitely reinterpretable) to obscure what is specific and historical.

9. Donneau de Visé, quoted from E. Lop and A. Sauvage, eds., Molière, *Le Misanthrope* (Paris: Edns. Sociales, 1963), p. 212.

10. For instance, Sganarelle replies, ". . . et vous parlez tout comme un livre," after Dom Juan's famous apology for change in Act I, scene 2. Ivan Barko has found the book, details of which (*RHLF*, 74, 1974) will help to show how Molière adapts a supplementary source to his subject, puts in his character's mouth a current (but not necessarily his own) line of argument, and makes an "in" joke while calling attention to the literary inspiration of his comic character.

11. W. G. Moore, "Molière et la sottise," in *Kentucky Romance Quarterly* 17 (1970): 335–43.

12. Gomberville, *La Doctrine des mœurs tirée de la philosophie des stoïques*, représentée en cent tableaux et expliquée en cent discours pour l'instruction de la jeunesse (Paris, 1646), dedicated to Louis XIV, but with letters also to the Prime Minister Cardinal Mazarin and to the Queen Regent Anne of Austria, reprinted a number of times in the last third of the seventeenth century. There is much interest in this book with a preliminary sonnet by Tristan L'Hermite, the first playwright staged by Molière's Illustre Théâtre: the allegorical Virtue who reminds the king that royalty is worth little without virtue, the parallel of miser and prodigal (fol. 9), the perfective role of love ("L'homme est né pour aymer. . . ," fol. 21; 'En aimant on se rend parfait," fol. 22), etc.

13. M. Michel Aumont, in *La Troupe du roi*, a spectacle by P.-E. Deiber incorporating elements from *L'Avare* and some fifteen other plays, at the opening of "Un Chapiteau pour Molière" in the Tuileries, December 1972.

Notes to Chapter 8

1. See Georges Mongrédien, ed., *La Querelle de l'Ecole des femmes, comédies de Jean Donneau de Visé, Edme Boursault, Charles Robinet, A. J. Montfleury, Jean Chevalier, Philippe de La Croix*, 2 vols. (Paris: STFM, 1971).

2. Molière, *L'Ecole des femmes* and *La Critique de l'Ecole des femmes*, ed. W. D. Howarth (Oxford: Blackwell, 1963), p. xii.

3. Raymond Picard, "Molière comique ou tragique? le cas Arnolphe," *Revue d'histoire littéraire de la France* 72 (1972): 69–85.

4. Some of the following points are adapted from my article on "Scarron and the Travesty of Vergil," *Yale French Studies* 38 (1967): *The Classical Line: Essays in Honor of Henri Peyre*, 115–27.

5. Géruzez, quoted by Victor Fournel, "Du burlesque en France," in his edition of Scarron's *Le Virgile travesti* (Paris, 1858), p. x.

6. D'Urfé, *L'Astrée*, Deuxième Partie, (Paris, 1616), pp. 569ff. These "loix d'amour" are given to Céladon, a faithful shepherd, by the Druid Adamas and are quoted from *L'Astrée*, ed. Maurice Magendie (Paris, 1928), pp. 161–63.

7. See Franco Simone, *The French Renaissance* (London: Macmillan and New York: St. Martin's Press, 1970), pp. 198–206. Something of this Renaissance tradition continued evidently into Molière's time. The Griselda parody begins as early as Arnolphe's explanation to Chrysalde in the first scene: "Choisir une moitié qui tienne tout de moi, / Et de qui la soumise et pleine dépendance / N'ait à me

reprocher aucun bien ni naissance" (ll. 126–28), which may be compared with Alceste's wish to see Célimène in a similar position, in *Le Misanthrope*, act 4, sc. 3, lines 1424ff.

8. *Oxford Book of Medieval Latin Verse*, p. 23.

9. Racan, *Poésies*, ed. Louis Arnould (Paris: STFM 1930), 1:9.

10. Du Perron, quoted by Odette de Mourgues, *Metaphysical, Baroque and Précieux Poetry* (Oxford: Clarendon Press, 1953), p. 63.

Notes to Chapter 9

1. Cf. notably H. P. Salomon, *Tartuffe devant l'opinion française* (Paris: Presses universitaires de France, 1962); Jacques Scherer, *Structures de Tartuffe* (Paris: SEDES, 1966); and Molière, *Œuvres complètes*, ed. Georges Couton, 2 vols. (Paris: Gallimard, 1971). The "Background" chapter in my own *Molière: Tartuffe*, "Studies in French Literature," 2 (London: Edward Arnold, 1960; New York: Barrons, 1962), is best read in the revised form for the 1976 and later reprints.

2. Saint-Amant, *Œuvres* (Paris, 1661), p. 190. Italics ours. Spelling modernized in this and later quotations from seventeenth-century editions in this chapter.

3. Molière, *Le Tartuffe* and *Le Médecin malgré lui*, ed. Jacques Guicharnaud (New York, Dell, 1962), p. 18.

4. Jacques Birnberg, review of Rachmael Brandwajn, *Twarz i Maska* (Warsaw, 1965), *Studi Francesi*, 1970, no. 41:304.

5. Du Bosc, *L'Honnête Femme*, 3 vols., (Paris, 1636; rpt. Rouen, 1643), 3:113.

6. For an expert and richly illustrated evocation of this strange but exciting production, see Tadeusz Kowzan, "*Le Tartuffe* de Molière dans une mise en scène de Roger Planchon," in *Les Voies de la création théâtrale*, vol. 6 (1978), pp. 279–340.

7. Cf. Bernard Dupriez, "Tartuffe et la sincérité," *Etudes françaises*, vol. 1, no. 1 (1965).

8. Gabrielle de Coignard, *Œuvres chrétiennes* (Paris, 1595), sonnet 3, p. 10.

9. Jacques Scherer, *Structures de Tartuffe*, p. 159.

10. Cf. A. H. T. Levi, "The Neoplatonist Calculus," in Idem, ed., *Humanism in France* (Manchester, England: Manchester University Press; New York: Barnes and Noble, 1970), p. 238.

11. Cf. Fleuret and Perceau, eds., *Le Cabinet satirique*, 2 vols. (Paris, 1924). For example, the epigram and quatrains "Sur les femmes qui montrent leur sein," 2:339, or Guillaume Le Breton's "Stances sur la défense des gorges découvertes," 1:85–88.

12. (London: Oxford University Press, 1974), pp. 58–61.

13. J. L. Kasparek, *Molière's "Tartuffe" and the Traditions of Roman Satire*, Studies in the Romance Languages and Literature, no. 175 (Chapel Hill, North Carolina: University of North Carolina, 1977).

14. In her *Astraea, the Imperial Theme in the Sixteenth Century* (London and Boston: Routledge and Kegan Paul, 1975); first published in *Journal of the Warburg and Courtaluld Institutes* 10 (1947).

Notes to Chapter 10

1. It is common practice to preserve the spelling *Dom Juan* when referring to Molière's character and play, while using the English form *Don* to refer to the legend, to which one can find a convenient introduction in R. Grimsley, "The Don Juan Legend," in *Modern Languages* 41 (1960): 135–41.

2. René Pintard, "Temps et lieux dans le *Dom Juan* de Molière," in *Studi in onore di Italo Siciliano* (Florence, Olschki, 1966), 2:997–1006. It would be proper to acknowledge here also a general debt in this commentary to the well-known books

on Molière by R. Fernandez, W. G. Moore, D. Romano, M. Descotes, and J. Guicharnaud.

3. M. Jurgens and E. Maxfield-Miller, *Cent ans de recherches sur Molière* (Paris, Imprimerie Nationale, 1963), p. 399.

4. Saint-Simon, *Mémoires*, ed. G. Truc, vol. 4 (Paris, Gallimard, 1953), p. 1005.

5. The theatrical fantasy is based on the doctor's black assembly gown and may involve satire of provincial practice. Except at official gatherings (and perhaps in the provinces?), writes François Millepierres, ". . . à la ville, [le médecin] s'habille à peu près comme tout le monde, selon la mode, avec discrétion cependant, sans y mettre de fantaisie outrée" (*La Vie quotidienne des médecins au temps de Molière* [Paris, Hachette, 1964], pp. 40–41).

6. Quoted in John Lough, *An Introduction to Seventeenth-Century France* (1954; rpt. London: Longmans, 1966).

7. Raoul Allier, *La Cabale des dévots, 1627–66* (Paris: Colin, 1902), p. 416.

8. It is as well to remember, however, that in the generation preceding the Revocation of the Edict of Nantes in 1685, it was government policy in France to buy consciences (the conversion of Huguenots). As an illustration of the word *pistole* in his *Dictionnaire*, Littré cites from the correspondence of Colbert the observation that "le nombre de ceux qui se convertissent ici (à Rochefort) est très-grand, et il est arrivé fort souvent de rendre catholiques des familles entières pour une pistole"—just half the amount which Dom Juan offers to Le Pauvre.

9. N. Faret, *L'Honnête Homme, ou l'art de plaire à la Cour* (Paris: Nicolas et Jean de la Coste, 1639), p. 56.

10. Comic treatment of religious questions in this play offended not only those who considered the theatre as a whole a wicked waste of time and those who thought playwrights should not touch upon any religious subject, but also those who, while accepting the theatre in principle and even religious themes reverently handled, objected to their comic presentation.

11. "Il observera particulièrement de n'attaquer jamais de ses brocards . . . les misérables. . . . Pource que l'inclination naturelle qu'ont presque tous les hommes à se laisser toucher de pitié des pressantes calamités dont ils voient ces malheureuses gens affligés, empêche qu'on ne puisse rire d'eux . . ." (Faret, p. 173). My argument is that Molière's polyvalent satire liberates the spectator from the anxiety diagnosed by Faret.

12. Molière, *Oeuvres*, ed. Despois and Mesnard (Paris: Hachette, 1873–93), 5:231.

13. The case for a comic Dom Juan is argued by R. Laufer, "Le Comique du personnage de Dom Juan," in *Modern Lang. Review* 43 (1963): 15–20.

14. Molière remarks in the first scene of *L'Impromptu de Versailles:* "Le marquis aujourd'hui est le plaisant de la comédie . . . dans toutes nos pièces de maintenant il faut toujours un marquis ridicule qui divertisse la compagnie."

15. Rochemont complains that Dom Juan's punishment is only "un foudre imaginaire et aussi ridicule que celui de Jupiter . . . et qui, bien loin de donner de la crainte aux hommes, ne pouvait pas chasser une mouche ni faire peur à une souris," a point not satisfactorily answered in the *Réponse aux Observations* (Molière, *Oeuvres*, ed. cit., pp. 227, 234, etc.).

16. Louis XIV, quoted ibid., 5:246.

Notes to Chapter 11

1. P. Bourdat, *Une Source cornélienne du "Misanthrope": "La Veuve,"* L'Information littéraire, vol. 20, no. 2 (1968), pp. 129. Lines from *La Veuve*, Act 3, sc. 2, are cited as a source for *Le Misanthrope*, act 1, sc. 1.

2. See also *Alceste et l'absolutisme* (Paris: Galilée, 1977), especially the paper by J.-P. Vincent, "Lire en 1666," pp. 127–30.

3. H. C. Lancaster, *A History of French Dramatic Literature in the Seventeenth Century*, Part I, vol. 1 (Baltimore: Johns Hopkins University Press, 1929), pp. 268–69.

4. Alceste—son of the King of Cilicia—is the name of a character in an episode of F. H. de Molière d'Essertines' novel *La Polyxène* (1623), books 2 and 3. In this connection, the title of Des Escuteaux' novel *Les Admirables Faits d'armes d'Alceste servant l'infidèle Lydie* (Saumur, 1613) is suggestive in a way that the title given by Rudler (doubtless a faulty transcription) is not: *Le Fils d'Alceste* (of which I find no other evidence), ed. cit., p. 69.

5. M. Descotes, *Les Grands Rôles du théâtre de Molière* (Paris: Presses Universitaires de France, 1960), p. 95.

6. Mairet, *La Sophonisbe*, ed. C. Dédéyan (Paris: Droz, S.T.F.M., 1945), lines 55ff.

7. *Annales Dramatiques* (1811), quoted in Voltaire, *Œuvres complètes*, ed. Moland, *Théâtre* (1877), 6:32.

8. *Les Morales de Plutarque [,] Seneque, Socrate, et Epictete* (Paris: Sommaville, 1659). There were several editions of this book, attributed by Tchemerzine and the Bibliothèque Nationale to Desmarets de Saint-Sorlin, but probably compiled by Cardinal Alphonse de Richelieu and originally published in a different form and with a somewhat different title at the Château de Richelieu in 1653.

9. La Rochefoucauld, *Maximes*, 1666 ed., no. 231, from *Maximes*, ed. J. Truchet (Paris: Garnier, 1967). M. Truchet suggests a relation between La Rochefoucauld's *Maxime*—which is also reminiscent of Gracián—and the indicated lines of *Le Misanthrope*, p. 59.

10. Cf. Adam's brilliant remark on Sganarelle of *Le Cocu imaginaire:* "Il exprime par la parole et *par la mimique* ses colères impuissantes et refoulées, ses humiliations rageuses, sa lâcheté" (*Histoire*, 3:267, our italics).

11. F. Maynard, *Poésies*, ed. F. Gohin (Paris: Garnier, 1927). Lop and Sauvage are of course right to note against Alceste's first mention of 'désert' a remark in Furetière's *Dictionnaire* (1694) to the effect that the word is used "en contresens d'un homme, qui, aimant la solitude, se fait bâtir quelque jolie maison, hors des grands chemins et éloignée du commerce des hommes pour s'y retirer" (ed. cit., p. 118). In the poetic tradition evoked, we could cite also Racan's famous *Stances sur la retraite*, especially the fifteenth:

> Agréables deserts, séjour de l'innocence,
> où loin des vanités, de la magnificence,
> commence mon repos et finit mon tourment;
> vallons, fleuves, rochers, plaisante solitude,
> si vous fûtes témoins de mon inquiétude,
> soyez-le désormais de mon contentement.

(cited from L. Arnould, *Un Gentilhomme des Lettres au XVIIᵉ siècle: Honorat de Bueil, Seigneur de Racan*, nouvelle éd. [Paris, 1901], pp. 116–17). It is striking to note from the opening *stance* that the Thirsis whom he invites to return to such a pastoral setting is no longer twenty:

> Thirsis, il faut penser à faire la retraite:
> la course de nos jours est plus qu'à moitié faite (p. 114).

12. Bussy-Rabutin, "Epigrammes choisies de Martial", in *Histoire amoureuse des Gaules*, ed. A. Poitevain, 2nd ed. (Paris: Delahays, 1857), 1:260.

13. Sarasin, quoted from *Les Précieux et les Précieuses*, ed. G. Mongredien (Paris: Mercure de France, 1963), pp. 159–60.

14. D. Dalla Valle, *De Théophile a Molière: aspectos de una continuidad*, Santiago de Chile, "El Espejo de Papel," Cuadernos del Centro de Investigaciones de Literatura Comparada, (Universidad de Chile, 1968), 2:84.

15. Bouhours, quoted by Ménage, *Observations sur la langue françoise*, seconde partie (Paris, 1976), p. 15.

Part II

16. "Lettre sur la comédie du *Misanthrope*," quoted from E. Lop and A. Sauvage, eds., Molière, *Le Misanthrope*, p. 212.

17. Saint-Evremond, *Œuvres en prose*, ed. R. Ternois (Paris: Didier, 1965), 2:167–68.

18. Du Bosc, *L'Honnête Femme*, part 1, first publ. 1632, quoted from the Rouen ed., 1643, 1:75. I pointed to this text as to the sort of source that researchers might discover and analyze in Part I.

Notes to Chapter 12

1. See John Loftis, ed., *The Works of John Dryden*, vol. 9 (Berkeley, Los Angeles, London: University of California Press, 1966), "Commentary" on *Sir Martin Mar-All*, pp. 352–75; and Susan Staves, "Liars and lying in Alarcón, Corneille, and Steele," in *Revue de littérature comparée* 46 (1972): 514–27.

2. See Orjan Lindberger, *The Transformations of Amphitryon* (Stockholm, 1956); L. R. Shero, "Alcmena and Amphitryon in ancient and modern drama," *Transactions and proceedings of the American Philological Association* 87 (1956): 192–238; and (without prejudice to numerous other studies) H. G. Tan, *La Matière de Don Juan et les genres littéraires* (Leiden, 1976).

3. T. E. Lawrenson, "Timon of Athens, Alceste of Paris, and Old Manly of the sea," *Comparison*, 1976, no. 4: 47–70. A first version of my paper was given at a conference on "Problems and Methodology of Comparative Literature" at the University of East Anglia, Norwich, England, in December 1975. Quotations are from the edition of *Le Misanthrope* by G. Rudler (Oxford, 1952); from L. Hughes, ed., *The Plain Dealer*, Regents Restoration Drama Series (University of Nebraska Press, 1967; rpt. London, 1968). For *La Prude*, see *Oeuvres complètes de Voltaire*, ed. L. Moland, vol. 3 (Paris, 1877).

4. See E. L. Avery, "The Reputation of Wycherley's comedies as stage plays in the Eighteenth Century," *Research Studies of the State College of Washington* 12 (1944): 132–54.

5. Pepys, quoted in Ben Jonson, *Epicoene, or The Silent Woman*, ed. L. A. Beaurline, Regents Renaissance Drama Series (University of Nebraska Press, 1966; rpt. London, 1967), p. xii. U. Chevreau, *L'Ecole du sage*, rev. ed. dedicated to La Comtesse de La Suze (Paris, 1652), pp. 70–71, quoted in Chapter 7.

6. Pierre Cerou, *L'Amant auteur et valet*, Textes littéraires, no. 29, (University of Exeter, England, 1978), pp. vi–vii. On its later fortune see my articles "From extravagant poet to the writer as hero: Piron's *La Métromanie* and Cerou's *L'Amant auteur et valet*," *Studies on Voltaire and the Eighteenth Century* 183 (1980): 117–32. "New Orleans' first comedy: celebrations in 1764," *Theatre Survey* 21 (1980): 186–89. "Two unlisted editions of Cerou's *L'Amant auteur et valet*," *Australian Journal of French Studies* 18 (1981): 13–15.

7. Maurice Descotes, *Les Grands Rôles du théâtre de Molière* (Paris, PUF, 1960), pp. 90–104.

8. R.-A. Weigert, "En marge des *Proverbes* de Lagniet," *Gazette des Beaux-Arts*, Sept. 1967, p. 177.

Bibliography

This is not a list of editions and works consulted, which are documented in the notes. It is limited to (a) major documentary sources, (b) books to which I am particularly indebted, (c) my own writings on Molière not included in the present volume, and (d) titles for further reading, especially several published too late for inclusion in the works edited by Baader, Johnson et al. and Lawrence *(Visages de Molière)*, and *A Critical Bibliography of French Literature*, Vol. III A—each of which contains a detailed critical guide to, and/or an extensive list of, the literature of Molière studies published since Cioranescu's work and the Cabeen-Brody-Edelman volume to which Volume III A of *A Critical Bibliography* is a supplement.

Various separate editions of different comedies are discussed in the text, especially in chapters 4, 6, 10 and 11. Since even the most serviceable paperback editions of Molière tend disconcertingly to go out of print without notice, let the standard edition suffice: Molière, *Oeuvres complètes*, ed. Georges Couton, Paris: Gallimard (Bibliothèque de la Pléiade), 1971, 2 vols.

Albanese, Ralph, Jr. *Le dynamisme de la peur chez Molière: une analyse socio-culturelle de* Dom Juan, Tartuffe *et* L'Ecole des femmes. University, Miss.: Romance Monographs, 1976.

Baader, Renate, ed. *Molière*. Darmstadt: Wissenschaftliche Buchgesellschaft, 1980. A collection of articles with extensive enumerative bibliography.

Chevalley, Sylvie. *Molière en son temps, 1622–1673*. Geneva: Minkoff, 1973.

Cioranescu, Alexandre. *Bibliographie de la littérature française du dix-septième siècle*. 3 vols. Paris: CNRS, 1965–66.

Collinet, Jean-Pierre. *Lectures de Molière*. Paris: Colin, 1974.

Defaux, Gérard. *Molière, ou les métamorphoses du comique: de la comédie morale au triomphe de la folie*. Lexington, Ky.: French Forum, Publishers, 1980.

Descotes, Maurice. *Les Grands Rôles du théâtre de Molière*. Paris: PUF, 1960.

Emelina, Jean. *Les Valets et les servantes dans le théâtre comique en France de 1610 à 1700*. Cannes: C.E.L.; Grenoble: P.U.G., 1975.

Eustis, Alvin. *Molière as Ironic Contemplator*. The Hague: Mouton, 1973.

Fernandez, Ramon. *La Vie de Molière*. Paris: Gallimard, 1929.

Garapon, Robert. *Le Dernier Molière*. Paris: S.E.D.E.S., 1977.

Guibert, Albert-Jean. *Bibliographie des oeuvres de Molière publiées au XVIIᵉ siècle*. 2 vols. Paris: CNRS, 1977. (First published 1961–65).

Guicharnaud, Jacques. *Molière, une aventure théâtrale*. Paris: Gallimard, 1963.

Gutwirth, Marcel. *Molière ou l'invention comique: la métamorphose des thèmes et la création des types*. Paris: Minard, 1966.

Hall, H. Gaston, ed. *A Critical Bibliography of French Literature, Vol. III A, The Seventeenth Century, Supplement (1959–79)*. Syracuse, N.Y.: Syracuse University Press, 1983.

———. Molière, *Le Bourgeois Gentilhomme*. London: University of London Press, 1966.

———. ed. Molière, *Les Femmes savantes*. London: Oxford University Press, 1974.

———. "A Comic Dom Juan," *Yale French Studies* 23 (1959): 77–84. (Reprinted in *Molière: a Collection of Critical Essays*, ed. J. Guicharnaud, 103–110. Englewood Cliffs, N.J.: Prentice-Hall, 1964.)

———. "Molière." In *Dizionario critico della letteratura francese*, ed. Franco Simone, vol. 2, 809–18. Turin: UTET, 1972.

———. *Molière: Tartuffe* (Studies in French Literature, 2). London: Arnold, 1960.

Herzel, Roger W. "The Decor of Molière's Stage: the Testimony of Brissart and Chauveau." *PMLA* 93 (1978): 925–54.

———. "Much depends on the Acting": the Original Cast of *Le Misanthrope*." *PMLA* 95 (1980): 348–66.

———. *The Original Casting of Molière's Plays*. Ann Arbor, Mich.: UMI Research Press, 1981.

Howarth, W. D. *Molière: a Playwright and his Audience*. Cambridge: Cambridge University Press, 1982.

Hubert, Judd. *Molière and the Comedy of Intellect*. Berkeley and Los Angeles: University of California Press, 1962.

Jasinski, René. *Molière*. Paris: Hatier, 1969.

Johnson, Roger, Guy T. Trail, and Editha Neumann, eds. *Molière and the Commonwealth of Letters: Patrimony and Posterity*. Jackson, Miss.: University Press of Mississippi, 1975. A collection of articles with extensive bibliographies, critical and enumerative.

Jurgens, Madeleine, and Elizabeth Maxfield-Miller. *Cent Ans de recherches sur Molière, sur sa famille et sur les comédiens de sa troupe.* Paris: Imprimerie Nationale, 1963.

———. *Revue d'histoire du théâtre* 24 (1972): 325–440. Special number continues *Cent ans* for a further decade.

Klapp, Otto. *Bibliographie der französischen Literaturwissenschaft.* Frankfurt-am-Main: Klostermann, 1960. Excellent current enumerative bibliography.

Knutson, Harold C. *Molière: an Archetypal Approach.* Toronto and Buffalo: University of Toronto Press, 1976.

Lawrence, Francis L. "Dom Juan and the Manifest God: Molière's Antitragic Hero," *PMLA* 93 (1978): 86–94.

———. *Molière: the Comedy of Unreason.* New Orleans: Tulane University, 1968.

Mongrédien, Georges. *Recueil des textes et des documents du XVIIᵉ siècle relatifs à Molière.* 2 vols. Paris: CNRS, 1965.

Moore, W. G. *Molière: a New Criticism.* Oxford: Clarendon Press, 1949.

Veyrin-Forrer, Jeanne. "A la recherche des Précieuses," *Bulletin du bibliophile* 3 (1982): 287–320.

Visages de Molière. Oeuvres et critiques 6, no. 1 (1981). A special number ed. by F. L. Lawrence presenting several "present state" and other articles on Molière.

Wadsworth, Philip A. *Molière and the Italian Theatrical Tradition.* Columbia, S.C.: French Literature Publications, 1977.

Index

For references to literary works and plays whose authors are known, see under the author. References include a few themes and topics to assist the reader, both in the general list and under Molière. But these are selective rather than comprehensive. Place names are normally omitted. The author wishes to acknowledge the assistance of Mrs. Pearl Moyseyenko of the Humanities Research Centre, Australian National University, Canberra, in preparing the typescript of the Index.